On the
Vineyard

Also by Jane Carpineto

R.N.
On Call

On the Vineyard

A Year in the Life of an Island

Jane Carpineto

St. Martin's Press ✿ New York

A THOMAS DUNNE BOOK.
An imprint of St. Martin's Press.

Design by Nancy Resnick

Library of Congress Cataloging-in-Publication Data
Carpineto, Jane F.
    On the Vineyard : a year in the life of an island / by
Jane Carpineto. — 1st ed.
        p.   cm.
    ISBN 0-312-15584-0
        1. Martha's Vineyard (Mass.)—Social life and customs.
2. Martha's Vineyard (Mass.)—Biography.   3. Carpineto,
Jane F.   I. Title.
F72.M5C38   1998   98-5546
974.4'94—dc21   CIP

First Edition: June 1998

10   9   8   7   6   5   4   3   2

*To Tony Lombardi in gratitude
for everything he did for me and
everything he does for Martha's Vineyard*

Contents

Acknowledgments

*M*uch of this book was written away from the Vineyard on other shores, thanks to the generosity of my friends Ginny and Harold Shuster on Maryland's Eastern Shore and Peggy and Tom Rothschild on Chebeague Island, Maine. I will be forever grateful to them for offering me the use of their houses when I was most in need of writing hideaways.

Needless to say, I am deeply grateful to more people than I can name on the Vineyard for their help with this project, but especially to all those who agreed to be interviewed. Without some Vineyarders, the book wouldn't have happened. Special thanks to Tony Lombardi, Anne Shepherd, the Goodmans (not their real names, but they know who they are), Pat at the Artcliff Diner, Bruce Eliot, Q.T. Bowles, and Johnny Seaview for their tolerance of my many intrusions and for all their support and assistance. Finally, I am indebted to Vineyard photographer

Betsy Corsiglia for agreeing to include her wonderful portraits in the book.

Thanks, too, to my husband, Joe, who tolerated, with grace and humor, my frequent absences from home. And, finally, thanks to Melissa Jacobs for her invaluable editorial help and to my agent, Jane Dystel, for seeing me through another book.

Introduction

An island in the summertime and Christmas are linked in my mind. Although adults *celebrate* both, the unadulterated joy of them *belongs* to children.

Every summer day growing up on an island was Christmas for me. It was the greatest gift of my childhood, endlessly unwrapping. Those island summers allowed me to be a child and speak as a child without interference, without the invasiveness of adult constructs: wake-up times, immutable bedtimes, schedules for reading and arithmetic and homework, doctors' and dentists' appointments, prearranged activities of one sort or another. There, through years of unfolding summers, I was released from the necessity to color within someone else's lines. I was Free to Be, as Marlo Thomas put it.

No doubt, this is the reason why people of all ages are drawn to island living. Many of those whom you will meet in this book have never lived anywhere else, and have never wanted to;

others were pulled back to Martha's Vineyard by memories of carefree childhood summers there, and by the hope that the remembered freedoms would rematerialize in grown-up guise. Still others, the "transplants," came seeking a composite of freedoms, a package containing freedom from the daily stresses of mainland life, freedom from restrictive social and professional demands, freedom from fear: of crime, of the every-man-for-himself, dog-eat-dog mainland culture. But, whether rooted or transplanted there, for these residents, the theme was the same: the desire either to recapture the security and freedom that was lost in childhood, or to find it for the first time. Alice DuBois, one of the women interviewed for this book, described it best: "If you're on the edge here, there's always someone who will come to your rescue. I never have to worry about my kids' safety or my own. I don't have to lock my doors at night." Unlocked doors, safety, a caring, helping hand, the Freedom to Be. These are the things of which island childhoods are made.

I grew up on an island in Maine in the summertime. I am neither a native, a regular or resident of, nor a transplant to Martha's Vineyard. Because I know who I am not, there is much that I did not try to do in this book. I am not a historian; better to leave Vineyard history to its many able historians, some of whom have already published comprehensive works. I am not a naturalist. Except for having an aesthetic appreciation, I lack the breadth of knowledge and the fine-tuned eye for detail that is required of a good observer of nature. I am not a biologist, an oceanographer, an ornithologist, a botanist, or an environmentalist (except in sentiment). For each of those fields and their experts, Martha's Vineyard does and will continue to offer rich resource material. Finally, I am not a sociologist or a census taker, and therefore am disinclined to knock on doors at random. Thus, I have little to say about the people of Chappaquidick, the infamous, bucolic little Edgartown island, not because they are unworthy, but because theirs is not a curbside community. Most Chappaquidick houses are set back from the street, making casual encounters with its residents rare. The same can be said about West Tisbury, with its lovely rolling hills and farms. Unfortunately, though I went often to both on foot and by bicycle, I never found "the man (or woman) on the street." At Alley's General Store, the logical lookout post for West Tisbury citizenry, an outsider like me could not distinguish a West Tisburian from a Chilmarkian, and without an opportune encounter or an introduction, I was reticent to approach anyone. In the majority, the people on these pages were culled by using the old reliables: personal referrals and the grapevine. The others I came across by accident.

The reader will note that I tell this story in the present tense. I do so to give it immediacy and intimacy even though most of my meetings with people, and most of the activities I engaged in, occurred some time ago.

What I am is a chronicler of people. It is my work in this field that fills these pages. From the outset, it has been my fervent wish to tell the *other* Vineyard human-interest story. This story is the one that hasn't appeared in the newspapers or popular magazines, been seen on television (public or otherwise), or traveled through the social circuits. It is a contemporary story transcribed by me, but told by them—the free-spirited people who live on Martha's Vineyard.

1

An Island Childhood

*I*f we don't step on it, we'll miss the five-twenty," my father would say once we had crossed the state line from New Hampshire to Maine on our annual trek from Washington, D.C., to our summer place on Little Diamond Island, one of the 365 "Calendar" islands of Casco Bay just out of Portland harbor. Dutifully but nervously, my mother would step on the gas pedal of the blue Hudson sedan, and the speedometer needle would jump from forty to forty-five. (Highway travel made Mother anxious; traffic did too, but speed more than anything. The only way she could tolerate all three was to be in the driver's seat.) No one in our family, least of all my sister and I, wanted to arrive on the 6:15—a slower boat which stopped first at another island, and challenged our need for gratification beyond capacity. Most years we made the 5:20 ferry.

Our friends had been forewarned of our arrival date and time. They were already settled in for the summer. We came from the greatest distance, and were always the last family to arrive. Over the years, it had become a ritual for the islanders to greet us en masse at the 5:20 on the designated day. If we missed the boat, we missed the hoopla on the island pier, the view from the upper deck of waving handkerchiefs on the pier below, the sounds of welcoming shouts and cheers, the lineup of freshly painted wheelbarrows ready to receive a summer's worth of our belongings.

The 6:15 would never do. Our friends would have given up on us, retired to their supper tables and denied us our coveted moment in the limelight.

Sunset time was grown-up time on Little Diamond. Cocktail hour. You could hear glasses clinking and ice buckets rattling on the porches, see the trays coming out from the kitchens adorned with little bowls of cherries, olives, and orange slices; with plates of canapés; with ashtrays and napkins, silver shakers and stirrers. The grown-ups would settle into their chairs, facing the sunset, saying "Glorious, isn't it glorious?" while smoking and sipping. The children each could have one of the canapés and one drink of ginger ale in a very tall glass with two cherries and one orange slice to float on the bottom. After sunset, the fireflies came out and the children would run from the porches and catch them in jars to be stored in the pantry before bedtime. Upstairs in their beds, they could hear the grown-ups laughing and bidding their bridge hands, and the sound of the waves kissing the shore and sometimes the foghorn off in the distance. And just before sleep, they could have been wondering why grown-ups were nowhere near as cheerful and nice in wintertime Washington or Boston or a place called New Jersey. And, in the daytime, they might wonder again down at the beach when their mothers, in short-skirted bathing suits, would patiently teach them the dog paddle first, then give them crisp dollar bills when they'd mastered the crawl. Or spend all afternoon helping them dig in the sand, as far down as China, if their little hearts wished. And what to make of their fathers, so generous and kind, holding their small quivering hands as they tried casting from rods, guiding their short arms around the wheels of the speedboats? And at suppertime, down on the rocks by the shore, singing and laughing in front of the fire, then serving up lobster and corn on the cob and letting them roast marshmallows to put in s'mores.

Saturday night was family time. We washed and dressed, and carried our baskets of dishes and flatware down to the casino for the Saturday-night supper. The whole island community fit around three long tables, each family in seats that they occupied, year after year, generation after generation, until some vagary of fortune forced their replacement. When dinner had been served and digested, the president of the island association clinked his glass with his knife and called for attention. "Are there any announcements?" he'd bellow. And someone would stand to remind the women about the next Cogaswesco Club luncheon or a child would rise (nervous and blushing) to announce the date of this season's play. And another clink of the glass for introducing the guests: the Fullers from Philadelphia (applause), the Bennetts from Portland (applause), the Warners from Vermont (applause), and our family's guests, typically from some other continent, like the Gyan-Chands from New Delhi (loud applause followed by curious stares and whispers of "Look at those costumes" and "My, that's far away"). And now let's have a hand for the Supper Committee (longer and louder applause as the committee entered from the kitchen in aprons). The last sound was the clanging of dishes going back in their baskets. I liked it when our family was the last to depart. Then I could watch the procession of people and baskets wending their way uphill and homeward, hear their voices fading into the darkening air, see the sun setting behind them. And, the next day in the *Portland Press Herald*, you could read all about it: the menu, the guests, the committee, all the upcoming events.

All day, every warm, sunny day, was children's time. Playtime. You'd hear the screen doors slamming all over the island. It meant that the children were coming out to play. We'd hear the echoes of each other's voices and we'd converge, barefoot, upon the noisiest location: the beach, someone's lawn, or, when we were older and could swim, the island pier. When we met, we'd decide on the day's activities. We might rehearse for our annual children's theatrical event; spend the day excavating the sand, finding shells, collecting and painting starfish and sand dollars; or playing hide and seek, Ollie, Ollie in Free, and games of our own invention. On the back side of the island, there was an empty lot bordered by a narrow metal railing, and we spent many an hour there practicing tight-rope walking on the railing. We had a playhouse all our own and a village we made in a goldenrod meadow, decorated with castoffs from our houses. Adolescence was hard on us, when it came, because it forced us to abandon these pleasures, and I think we knew even then that we were losing something precious, and losing it forever.

It was the annual midday Labor Day clambake that closed the season. It was not an entirely joyous occasion as the return to winter homes and schools loomed on the horizon, but I remember fondly the scenery of the day: the men on the Front Beach, sweating under white hats, cotton trousers, and shirtsleeves rolled above their elbows (T-shirts and shorts not yet in fashion); digging the pit, filling it with wood, standing around stoking the fire in turns, heaping seaweed on it, then clams, eggs, and corn, and finally dark-green lobsters hurled to sudden red deaths; the smoke wafting high in the air, blowing with the wind. I remember the smells of the day: the mixed odors of food and fire, and after the meal, the smell of singeing seaweed on dying embers. And, I remember sadly, bedtime on that last summer night, hearing the waves come in to shore for the last time, the wind rustling in the leaves of the big oak tree, the drone of the foghorn, the whistles of boats and the clanging of buoy bells, all for the last time. I often cried myself to sleep feeling truly that this might be my last time, that anything could happen between now and another summer—a string of D words—death, disease, disaster (but not divorce, because it, like cancer, was so removed from common parlance that a child could not imagine it). And my spirits were no brighter in the morning when I awoke to furniture covered up with old blankets and sheets, windows shuttered, playthings put away. From a child's perspective, an ominous, funereal air permeated these rites of departure which all of the shouts from the pier of "See you next summer" were insufficient to assuage.

A long time passed, but finally the wisdom of age, the neutralizer of distance, and the fortuitous emergence of a recurrent dream combined to rid me of my Little Diamond separation demon. In the dream, I still summer there, it's the day after Labor Day, and I am closing up the old house, working against the clock, conscientiously covering the furniture, coaching my husband on the proper procedures for installing the shutters. In spite of our best efforts, we're unable to complete our tasks in time to catch the boat. Our daughters' toys are still on the unrolled, unwrapped, unmothballed living-room rug which is spread out, like a banquet, for winter's rodent guests. I sprinkle mothballs hastily over the rug but am overcome by a fulminant, heart-pounding panic. My husband's eyes meet mine and I ask him fearfully (hoping for reassurance, expecting objectivity at least, because he doesn't have the history with the place that I do), "Will something terrible happen if we don't do all this? I mean, the house will still be here, maybe a broken window from a winter storm, but the furniture will still be standing next summer, won't it?" "Of course," he replies, amazed that I would ask such a ridiculous question, and we both burst into laughter, leaving the house in its incomplete cold-storage state, closing tightly but not locking the door behind us (we've misplaced the old-fashioned skeleton key) and dashing for the boat.

One family, the Rands, lived on Little Diamond all winter, their five children commuting by ferry to school on the mainland. The rest of us grudgingly returned to our suburban existence after Labor Day. We didn't mingle much with the Rand family. We had no real conception of their lives, no way to fit their experience into ours. They were winter people and we were summer people, and that distinction set us apart. But this was not the only divider; there was another. Their entrance into island life in the early fifties brought a sense of foreboding to the summer people. Except for a little food store staffed and managed by the island children, there had never been any commerce on the island. The Rands intended to change that. They had bought the old Coast Guard station and pier at the eastern end of the island, and planned to open a marina, a small lobstering business, and another food store. The islanders were wary. Meetings were held, angry words exchanged. "This will change the character of this place forever. It will never be the same. Before you know it, we'll have cars here and undesirable people coming over by the boatload for the day. God only knows what else after that. No one will want to live here any more," they shouted in turn.

The Rands weathered the storms of protest and opened their marina and store in the dual names of Change and Progress. Nothing much changed, though. Life went on as before except, as memories of battle faded, the Rands' former enemies became their customers. They came to buy lobsters, make purchases at the store, or pull their boats up to the fuel pumps at their pier.

Progress did come gradually, and things did change, but it was so slow as to be barely discernible. It would have come anyway, but the Rands were its first ushers. They recognized

6

that summer was a consumptive season with its own market demands. For them, earning a living catering to these seasonal whims took precedence over belonging to the community. Step by step, summer by summer, the island lost its innocence and its citizens their habit of share and share alike. Bigger boats from off-island pulled into the marina carrying people with deeper pockets than the islanders'. Some of the new visitors bought land and constructed glassy summer houses. Au courant and out of character. The Rands built themselves a new one, too. The word spread, the island's popularity and its property values rose, and many of the old houses changed hands.

I go back to visit now and then. Most of my playmates, now middle aged, have remained in the houses they occupied as children, but progress has touched them all. My eyes seek out the old, familiar, ramshackle household effects. A few are left, but most are gone. Nowadays we sit together in living rooms that look like Crate and Barrel showrooms, and I listen to them complain vociferously about their taxes.

I left Little Diamond for good when I was in my thirties. As an adult, I didn't have the need of it that I had as a child. Maybe it was the old culprits, Change and Progress. Whatever it was, the place just didn't bounce for me the way it used to. Maybe I needed the memory of it more than the continuation of it, or had some vague premonition that the latter might contaminate the former. Maybe it was simply that I had changed. Yes, I know that's true because I now recall that shortly before I left, I had an apparition in which I came to view owning more than one house as a kind of imprisonment. A winter house and a summer house, too many properties to attend to. By then, I had two children to attend to, and that was enough attending for me. I wanted new faces in new places. I wanted to occupy other people's rooms. And so I have.

2

A Calling

*I*f there were an axiom that you could take the child from the island, but not the island from the child, then my wanderings in the last quarter century would not lend credence to it. Judging by the facts of my life after Little Diamond, I would seem to be a mainlander mostly, an islander only occasionally—an island-hopper. I've been a weekend guest on several islands in Maine, a vacationer on Martha's Vineyard and Nantucket, a tourist on islands in foreign countries. But the earth hasn't trembled anywhere on or off an island. No place has called to me (which is disappointing, because I've been hankering for someplace to "call" to me since the onset of middle age—a place that screams "You can live nowhere else but here"). I am surprised that the call hasn't come, because history supposedly repeats itself. But because I still believe in the axiom (even without the supporting evidence), I have been primed for some time now for the call of the isle. If I haven't heard it yet, it must mean that I haven't stayed put on any island long enough.

Returning to a place is not the same as being called by it. Of all the islands I have visited, I've returned most often to Martha's Vineyard. For a Bostonian, this is not unusual. A couple of hours on the highway, a forty-five-minute ferry ride, and one is on-island. So, over the course of twenty-five years, I've been there seven or eight times. I've gone like any ordinary tourist for a summer vacation or a weekend, for the fun of it, for warm water, good beaches, and sunshine. At least, these are the reasons I would have offered had anyone inquired. But there must have been more to it.

In the summer of 1993, thanks to a friend's invitation, I find myself there again after a few years' absence. I arrived midway through President Clinton's first Martha's Vineyard vacation. His choice of vacation spot has inspired a media feeding frenzy. Every newspaper and magazine I pick up extols the island as if was a hidden treasure just unearthed, a major archaeological discovery. It's close to heaven, the stories say. Beautiful, serene, an unspoiled summer retreat, a winter haven, a secure and happy colony of mixed races, classes, and livelihoods. So heavenly that it's not just presidents, but movie stars and other politicians, writers and artists as well who are tripping over each other in their haste to summer there. A new wave of winter residents is coming, too, and tourists by the thousands. The excitement is contagious.

How has the apparent fact of Martha's Vineyard's supremacy escaped me? I wonder. My receptivity to this form of media inducement rankles. I like to think that I'm impervious to it, but now I think it likely that these intrepid reporters have seen things that I have missed. Heretofore, my stays on-island have kept me far more attentive to family recreation than to cultural immersion. To be sure, I haven't been blind to some of the island's most heralded attributes: its multiethnic population, its celebrity draw, and its natural and architectural splendor, but these have been passing observations, secondary to recreational imperatives.

So, I'm wooed there by the media. I confess all of it—the attraction, the arousal, the lure, and the anticipation of the seduction. This very special place, this breeding ground for special people, comes almost with a guarantee that its specialness will rub off on me once I've settled in.

You might be thinking that I suffer from low self-esteem, and you might be right, but I trust that you know that I am not alone. You've seen the articles and the TV shows, too. Some of you, I daresay, have been thus driven to the island yourselves. Why? Because the media, collectively, is an agile courtier who nurtures your desire and rations your contentment. In a state of desire, are you ever as good as good can be? No, you need new products and new places; by implication, better products, better places.

So, I'm going to Martha's Vineyard because those in the know say that it's the *best* place. I'll submit myself to the island's deep-penetration regimen. It won't be like going to a body spa into which one enters fat and exits thin, but to a heart-and-soul spa into which one enters ordinary and exits special (or never exits at all). I can't say that I've been called there, because this has none of the atavistic feel of a calling. It feels more as if I'm responding to a personal ad, readying myself for love. I will be ready for Martha's Vineyard. Not yet fallen as in love, not yet called, but open to it, ripe for the calling. This time I won't go there in my typical here-today, gone-tomorrow mode. I will stay awhile, take my happy island memories out of psychic storage and set them free, watch to see if a reincarnation takes hold. A mood of anticipatory exuberance carries me to the following spring when I begin to prepare my residency. Soon I will rent a house for the coming summer and make plans for part-time off-season accommodations. I want to stay full time on-island, but I have another life I can't abandon altogether: a job, a husband, a home, children for whom college tuition must be paid.

I will begin my time on the island in the spring when trees and flowers bloom but tourists don't. In early spring, Martha's Vineyard looks like one of those paradises evoked in prose, a long paragraph of blue and green with pink and red, orange and yellow punctuation marks. I can get my bearings and soak up the island's natural beauty before the swarms of summer come.

3

Getting There

From May through September, the big ferries carrying passengers, cars and trucks, and sundry cargos to Martha's Vineyard from Woods Hole run almost hourly. Even in the dead of winter, they make twelve trips a day. But for one like me, conditioned over my formative years to catch the boat of my choice, it is with this peculiar genetic mix of anxiety and anticipation that I set out for The Vineyard (the moniker preferred by those in the know and those who want to be).

"Let's go, let's move," I shout, in sublime rendition of the nagging wife, to my innocent husband, Joe, who is scurrying to complete the business of departing our Boston household this April morning for what will be the first of many succeeding trips to the island. He's forgotten to put out an extra bowl of cat food to prevent our pet's starvation during our two-day absence.

"We're not going to make the ten-forty-five if we don't leave now," I hear myself say in an agitated voice.

Echoes of bygone departures, the replay of the family exit tape, with one alteration—a nod to the customs that have evolved over a quarter century of marriage: Joe drives. My stress tolerance is inadequate to navigate, worry about making the boat, and anticipate our arrival simultaneously.

Buckled into the passenger seat, I worry and anticipate with abandon. Joe keeps his eyes on the road and his voice on complaint frequency. Don't I know how much he hates going to places that require catching boats? No, in fact I do not. Silently I recall that he hadn't objected at all that summer when we dropped off our rental car in great haste at the mainland port of Piraeus in just enough time to keep our reserved cabin on the boat bound for the Greek island of Naxos. For several years afterward, he'd spoken of how nice it would be to have a house on Naxos someday. He had it worked out in his head. He'd spend his mornings sitting with the men at a sidewalk table drinking strong coffee and his afternoons in the same location drinking retsina.

"This reminds me of all those horrible Friday-night trips to Little Diamond rushing to catch the last boat. Thank God, we sold that house," Joe says, and adds for insurance, "No way you'd ever get me to buy a place on Martha's Vineyard. If there's another summer place in the cards for us, it will have to be no more than two hours away by car, a place you could just drive up to, open the cottage door, and unload your stuff."

This trip is a first in our record book. We've made it to the Woods Hole terminal with a full twenty minutes to spare to get our car in the standby line for the 10:45 ferry. At this time of year, we would have no trouble boarding with our car, but on a summer weekend, we would have waited for hours. Waiting gracefully is not in our repertoire. Now I have just enough time to pick up a lobster roll.

The tradition of requiring a *specialité de la region* before a boat trip goes back to my childhood, too, back to Portland, Maine, the only place in the *entire* world where you could get a real Italian Sandwich made a special way on a family assembly line at Amato's Italian Sandwich shop. With special ingredients like sour pickles and soft bread, much tastier than ordinary submarines; or a very special kind of chocolate doughnut (a Mrs. Watson's doughnut packaged by the half-dozen in plain white boxes with red lettering and cellophane windows) topped with granulated instead of powdered sugar like they served up everywhere else. At the food stand by the boat terminal in Woods Hole, they have *my kind* of lobster roll (although I cannot say precisely what makes the Woods Hole rolls better than the Vineyard rolls), and it matters not at all that I've just had breakfast and am not hungry.

This is contentment. A lobster roll. No waiting in lines because April is a much kinder month than June, July, or August on standby.

Even the most innovative minds could not devise a better way to spoil a summer weekend on Martha's Vineyard than coming to Woods Hole on a hot and muggy Friday or Saturday (or a cold and rainy one) with your kids, your gear, your pets, and your car; or without much of anything but yourself, a suitcase, and a car—minus a boat reservation for your automobile. But people do. They even do it on holiday weekends, forming a line of cars that extends clear back four miles to Falmouth center, with precious little hope of boarding any time in the near or distant future. They come from all over New England and from places farther flung, apparently unaware of the standby nightmare or in total denial of it.

Why, they wonder when they arrive at port, is it so damned difficult to get a car to Paradise?

The very rich and very famous fly to the Vineyard, and have cars awaiting them when they arrive. The regular, unrecognizable rich do the same, or they remember in February to book their summer arrival and departure reservations. The not-as-rich but obviously comfortable reserve early, too, as do the renters whose boat passages are included by their landlords in their rental packages. The ordinary, the curious, the sensible, otherwise known as tourists or "day-trippers," take the bus down from Boston or park their cars at one of the four oversize parking lots that consume hundreds of acres of valuable real estate in the Cape Cod town of Falmouth. They load themselves, their luggage, and perhaps their bicycles onto the free buses that shuttle continuously between the parking lots and the terminal. The truly sensible rent bikes, cars, or mopeds (though, in the case of mopeds, "sensible" might be malapropos) at ridiculous prices when they reach "the other side." There, all the newly arrived passengers and vehicles converge with the already arrived on the island's narrow roads and bike paths. Together, they will create enough gridlock to dominate the front page and the letters to the editor columns of both local newspapers' summer editions, and enough injuries to fill the hospital's emergency room to overflowing.

But in April, there are none of these problems. I buy the ferry tickets from an idle agent who has a smile on her face and plenty of time on her hands. Meanwhile, Joe stands by the car chatting with the neighboring drivers, all of whom are cheerful in the knowledge that they are assured a space on the 10:45. The round-trip fare is sixty-four dollars for two passengers and the car. It would have been more if we were hauling a boat or had bicycles on a car rack. That's all Joe needs to hear.

"Can you beat that?" he says, well within earshot of our

fellow travelers. "Sixty-four dollars for a forty-five-minute ride, and that's only in the off-season. Imagine the price tag in the summer. If we had a place there, we couldn't afford to go to it."

"You can say that again," replies Sam, a portly middle-aged man standing by an adjacent car whose acquaintance Joe has apparently made while I've been off buying the tickets and lobster roll. "That's why Helen and I come down in the spring and the fall and rent out our place during the summer. We like it at this time of year, though. It's relaxing. Quiet, too. None of that traffic and noise they get in the summer. A better class of people in the off-season. You don't get nearly as many of those damn day-trippers riding around on mopeds, revving their engines, pretending like they know how to drive 'em." In her seat in the car, Helen is smiling and nodding approvingly.

We wave good-bye to Helen and Sam when we're directed to drive onto the boat by an attendant in a red shirt with a Steamship Authority insignia imprinted on the right breast. We park in our space belowdecks as instructed by the vigorous hand signals of another attendant, and soon settle into seats upstairs in the spacious and underpopulated passenger area. Thus situated, we doze off and awaken to the captain's voice asking all drivers to return to their cars. As we drive off the boat and onto the pavement in Vineyard Haven, Sam pulls up alongside us, waves, and says, "Now you two have a good weekend, ya hear!"

The Vineyard Haven dock has its greeters-in-waiting. Attractive people dressed in attractive sweaters and slacks, waving and smiling at passengers on the gangplank, hugging others who have disembarked, but the welcomes are decidedly subdued. For us as for most other passengers, no attention at all hails our arrival, nobody on hand making an occasion out of it. My heart sinks momentarily, as if directed to do so by memory's automaton. On the short drive down the Edgartown Road to our hotel, I mourn for the way things were and will never be again. Later, after many weeks and months on Martha's Vineyard, I will come to see nostalgia as more endemic to islanders than to any other breed of humans.

My mood lifts gradually, propelled by the warmth of the day, the smell of the sea, the fragrances and colors of the flowers and trees, the quietness, the scale of the buildings. I like the miniature effect that Martha's Vineyard gives to the arriving urbanite (in the off-season)—like a series of doll villages full of small stores, small houses, small streets. Even the people look smaller. No wonder city folk want to come here, I think. The smallness of it hints at an ease of intimacy and pleasure. None of the reaching and grasping that the enormous, horizonless, vertical cities demand.

"I am going to like it here," I tell myself. Soon I will know the shopkeepers, the householders, the citizenry. I will greet them by name as we pass in the street.

In places where my stays have been short, I have enjoyed being the muddled, dislocated tourist at the natives' mercy, but not in places where I plan to stay awhile. Then I feel an urgency to get my bearings. Everyone tries, but not everyone succeeds. Once, my husband and I stayed for six weeks in a Mexican hill town. For a week before our rental house became available, we were housed in a hotel along with Canadian and other American guests who were staying for a month or more. Every morning after breakfast, we noticed that our fellow inmates rushed with books and pens to Spanish classes. Every afternoon after lunch, they returned, and the hotel garden became a Spanish study hall. One of the students was a retired Canadian businessman who worked as earnestly at denigrating Mexican business practices as at mastering the native language. "I like to be able to converse with the people when I'm here. That's why I'm learning Spanish," he said, "but when I can finally talk to them, I'm going to tell these people that they don't do anything right. Look, the swimming pool filter system doesn't work. The phones don't work. Nothing works in Mexico."

Back in Toronto or New York, these students' hard-earned *hays* and *hablos* would doubtless be forgotten, but they were very useful in Mexico.

"I think it's terrific that they are learning Spanish. It helps them get their bearings," I remarked to Joe, "to be able to order their food and conduct their business in complete Spanish sentences." In short order, I, too, was enrolled in a Spanish class and completing my assignments in the garden.

But I have a leg up on this Vineyard excursion. I speak the language, and I am not a complete stranger to the territory. I want to regain my bearings, to feel a sense of place, a visceral connection to the island. I am glad that Joe is with me to help with the acclimation. My recognition responses fail me more often than not, and before long, I discover that Joe's are no better. Over the previous twenty-five years, I have come here for varying lengths of time. In March 1970, thanks to a friend's wedding present of a week in a Vineyard Haven motel, my husband and I honeymooned there. Although there are several motels near the center of town, on this occasion we can't place it. (A year later, we stayed a night there, and then realized why it had been so easy to forget. Except for its water views, it had nothing to recommend it.) Then, some years hence, when our daughters were elementary-school age, we returned to the island *en famille* for a vacation. For two weeks that summer, we occupied a dark, poorly constructed ranch house in a wooded development off the Edgartown Road. Now Joe and I try to find it, but every side street we take is marked by a boulder announcing a community. Nothing familiar. One boulder invites us into a community that is subsequently described disparagingly to me by local builders as "one of those seventies' developments." "This looks vaguely familiar," Joe says and remembers aloud that our "cottage" was a brown split-level with a deck on the side surrounded by tall trees. Unfortunately, excepting some variations in exterior paint color, these appeared to be the distinguishing features of most of the residences.

Feeling downhearted again and out of place, like homesick tourists eager to go home, we drive out the Katama Road toward South Beach. As we approach the end, up ahead and off to our left, we see the gray, angular outlines of the Mattakesett Condominiums.

"Remember that place," I exclaim. "Remember, Amy was only a baby, and we came there for a week. The first night, she was colicky, remember, and you and I took turns pacing back and forth across the living room, but mostly you did it. Finally, when that didn't stop her crying, we put her in the backseat of the old Peugeot and drove around for an hour until she fell asleep. And, over there, that's where we played tennis, and look, there's our unit, the second one in from the left. We had a gin and tonic on that deck every night, and so did all our neighbors on their identical decks."

We pull over to the side of the road adjacent to the complex and sit for an hour, staring at it, laughing ourselves silly. Remembering.

By dinnertime on this first day of what will be a two-year odyssey on the Vineyard for me (and, intermittently, for Joe), my bearings are intact. I feel ready to venture out into my new world. Later that night, we attend the sixth annual Martha's Vineyard lip-synch contest in an Oak Bluffs nightspot. It's a benefit for the Martha's Vineyard after-school program. The dance hall at The Atlantic Connection on Circuit Avenue is full. Except for a few black faces interspersed throughout, the audience is young and white. Barbara Dacey, the program director of the island's radio station, WMVY, is the evening's MC. The first words out of her mouth are a reminder that Martha's Vineyard is a winter place most of the time and a summer place some of the time.

"There are lots of people on the Vineyard this weekend," she begins. "Seems earlier than usual. Is there anyone in the audience who is just visiting?" About a third of the available hands in the room are raised, including ours.

"I want to know *before* we start talking about you."

Laughter erupts from every corner of the room.

"Well, what's the latest word? Is he or isn't he?"

The people who know what she means laugh heartily. Those who don't look appropriately confused.

"OK, I'll give you a hint. Is Bill coming back this summer or not?"

The audience response is a resounding (and as it turns out, accurate) Yes. As the whole world soon learns, President and Mrs. Clinton will return at the end of the season for their second island vacation.

Barbara announces what the first five performers will take home for prizes—five hundred dollars for the winner and a dinner for two at the Black Dog Restaurant for the fifth-place performer. She introduces the judges. One is a screenwriter of some renown about whom she quips, "He's using his position here as a judge as a stepping-stone to the Supreme Court."

Then the show goes on. The winner is a male, a Julie Andrews impersonator, who brings down the house with his rendition of "Supercalifragilisticexpialidocious," and again in his encore, a sped-up number by Barbra Streisand. But for me, the real show-stopper is a Vineyarder named Taffy McCarthy lip-synching Marilyn Monroe, wearing a white halter dress plunged low at the neck, a blond wig, and strapless white pumps. Twice in her routine, Marilyn-like, she protrudes her derriere and lifts her skirt up to teddy and garter height. The audience loves it. Taffy McCarthy must have remained in some subliminal corner of my consciousness. A year passes before I see her again. I walk in midset on a Sunday afternoon jazz session. A tall brunette is singing Duke Ellington classics to the accompaniment of a band, and even though the authentic Taffy bears no resemblance to the faux Marilyn, I recognize her at once.

For the rest of the weekend, I spend my time looking for a house to rent for the summer season. (In the off-season, I can stay in friends' houses or at bed-and-breakfasts.) There are plenty of available rentals, but only a handful in my price range. The real-estate agents are kind and eager to oblige, but most of what they have to show costs more for a week than I can spend for a month. The houses I can afford look drab and light-starved. It will take additional time on succeeding trips to the island, careful probing of the classifieds, and consistent inquiring through the grapevine before I find something. I leave the island with mixed emotions: dispirited about the necessity to put my assimilation into island life on the back burner while I keep house-hunting on the front burner, but eager and excited by the prospect of being there.

4

Spring

*I*n late April, thanks to the *Boston Globe* classifieds, I find my hacienda. "Small house in Edgartown. Two bedrooms. Convenient to town. Ferry tickets included." The price is right—five thousand dollars for the summer (excluding Labor Day weekend). Without seeing it, I sign the lease. For that price, I know it will be a humble dwelling, but well suited to my pocketbook and my purpose. If it had charm, character, beach frontage, and an ocean view, I'd be tempted to stay put—to get my money's worth, so to speak. This house would offer no such temptation. I would rarely be at home. I would be out, busily injecting myself into island society.

But to my astonishment, a certain reticence, an odd shyness, grips me on succeeding visits to the island in the spring. I feel compelled to stay to myself. I walk alone on pristine white beaches, down quaint village streets in full foliage, through damp, verdant woodlands. I eavesdrop on conversations in restaurants and other gathering places, watching and listening, but speaking only when spoken to; and all the while, I am meeting a side of myself that I haven't met before, at least in a very long time. Is this the same me? I wonder. The woman who approaches strangers with ease wherever she happens to be—at parties in Boston, in foreign countries, in commercial establishments. The same woman who prides herself on what she regards as her God-given ability to communicate across social classes, races, and cultures. Suddenly, on this little island, I'm not that woman anymore. No, instead I am like the new girl in the high-school class involuntarily transplanted here from some beloved location. I'm all awkwardness and timidity. I stand apart—off to the side, praying that I won't be ridiculed by the rowdy boys nearby, longing for home.

Not only do I feel ill at ease and out of place, but I develop an instantaneous sympathy for professional journalists. The American public must not understand how difficult it is to master the art of invasion, to muster the courage and the skill to impose oneself upon strangers, I think. But how could they? As a nation, we worship at the shrine of privacy. Barely out of diapers, we are taught to pay homage to all that is private: private parts, private property, individual privacy. We shalt not trespass. But now I must trespass, not onto property (unless by accident) but into people's privacy. Obviously, I will have to undergo a reconditioning.

To compound my problem, I tell myself that is easier to intrude upon a mainlander than upon an islander. The promise of privacy is the lure that draws people to island habitats in the first place. I know that from my own island experience, but even without benefit of personal experience, I would have discerned that Vineyarders are the same. Eavesdropping elicits that kind of information. Whether direct or indirect, references to outside invasions are, like idioms, on the tip of every tongue. *"They're* [the tourists] coming earlier this year." "Better stock up now [May] 'cause pretty soon you won't be able to get to the supermarket." (Thanks to increased traffic from off-island vehicles.)

And, more than the rest of us, islanders prize their individual and collective independence, and resent outside interference. On Martha's Vineyard as on other islands of comparable size and proximity to the mainland, outsiders may be defined as narrowly as the citizenry and its elected representatives from a neighboring town, or as broadly as all off-islanders of any stripe. Among the latter, there are subcategories and hierarchies of the untrustworthy. High on the list are representatives of the state and federal governments who occupy positions empowering them to issue edicts. Close on their heels come the city slickers/developers—the big-money people with their cadres of big-name lawyers. They are followed summarily by tourists—people with no long-term interest in the island, and among them the least favored ranking is reserved for "day-trippers."

Yet for all his pride in it, the islander's notion of independence is more illusory than real, more ambivalent than definite. That I also remember from my island years. Sometimes the suspect "outsiders"/government officials turn out to be extremely island-friendly, more protective of the island's ecology than many of the local elected officials are. Similarly, the city slickers/developers/luxury home builders, while they had their day, incidentally put their bulldozers to their neighbors' advantage, elevating neighboring property values along with their own. Tourists help the island economy, too. What does it matter whether they come today and leave tonight, tomorrow, or next week—as long as they spend money on some or all of the following: island food or trinkets, rental bicycles or vehicles (at least some of the proceeds from which do remain on-island), island beds or island entertainment?

Now here I come, an outsider cut from a different mold, but still an outsider, and a very nosy one at that. They won't take kindly to my questions. They will be suspicious of me and my motives. I will be persona non grata. And so goes self-pity, knowing no boundaries, banishing its victims to a black hole. But just before I submit to the pull of the black hole, I come across a note from a friend written a few months previously. It contains the name and phone number of one of his friends, a year-round islander. "He knows lot of people there, and will be happy to talk to you about the island," the message reads. With some trepidation, I make the call. To my surprise, the voice at the other end is friendly and receptive. He has been looking forward to hearing from me. That's all I need. I feel a surge of renewed energy and optimism which emboldens me to ask for more. "Would it be possible," I ask, "for you to gather a group of Vineyarders in your home, people who would enjoy talking with me about the island?" He responds that he will see what he can do, and will get back to me within a day or two. True to his word, he calls back. Yes, the request is granted, but with one condition—that I will not use the participants' names or identify them in any way. "It's a deal," I say elatedly and grate-fully, cognizant that I've stepped right into it—into the sacred zone of *privacy*.

A few minutes after the appointed hour on a warm Sunday afternoon, I arrive at my host's pleasant up-island home. Its appearance relaxes me. It is set back from the main road, bordered by trees. The front yard is littered with children's toys and a helter-skelter assortment of outdoor furniture and objects with no obvious purpose. On the exterior, the house is of weathered shingle and looks as if it might have been a farmhouse once. I enter through the kitchen, which smells, like a farmhouse kitchen, of baked goods and freshly brewed coffee. Around a big table adjacent to the kitchen, five people holding coffee mugs await me—three men and two women. I judge them to be in their mid-thirties to early forties. Collectively, they have a sixties' aura about them, an appealing artsiness. The men wear longish hair, the women sandals and jeans or gauzy skirts. The atmosphere is relaxed and unpretentious. For the next two hours, we sit together in the living room. I ask questions, they talk, and I take notes in which I am careful not to identify the speakers. (Afterward, too, I do my best to forget their names and appearances.) Here, then, is the essence of what was shared with me that afternoon:

It used to be so peaceful and quiet. We had a few thousand people living here in the winter and a few thousand more in the summer. We all knew each other and got along real well. We had our characters, too, people you'd never forget, but only a few of them are still around. Johnny Seaview is one. You'll run into him while you're here. Can't miss him. He wears a red baseball cap on his head and tree-climbing gear around his waist. He's always hanging around Vineyard Haven and Oak Bluffs when he's not climbing trees. That's what he does for a living. He reads all the time and quotes poetry to you while you're talking. When you meet him, ask him how he got his name. Johnny Seaview's not his real name. He'll tell you who he really is. Anyway, back then, in the good old days, we had everything we needed, right on Main Street in Edgartown, all the stores we needed, the grocery, the hardware and clothing stores, the repair places. You could just pull up and park out front. Hardly any traffic. Then that thing happened over on Chappaquidick with Ted Kennedy and that young girl. And, after that, they filmed *Jaws*, here on the island. All of a sudden everybody from everywhere wanted to come here. At first, it was just tourists wanting to go over to Chappaquidick and look at the bridge where the accident happened, or wanting to see where the movie was filmed. But then people started building houses one on top of the other. Houses and condominiums were thrown up overnight. It was worse down-island, close to the towns, but it happened up-island, too. People just kept coming. They came from Boston and New York and Washington, D.C., and later on from places as far away as Texas and California. After these big influxes, the character of the towns changed. The rents on Main Street in Vineyard Haven and Edgartown and on Circuit Avenue in Oak Bluffs went sky high, so most of the small service businesses moved out of the towns or closed altogether, and in came the big supermarkets and all these high-priced boutiques you see now and all the T-shirt shops, the galleries, and the trinket stores. Most of the owners live off-island, so the island never sees the money from their enterprises. The money goes where they go. None of these shopkeepers are riparians. The scallopers, the conch fishermen, the clammers; the shell fishermen and the deep-water fishermen, they're the people who keep the money circulating on the island. So do most of the restaurants, the boat builders, and the local tradespeople, but those shopkeepers who do a quarter of a million in inventory selling to day-trippers in the summer, they pay their debts off-island.

No doubt about it, capitalism has corrupted this place. Like so many nice places, it started out artsy and quaint. This is one of the nicest places on the East Coast. Warm in the summer, mild in the winter. The Vineyard was a well-kept secret until the sixties. Now it's mostly rich people and the people who work for them. Year-rounders are a strange breed, too. We're escapists. We're escaping the real world. You have to do some horrible work to live here. We live off what we hate. All of us are just scraping by. A lot of us are struggling, service-sector artistes—part-time artists, full-time and overtime service-sector wage slaves.

These are their words, not mine. I understand the words, but the message sounds strange. It reminds me of my early-morning arrivals in foreign lands, when, groggy from a sleepless flight, I'd be jolted into consciousness by the shrill sound of native speech and the cultural disconnection between my home port and my new port. We call this "culture shock." Listening to these Vineyarders, I feel a kind of culture shock. In mainland America, the talk is all violence and crime and how poor people, mostly those of color, are causing it, bringing down property values in the cities, making them unlivable, wrecking the fabric of our families and threatening our American way of life. But in this island culture close to home, the culprits responsible for the island's decline are different. Not poor minorities, but rich white Americans—capitalists. If my informants are correct, these new rich are to be distinguished from the old rich, the moneyed summer people who have been coming to the island for generations of summers. The latter are the *good* rich. They keep to themselves in seafront houses, hire the locals to prune their hedges, paint their porches, modernize their electrical systems, roll their tennis courts. It is not they. It's the *bad* rich—the T-shirt rich, the four-wheel-drive vehicle, Saab, BMW rich, the ones with the New York, Illinois, Texas, New Jersey license plates, the let's-see-it-all, do-it-all, buy-it-all, short-stay-get-out-of-my-way rich. They are to blame. They aren't bringing down the property values. *Au contraire*, they are elevating them so high that the natives can barely afford to stick around. Some have to move out of their places come May when a month's off-season rent might, if they're lucky, give them a week's worth of in-season roof over their heads. And who is clogging the roads so you can't even get to the supermarket, except in the hottest part of a good beach day? These different, indifferent transient rich, who can be subdivided into categories of objectionableness, their ranks expanding or contracting depending on who is talking. It is these "outsiders" who are doing the damage. And not just wealthy vacationers, but well-heeled small-business owners from somewhere else who come in for the season, make a killing, and depart with the cash. And the day-trippers, too, regardless of their means (though I'm soon to learn that it is a standard assumption that they come for the day because they can't afford to stay longer), don't do anything for the island. They buy T-shirts and rent mopeds. The money they spend leaves the island in the hands of the "outsiders"/entrepreneurs instead of remaining on-island for the hotelkeepers and landlords.

No less intriguing than the people that my new acquaintances include are those they omit from their list of undesirables. Black Americans (who have been coming to the island in increasing numbers for four decades) are noticeably absent. Could it be true that Martha's Vineyard is the one place in America where black people are not held responsible for social decline? Not only do I hear no such suggestion from my group, but neither do I hear any in my subsequent conversations with white islanders. The silence is refreshing, but I wonder if it is a veneer covering something more sinister. That question will wait until I can give it the attention it deserves.

The "stars"—the rapidly growing population of movie and television personalities—are not to blame, either. Hearing no mention of their much-publicized presence on the island, I ask the quintet what they think about Martha's Vineyard's conversion from secret hideaway to tabloid replica of Hollywood East. "Well," they say, "we're used to them. They've always been here, people like Carly Simon and James Taylor. They're old-timers. We've always had celebrities here. It's fine if they want to come." Soon I discover that I need only to say the word "celebrity" to be guaranteed a response that would include some reference to the *"right of privacy."* Apparently, the stars are not on the receiving end of the perennial interogatory about who is responsible for destroying this place. Slack is cut for them. They don't cause the traffic jams. Presumably, then, they just sit in their houses, stroll on their beaches, and wait for their victuals and other necessities to be delivered.

Later I learn from other people that although the celebrities' privacy is respected by permanent islanders, their contribution to enlarging the fleet of island tour buses is undeniable. They have given that business the kind of boost that less fortunate entrepreneurs would die for. Thanks to them, the tour guides have something to talk about. Tourists tire of beautiful scenery and historical landmarks, but show them the house where Jackie lived or the one where Goldie now lives, and their attention spans lengthen immediately. They're star-struck, pointing at the houses like children showing off chicken-pox scars, proud to have caught a disease that everyone should catch sooner, not later. And, swooning with fever, they carry the contagion home to their friends, who hasten to succeed them onto the mobile infirmary.

When I say good-bye and thank-you to the host and his friends, I feel satisfied that my reconditioning has been accomplished, that I have crossed over the line from reticence to renewal. Everyone has been kind to me, eager to talk, seemingly pleased that I am interested in their opinions. What's more, I think that inadvertently I've come upon one of the secrets of the journalist's trade: namely, that a notebook and a pen are her security blankets. With them, one need not feel so vulnerable about intrusion. Those simple tools make me appear as much a giver as a taker. Yes, I am *taking* cherished information from my sources, but in return I can *give* them something of more or less value—the sense that their words, dutifully recorded, may have an import and an audience.

From that day forward and throughout my time on Martha's Vineyard, I am never without my pen and notebook.

Nostalgia runs rampant on Martha's Vineyard. The bolder I become, the more Vineyarders I talk to spontaneously, and, one by one, they tell me how they pine for the low-profile days before the American and international invasions. America is anathema. Going to America, to a diehard Vineyarder, means going to the mainland, over to New Bedford (for the discount outlets) or Hyannis (for the malls), or, God forbid, to Boston (for the hospitals), or Providence (for who knows what). The Vineyard, to this kind of Vineyarder, is not America, but, like Cuba, is imperiled by its proximity to America. However, while Cubans fear our army, not McDonald's, Vineyarders fear McDonald's and would form an army to keep it at bay. In Oak Bluffs they've already got a Dunkin' Donuts, and another new one in Vineyard Haven (at least this time, the army, if not exactly of winning strength, is of sufficient force to prevent the trademark pink-and-orange sign from appearing on the store-front), and if this invasion of the franchises continues, so the argument goes, Martha's Vineyard and America will be indistinguishable.

But to my outsider's eye, it feels as if Vineyarders should worry less about franchises (against which they have legal recourse) and more about the influx of people. The place is on the map now, and conventional island wisdom holds steadfastly to the notion that the population waves have a pattern, like ocean waves that follow storms. These waves follow publicity storms generated by celebrities themselves, or by events surrounding them. So there was a wave after Ted Kennedy's accident at Chappaquidick, another wave after *Jaws* was filmed on the island, and finally a huge, incessant wave following a vactioning president and then a vacationing princess. They are curiosity seekers of all stripes: short-stay tourists, homeowners, and renters; preceded by paparazzi and columnists who flash their bulletins around the world. Pictures and words, all delivering the same subliminal message: "Here is an American treasure. The people you admire most admire it, and so will you."

Probably, most people coming over from America for the first time experience culture shock. Can't get there by super-highway. No malls within viewing range of the ferry slip, but soon enough you find them, mini malls to be sure, but there nonetheless. A good-size hospital, too. Once you've been around for a while, though, you know you're in America, mini America, the best and the worst of it. The best (in my opinion): that which is homegrown, homemade, unsullied, and supported by a civic ethos of preservation, fairness, and justice. The worst (again, in my opinion): that which is tainted by excess, mostly of money, but also of human encumbrances—trash and garbage, vehicular traffic and pollution, noise and space waste. An excess of new houses—tacky look-alikes without claims of distinction. These luxurious designer houses try too hard for uniqueness and leave instead an oddly indistinct aftereffect, like that which follows a tour of Beverly Hills—so much of a good thing that nothing stands out.

And, irony of ironies, some of the luxury houses are occupied by people who live most of the time in America, and are investors in, and creators and overseers of, all manner of enterprises including franchises and chains, the sight of which they presumably come to the Vineyard to escape. They are the most publicized of the new "capitalists" my five friends have talked about, and since they are poorly represented in my social circle, I'm as curious as George. How do their heads work? I wonder. In my imagination, I see them as people whose private meditations about their Vineyard vacations contain a common wish: Let us have our time in the sun, out of sight of the shopping strips, office parks, and real-estate developments we've built. Apparently, though, I don't have it right. Many of the Vineyard's titans of industry would like nothing better than to erect parking lots or housing developments right in (or nearby) their own backyards.

Ernie Boch is reputed to be one such. On Memorial Day, through arrangements I'm able to make with his secretary, I visit him at his palatial island residence. He has been at the center of much controversy on the island. According to the local (and Boston) newspapers, he owns land near the ferry terminal in Vineyard Haven and has envisioned it as the perfect site for a Subaru dealership. He has proposed the idea to the town, but its fathers have not shared his enthusiasm and have quashed his proposal. Apparently, a little opposition like that doesn't stop Ernie Boch. If not a dealership, why not a parking garage on the spot, a pretty parking garage, bordered by trees and fronted with the best brick and mortar money can buy? Alas, when this plan is brought to a vote, once again the Tisbury town fathers kill it, at least momentarily (though a court challenge will follow).

Contrary to the political wisdom which proclaims that "You don't solve public-sector problems by throwing money at them," Ernie Boch's experience on Martha's Vineyard is proof that you *do* solve most private-sector problems by throwing money at them. All you need is a lot of it to throw, and the perseverance to keep throwing.

Boch's is a household name, not just to Vineyarders, but to anyone who has ever lived in Massachusetts. "Come on down," he implores us ebulliently, grinning and gesturing on our TV screens like an old pal inviting us to the party of a lifetime, when, in fact, this hortatory exercise is meant to lure us to the Boch Automile out on the old Route 1, where Boch car dealerships line the strip like casinos line Las Vegas. Boch Subaru,

Boch Toyota, Boch Honda, Boch Oldsmobile. There is hardly a car that Ernie Boch doesn't sell, and hardly anyone, so it seems, who doesn't come on down and buy one from him. Those three little words have made him the vehicular Tsar of New England. So appreciative is he of his advertising agents and Japanese patrons that COME ON DOWN is emblazoned in bold Japanese lettering on the entranceway to his Vineyard retreat.

When I pull up to the Boch residence off the Katama Road, I know instantly that no one without prior arrangement "comes on down." Not a hint of spontaneity here, from the tall locked gates protected by an electronic intercom to the long, patterned-to-perfection stone driveway bordering an expansive groomed lawn on which Mr. Boch's pet llamas are grazing. (If not a spontaneous gesture, the animals are, at least, a whimsical touch, I think. Later someone insinuates to me that pet llamas make good tax deductions. (And sure enough; Boch has one named Chico sharing the spotlight with him on his television commercial.)

The driveway climbs upward for some distance before the house is visible atop a slope that descends to the waterfront. It is a colossus of glass and shingle, with multiple decks facing Katama Bay, Chappaquidick Island, and, in the distance, the Edgartown harbor. This is the house that Ernie built several years after he emerged victorious from World War I with Edgartown officials over renovations he made to the grand old Vineyard summer house he had bought originally, and from World War II (a longer, bigger war), after he tore it down.

Suffice it to say that among those who don't buy their cars from Ernie Boch are the tradespeople and town officials of Martha's Vineyard. Boch has nothing left in his account with them. In their book, his list of sins is long. He has torn down a historic house, brought in labor from off-island, destroyed a rip-rap (a jetty), filled in a wetland, put in moorings and used them for commercial purposes, buried fuel tanks without a permit. Rumor also has it that he charges his workers a fee for taking showers in his cabana.

Not loathsomeness but physical fitness frames my first impression of Boch. A tall and muscular man, wearing jogging apparel and looking slightly grayer and less enthusiastic than the TV Boch, greets me at the side entrance to his house. He ushers me into an immense kitchen where his wife, Barbara, is cleaning counters that are already spanking clean. While Mr. Boch and I seat ourselves at the kitchen table, she stands and chats with us intermittently. From where I sit, I can see the water and the Boch powerboat flotilla through the glass doors that front his spacious, cabinet-lined dining room. The room is crowned by crystal chandeliers dangling from above like jewelry from a royal neck.

"So why all this fuss about you?" I ask, cutting to the chase.

"The people in Edgartown resent me, especially the local officials. I guess they say 'Here's this guy with a big house, just some car dealer who probably gets his money from the mafia,' but I've done a lot for the locals. It's not true that I haven't hired them. I've hired a lot of them, but I couldn't use them for my driveway. No one here knows how to lay a driveway like that. I had to bring in a mason. That stone was imported from Italy, and it had to be put in just right. I believe in maintaining the work ethic here. When I have jobs the locals can do, I hire them."

The phone rings. "Hey, Greg, how are ya, where are ya?" Boch inquires into a portable instrument. "Oh, you're in Arizona. Must be nice there. Playing golf, I suppose. Well, it's really good to hear from you. Take it easy now." He hangs up. "That was Gregory Peck. He calls me on every holiday no matter where he is in the world."

Thankfully, someone is in his corner. A year earlier in a *Boston*

Globe article I happened upon, the Bochs had been portrayed as friendless on the island, snubbed not only by tradesmen and officials, but also by their prominent, wealthy Vineyard neighbors (Walter Cronkite among them), and excluded from high-profile island social events.

Now I ask both Bochs if the story is true and if it stings.

"Not at all," answers Barbara Boch emphatically. "We have our own social life here, a large circle of friends. We don't need any more friends. Our family keeps us busy."

"And," adds Ernie, "we have friends who've bought houses down here just to be near us."

But their most proximate neighbors, relatives of the original owner of the Boch estate, rue their proximity. "They don't like us much," says Ernie Boch. "We got this place for a good price from Reverend Brainerd, a better price than they got for their properties. He was the CFO of a church in Baltimore. We flew down and made the deal on a handshake. The deed said we couldn't change the house, but Reverend Brainerd didn't really care. Whenever we changed something, the neighbors complained. Sometimes they'd call the police. And we also complained when they cut across our lawn on their bikes. Eventually, there was a truce of sorts. We went ahead with our plans, and finally got carte blanche to do whatever we wanted."

That they wanted it all and then some became indisputable once Boch had shown me the house (pausing by a picture of the reverend's original roomy, classic summer house, which bore no resemblance to the present one).

"Now the place is so big I can get lost in it," he remarks with a chuckle as we begin our house tour.

Down a corridor to a guest bedroom with black lacquer bed in the shape of seashells with companion pieces of the same material, all imported from Japan: one is a bureau with a hidden TV that magically appears with the touch of a button. On into the foyer with a hotel-size chandelier glittering overhead, and into a living room the size of a Boch showroom, enlarged by its white decor. Massive white couches and chairs fill the space, and enclosed in a bay sits a white grand piano (for guests to play). Another huge push-and-pop TV set appears again on command, this time from behind the doors of a cabinet. Back to the foyer, under the chandelier, up a wide curving stairway and into the second-floor master bedroom, an impressive display of square footage. Here is more black Japanese furniture on a larger scale, but the button prompts the television not to pop out but to rise up like Lazarus from the foot of the bed. We visit closets as big as rooms and a bathroom the size of a suburban kitchen, and then an honest-to-God, fully applianced kitchen. More bedrooms and sitting areas, off limits today to avoid intruding on Boch's sons and their friends.

"I've got three kitchens in this house," my host explains proudly, "but you wouldn't believe the grief I got from the town about them. I guess they thought I was going to rent out rooms or something crazy like that. I've got another kitchen and entertainment area down in the basement. It's great to have them. We don't have to keep lugging food and drinks up and down stairs."

Charity, after all, begins at home, and one imagines that the extra kitchens come in handy when the Bochs host their annual July party for the island's Camp Jabberwocky—a camp for people with cerebral palsy. The camp is their primary Vineyard charity, but they also donate generously to other causes: to the Mayhew seminars, a highly regarded adult-education program on the island; to the Martha's Vineyard Historical Society, for whom they open their gates annually for a house-tour benefit. The sum of these activities, aside from their charitable purpose, make a statement to Boch detractors: "Yes, we take, but we also give back."

As I have taken a chunk from their afternoon leisure time, I leave them at last to their own amusement, and make my way down the expensive Italian driveway past the exotic South American pets, out the Japanese-lettered gates, and back onto the scenic American roadway. Amazing, I think, how islands are the microcosms of the world, showing us its ways with mind-expanding immediacy. So it must be the island Bochs, not the Automile Bochs, who deliver me an epiphany, alerting me to the fact that I have just visited not only a home and a family, but also that amorphous locality called the global marketplace, where it matters not from whence come the goods or the labor as long as both can be procured from somewhere.

The Wallace brothers live during the summer in Boch's Edgartown neighborhood. Herring Creek Farm is the site of their immense oceanfront edifice erected alongside the Great Pond on the coastal Katama Great Plains—a vast swath of land designated as fragile by environmentalists. The Wallaces, Boston real-estate developers by trade, use some of their land for cattle farming, but their agrarian instincts play second fiddle to their development instincts. They have 215 acres of unused backyard. Perfect for a fifty-four-unit luxury-housing development and beach club. If they could bypass the three-acre zoning requirement in Edgartown ("snob-zoning" as they referred to it in one of their lawsuits), they could build many fine houses for fine people, and a few ordinary houses for ordinary people, all hankering for places in the sun.

Luck refuses to smile on the Wallaces. Their grand design meets defeat first at the hands of the Martha's Vineyard Commission, who reject it after a three-year review, and again in 1996, when that body's decision is upheld by the Massachusetts Land Court. The Wallace wars, then, have been fierce, protracted, and cumulative, waged against neighbors, the town of

Edgartown, and the Martha's Vineyard Commission. Next to these, the Boch wars look like mere skirmishes. The Wallaces, though short on luck, are long on lawyers, lawsuits, and money. For those of us watching on the sidelines, the fight is a sizzler from start to finish, nearly breaking the defendants' bank, a match between Davids and Goliaths, and providing oh-so-hot copy for the editors of the *Vineyard Gazette* who serve it up in weekly installments as a long-running serial replete with villians and heroes. And on it goes. An appeal of the Land Court decision is in the making. In the not-too-distant future, the battle will begin anew.

Naturally, I'm chomping at the bit to meet with the Wallaces, men with fire blazing in their bellies. With surplus confidence left over from gaining an interview with Boch, I call the Wallaces' Boston office and speak to their attorney. Although she is not especially sanguine about my chances, she gives me some cause for optimism when I say that I have no particular axe to grind with her clients. "In fact," I add, "this could be their opportunity to present their side of the story unedited and unadulterated." She signs off saying that she will see what she can do. A few anxious days pass before I hear from her with the bad news. My request is rejected unequivocally. I try not to reveal my disappointment, and instead make a gallant attempt to sympathize with the beleagured brothers who, she explains politely, have had too many negative experiences with writers and reporters to take a chance on me.

But, of course, I don't have to look far beyond the neighborhood to find people who have had their own negative experiences with the Wallaces. Michael Wild and his sister, Rebecca Baxter, are the heirs of the twenty-two acres that remain of their family's estate, property which abuts the Wallaces'. In the 1940s, the Wilds owned the entire area and farmed eighty acres of it, but in the late forties they sold most of it to a man who carried on the farming tradition until his death, when his property was bought by the Wallaces.

Michael, the eldest child and only son of the Wild family, is a lively, stocky man of early middle age whose finger has always been in almost every Vineyard pot. The man and the metaphor are a perfect fit. When he was a small child, he stuck his finger in a neighboring farmer's oilcan, where it remained until the farmer could be summoned to extricate it. "For years after that," said his mother in an article in the *Gazette*, "Orin Norton [the farmer] would point to the can and remark, 'There's the can that really held Michael Wild down.'" But nothing holds him down for long. He has a hurried, gotta-go manner more suggestive of an urbanite than an islander. Thus, I approach our meeting in a less expectant, less enthusiastic frame of mind than usual. I have wanted the Wallace brothers, but I've gotten Michael Wild instead—a second best, a substitute for the grand prize. We sandwich our time in between his appointments, and meet it in his car near the infamous property. It is a rushed encounter which, when it is over, impresses upon me the folly of counting chickens before they've hatched.

First Michael tells me that the Wallace brothers have kept him moving at city pace, to and from courtrooms, for several years. They have brought suits against him on access rights to his property and against him and the town planning board on a proposed subdivision of two five-acre plots on the property. He then digresses into autobiography. During Michael's young adult life, he has followed a typical summer Vineyarder's course: college (but no degree), a stint in the navy, then a return to year-round residency in the old summer homestead and a move into carpentry—the island's jump-start occupation. It's dead-end stuff, but lasts until his big break comes in the seventies with the inchoate conservation movement and the establishment of a local environmental body. He secures a position at the bottom of the ladder, and works his way up to the directorship of the Martha's Vineyard Commission, one of a handful of such bodies in the United States.

"It was an interesting and innovative time. Up to then, Massachusetts hadn't done anything to protect its jewels, and Vineyarders had just woken up to the destructive influence of development. We were a perfect location for the commission—a self-contained region and a jewel. The legislature passed the Islands Trust Bill and established the commission granting the six island towns authority to work cooperatively on regional planning and regulation of development. During my tenure, I researched wetlands, became an expert on them, in fact, and published my findings in a guidebook that was down-to-earth and readable. It helped to garner community support for wetland legislation. The six-town conservation partnership didn't always work, though. Each town had its pride and didn't want to take direction from a collective body. There was haggling. It was like working in paradise but living in the trenches. In 1982, I realized that the time had come for a new face for the commission and a new kind of life for me. By then, I was an on-the-job trained, but solid nature guy. Eventually I added the finishing touch—a bachelor's degree in social ecology."

Now the nature guy calls himself a jobber—a sometime artist, a dump runner, an island historical tour guide, a Realtor, and a site finder and production facilitator for movie, TV, and fashion shoots.

Eventually Michael delivers the happy ending to the Wild-Wallace story. All the courtroom time, the accumulated bills, and the endless wrangling have paid off. At long last, he has won the suits the Wallaces brought against him and his sister.

"This is high-end property we have here. It's right on the oceanfront," he says and adds, "Thank God, because my legal bills are high-end, too."

After Michael and I must part company (so he won't be late putting his finger in the next pot on his schedule), it occurs to me that he could be a box-office hit himself, the leading man in a Vineyard documentary. He has the site, the supporting characters, and the storyline for a chronicle of the island's struggle between preservationists and developers.

It has been a long ordeal for Vineyard attorney Ronald Rappaport, too. As one of the two attorneys representing the town of Edgartown to preserve the three-acre zoning requirement challenged by the Wallaces, he has been at the center of the struggle. That would seem to be enough work for one man to undertake, but apparently Rappaport has boundless energy. At this stage in my island immersion, he appears to my unknowing eye to be the most wanted man on Martha's Vineyard. He serves as counsel for five out of the six island towns, and on the board of directors of the Steamship Authority, activities which consume more than half of his time (the remainder, he spends in private practice). Already I have read all about him in the local papers, about the many battles he has waged on behalf of the island, and have determined that I must find my way to the end of the paper trail, to the man himself. I make several cold calls to his office, all to no avail. Finally, I discover that we have a mutual off-island friend who succeeds where I have failed in arranging an appointment for me. Before we meet, I surmise that even if he is overburdened, his must be rewarding work, the kind of lawyering that is loved, not loathed, by his fellow citizens, the kind that makes it easier to get to sleep at night.

Once I meet him in his office, I am certain that my hunch is correct. Mr. Rappaport is a slightly eccentric-looking man in middle age with a tall, lanky body, a full beard, and a generous, wiry head of hair. From all appearances, he is a modest, relaxed, and amiable person who is disinclined to revel in his glory.

Rather, he speaks of his appreciation for his fellow islanders. "People here care about this place. Sometimes the caring is too little, too late, but at least it's there and growing. And as we win more struggles, Vineyards are less intimidated by the big-money folks, the city slickers with their teams of pricey lawyers."

Ronald (Ron) Rappaport has solid island roots as the son of a Vineyard-bred mother and transplanted physician father. Until he went off-island in high school, he attended Vineyard public schools. For a long while thereafter, he took other roads—to California for college, to Boston for law school. After graduation he lived and practiced law in Boston, met and married his lawyer wife there, and might have stayed on had pregnancy not intervened.

"Once our daughter was born, my wife found out that she couldn't be a civil litigator and a mother." In 1986, they decided to practice on the island, and joined with a partner who was already established. "We were a little worried that our work would be routine, that we'd be trading intellectual challenge for calm and stability, but it turned out to be more exciting than we ever anticipated." Ten years after his resettlement, the firm grew from three to seven attorneys and a total staff of seventeen. "In addition to my private practice, I stepped into the town counsel's job in Edgartown not long after I moved here. Little did I know that I was walking into a boiling cauldron. Someone wanted to develop a huge public parcel of South Beach, the only beach on the south of the island without entry or parking fees. Well, I brought a lawsuit on behalf of the town and the public, and the state took the beach by eminent domain. It was a great political win, and brought us national publicity. Taking land by emiment domain made for a happy marriage between conser-vationists and governing bodies. Soon I was serving as counsel to four other towns besides Edgartown."

There have been many wins with the Rappaport stamp on them: the taking of the little airport in Oak Bluffs, the Nickerson property abutting another small airport in Edgartown, and that town's battle to own and operate a water company that had been in private hands. Ron fought for and won the preservation of Alley's General Store in West Tisbury as a historic landmark and institution. Now, in the Wallace case, another sweet victory. Thanks to his efforts, three-acre zoning in Edgartown is here to stay.

With characteristic modesty, Rappaport emphasizes his good fortune and eschews his good deeds. He sees himself as a man of privilege, able to lead an island life and raise his child in an island way. If such are the benefits he takes from Martha's Vineyard, then many are the benefits he returns. His place in local folklore is solidly on the side of the angels. He is the tortoise who outruns the hare.

By early June, my skills as an intruder have sharpened. With pen and paper always at the ready, I conduct "man-in-the-street" interviews with abandon. I inject myself into random conversations. As a result of my newfound bravado, I have a notebook full of names of more people (some obtained from friends—everyone knows someone on Martha's Vineyard—or from islanders I've intruded upon) to whom I *absolutely must* talk about the island. As the numbers accumulate, they eventually have a dizzying effect, enough to make me slightly regretful that I've cured myself of reticence. Now the problem is not who will talk to me, but to whom I will talk. With my head spinning from this conundrum, I am grateful for my home base in Boston, for the relief that distance can provide. There I should be able to devise a selection system, ready for implementation when I move to Martha's Vineyard for the summer.

The system, once devised, is a crude product whittled from the remnants of dreams and free associations. The Vineyard on my mind. Its flora and fauna painted in broad brushstrokes; its people in details—the lines in their faces, their smiles and scowls, their turns of phrase. In Boston, I paint a Rivera-like mural in my head of the Vineyarders I want to know. Year-rounders: fishermen, boat builders, craftspeople and tradespeople, retirees, merchants, professionals, struggling service providers, Native Americans, quirky characters. I think of summer people: old and new Vineyard white and black families, tourists. Celebrities come to mind, too, but I put them in the background because their island lifestyles have been rendered time and time again in many mediums.

I give myself a few basic instructions: Divide the names in the notebook into categories. Select a few people from each. Let my instincts guide me the rest of the way. Leave myself open for chance encounters. Find Johnny Seaview because the word on the street is that he's the prototypical island character, the last of a dying breed. He's middle-aged and healthy as far as I know, but his occupation—tree work—has its hazards. What if Johnny falls before I find him?

The mere thought of finding Johnny Seaview compels me to make an overnight trip to the island to find him before the end of June. I search in all the reputed right places—Cumberland Farms convenience store, Bruce Eliot's car-rental agency (where I, too, am becoming a regular), The Artcliff Diner in Vineyard Haven, at his apartment complex in Oak Bluffs—but at all the wrong times. No Johnny, but I know he's still alive because he's recently been seen in all his favorite hangouts. I breathe easier. I'll find him later if not sooner. Meanwhile, Bob Tankard, the principal of the West Tisbury School, will be easier to find. Unlike Johnny, he has an office, a desk, a sit-down job. School is almost out for the summer, and I want to see him while it's still in session in order to discover what, if anything besides location, distinguishes an island school from one on the mainland.

The school is a modern edifice on a quiet street just off the Tisbury Road. It looks like any rural school in the U.S.A. but spiffier, and the construction equipment outside suggests that it will soon be spiffier still. I enter into a spacious lobby filled with moving children and teachers. The school's student body and faculty appear to be overwhelmingly white, an unremarkable observation, except for the fact that its principal is black. The walls are decorated like school walls everywhere, with children's art. I follow the signs to the principal's office, the outer reaches of which are occupied by several female secretaries seated at desks behind a high protective counter. One woman ushers me into Bob's adjoining, glass-fronted office. From his desk, he has a good view of the bulldozers and the pedestrian traffic in front of the school. Sitting opposite him, I have a good waist-up view of a broad-shouldered man with a well-toned torso. I surmise correctly that he's tall, fortyish, and gregarious. With very little prodding from me, he launches into a monologue.

"This island isn't the real world. I went to high school here, left for a while, and came back to live. You know, I don't even lock my doors at night. I can leave my keys in the ignition of my car, and no one will touch it. It's some kind of utopia here on the Vineyard. You don't get stressed. Even the taxes are low. My God, the taxes in Chilmark are the lowest anywhere in the state, and you've seen some of those houses up there. I mean, those are some *big* houses. And look, we're building additions on all of our schools, expensive ones, too. We're getting fifty-two percent reimbursement from the state here in West Tisbury, and they're getting even more in Vineyard Haven and Oak Bluffs. Now where else in the United States are you hearing about that kind of thing? It's unreal."

47

Already, without asking for it, I have the answer to my question about how this island's schools differ from the mainland's. They're still being funded. Every one I happen upon later is either spanking new or in the process of major renovation.

In 1993, Bob Tankard became a school principal, but not without a struggle.

"A small group of people were against me because of this," he said, holding up his bare forearm, pointing at his dark skin, and anticipating my next question before it is uttered.

Doesn't racial prejudice bring you about as close to the real world as you can get? I ask.

"You gotta understand. In the wintertime, there's a small black and Cape Verdean community here, but most of those children live and go to school in Oak Bluffs. In the sixties and seventies, there were more black families year-round on the island than there are now. I'm not sure why. There might be thirty kids now in this school who are minorities—black or native American. Here most of the kids are white, from hippie families, trust-fund families, or just plain working families. They're watching everything we do in the schools. They have time for that kind of involvement."

Another distinction, I think, judging by newspaper reports of funding cutbacks at other schools, of declining parent involvement in the public schools and, concomitantly, increasing demands on school personnel to act in loco parentis and educate simultaneously.

Bob returns to the racial issue. He recalls his high school years.

"I think the adults felt that there was racism here on the island, but as a kid, I didn't feel it much even though I certainly stood out in my school. There was interracial dating when I was growing up, and there's more of it now. I know that the

Realtors didn't show houses to blacks in certain locations. No matter how much money they had, they were encouraged to look exclusively in Oak Bluffs, where a majority of blacks lived and still do. The most liberal whites have always lived in West Tisbury. I remember that several of them were members of the island NAACP. There are so many private clubs on this island. Every one of them had, and some still have, discriminatory practices. There's always some group or another that's excluded. I don't belong to any of them, but I've been to them all."

Finally, Bob has to concede that the real world does creep into island race relations. So real that he can't even do something as benign as sit comfortably in a bar like his mainland counterparts and have a drink, however respectable his companions or the establishment; he must project a pristine image. "It wouldn't look good," he explains. "I always have to think a lot about what kind of appearance I'm making. Everybody knows everybody's business."

So here's a page from an island principal's diary on which is recorded the novel suggestion that life in the unreal world might not be as good as it looks. Keeping up appearances, putting your every word and deed to a filter test. These take a toll. Sometimes he thinks that life might be better in the real world, not in the city (too real), but in a place like Cape Cod (a little unreal).

As spring eases into summer, I ease into Martha's Vineyard, especially into Vineyard Haven. In the winter all the ferries from Woods Hole dock there, and in the peak season the majority of them do. I arrive, stay awhile, and leave from Vineyard Haven. I have good friends there. And because I am not yet one of those who treat it as a checkpoint en route to another island destination, a certain intimacy between person and place has evolved. To ensure that I belong there, I've invented a new arrival ritual to replace my childhood one. Bruce Eliot, from whom I've rented cars occasionally, has become my designated greeter. Although he doesn't come to the ferry slip waving a handkerchief to celebrate my arrival, he is consistently happy to see me when I show up at his nearby Holmes Hole Car Rental storefront, either in my own car or in pursuit of one of his. At first blush, we are an unlikely combination. He is boyish and brash. I'm no longer girlish, but, give me the slightest provocation, and I, too, can be brash. So it's habitual now for me to take a seat on one of the store's streetside wooden benches, lingering long enough for us to banter in that folksy way that the greeters and the greeted in summer colonies always do. Light and easy, no pretension of profundity. Right away, Bruce gives me the local news in review, the latest tourist count, updates on businesses and romances (mostly his), and in return, I give him a rundown of my upcoming activities on the island. Thereafter, we throw lighthearted barbs at each other until it's time for me to leave. We have our favorites. I'll tell him that he's a hustler and a womanizer (characterizations he appreciates). "Maybe good for business, but definitely bad for health," I repeat. And he's fond of saying "So long, Mrs. Garcia" (he thinks my husband resembles the late rock star Jerry Garcia). And as I step into my ancient Volvo, he quips, "Must have been this car that made Jerry fall for you, otherwise it sure as hell beats me what it could have been."

Elsewhere on the island, I (alias Mrs. Garcia) feel like a tourist. Up-island I see storybook settings. Fields full of wildflowers. Horses grazing in delicious meadowlands. Here a quaint house, there a magnificent house, every one perched prettily. Giant trees, their lush branches swooping down to frame the road on either side like chorus-line plumes encircling a stage. For several miles, the scene before me forms a dreamy, lulling pattern and then breaks at unexpected intervals, at bends in the road or at the crests of hills. Great swaths of blue sea suddenly appear, lying in wait to surprise me, demanding to be noticed. I notice. Like a child, I am delighted by the illustrations in the storybook, but I wish it had some human characters. Because it's springtime in the storybook, most of the characters are somewhere else, I guess.

And down-island is storybook, too. A town storybook, more obviously New England than the up-island version. Edgartown's white whaling church and her streets of white houses and white fences. Oak Bluffs' multicolored carpenter's Gothic gingerbread houses. Bustling harbors and characters aplenty in both ports. Mix my fondness for characters with my deep New England roots, and it's no surprise my heart grows warmer to the down-island storybook.

Now, the reader may ask why I repeat this word—"storybook"—with its fictional connotation. It is because Martha's Vineyard—up, down, and all around—has the look of sweet innocence and fantasy. For symbolic evidence, look no further than the island jail. It is situated in a pretty white Edgartown house, and I find it a challenge to imagine it as a punitive establishment. Rather, it has the semblance of a homey bed-and-breakfast. A nice place to relax after a stressful round of criminal activity, I think. My illusionary attitude stays with me as I wander around getting acquainted with this pretty island. Any pretty place can have this effect on a newcomer—its picturesqueness leads you to the presumption that all its citizens are happy. You want to be included. You linger in front of real-estate offices, staring at the photos of houses on display. "I could be happy in this one," you say. Who but the blessedly happy could live in these wonderful houses, walk these clean, narrow streets, ride horseback over these luscious meadows, meander along these velvet beaches? Naive sentiment perhaps, because you and I know that this isn't Disneyland. It is a real place where people get sick, divorce, go bankrupt, and die as they do everywhere. I even find myself clinging for a while to the idea that when bad things happen to living Vineyarders, they leave for homelier, sadder places. Maybe not. Maybe suffering comes out from behind these beautiful facades, exposes itself boldly to the light of day, and receives a just and kind response. But so far, I have seen no suffering. Surely, time will tell me if it's there and how it's treated.

In a happy frame of mind, I later say good-bye to Bruce, warning him again to discipline his roving eye, letting him know that my time in Boston will be short and that I will soon return to take up residence.

During this off-island interlude, I happen to make the acquaintance of a former Vineyard official. He is the neighbor of a friend of mine. His story brings me down a notch about my prospects for becoming an *insider* on the Vineyard.

"When I took a town official's post there," Carl Walters, a soft-spoken, thoughtful man, recounts, "I visualized myself as an off-islander whose friendliness for the Vineyard would be rewarded in kind. I learned sooner than I wanted to that the islander's trust in an off-islander is given sparingly."

Carl is no stranger to Martha's Vineyard. Over the years, he and his family have rented a vacation house there for two weeks at the start of every summer. Over the years, he has been a consistently avid reader of the *Gazette*.

"I had a keen interest in the way local governments worked and professional experience with small-town governance in Massachusetts. In my regular readings of the *Gazette*, I noticed that the island towns were always governed by the same people who were forever fussing about the same issues and resolving none: The Steamship Authority brought over too many cars; the shell fishermen wanted to dredge barrier beaches and the naturalists were opposed; the developers were fighting the conservationists. Most of the dredging and development advocates were islanders. Most of the conservationists were summer people."

Carl pauses to pluck more memories from that time.

"I was enthused about my new job. I felt that the elected officials serving at the time were forward-thinking, progressive people who had enough off-island experience to understand how things got done in the world. I leapt in wholeheartedly, bought a house on-island, and prepared to settle in for what I anticipated would be many fulfilling years. Most of them were. We started a capital program, and planned a new police station, a town hall, the dredging of one of the harbors, and a new addition to the library. I thought we were accomplishing things, but the progressive officials were gradually being replaced by less progressive people. We just didn't see eye to eye. They wanted to do things the local way, not necessarily in a businesslike way. If they had better qualified out-of-towners to fill positions, they'd fill them with less-qualified locals. They thought I was a 'make-work' guy. I didn't fit into the local scheme of things. I think because I was an off-islander, it was easy to dispense with me. I felt like they hung me out to dry. In their eyes, I was an off-islander, pure and simple. That Mazer guy, the psychiatrist who lives on the island and wrote the book about it, had it right when he said that island insularity makes you feel separate from the world. That's great for vacationers— an escape from the hurly-burly—but islanders are too proud of their isolation. For the short run, they might bring in an off-islander to get things done, but in the long run, he'll be resented. They don't want to admit that they're part of the real world."

There they are again, those same references to the real and unreal worlds in one breath with Martha's Vineyard. Carl's words: "They don't want to admit that they're part of the real world."

Bob Tankard's: "This island isn't the real world." My own word: "storybook." Suddenly the words combine into a semaphore, a traveler's advisory: "Beware, you are entering a foggy zone. Visibility is difficult. Boundaries are poorly marked. You may experience optical illusions."

5

Summer

There has been a sea change. Now it is summer, and even when the water is out of sight, it is never out of mind. Boats whistle messages to each other, skis whisk blue liquid into froth, children laugh and shout along the shoreline. And the happy sounds waft into the warm air along the byways, into the open windows of moving cars and stationary houses and into gardens and shops. When the sea is in sight, it looks different than it did in spring. Close into shore, the water's aqua tone is richer. Farther out, its blue is bluer. The springtime sea looks casual, like a Sunday in the park. The summertime sea is hustle and bustle like an amusement park full of joy rides. Come one, come all, along for the ride. Ride the waves. Ride on your bodies or your boards. Ride on motorboats, sailing boats, rowing boats. Or ride vicariously. Sit under your beach umbrella or on a seaside bench and watch the locomotion in the great water park beyond.

My turn to ride will come, but first things first. Such as moving into my house. It is situated on a short, nondescript side street off the Edgartown Road. I have avoided the sight of it till now to afford myself an element of surprise. And there is an element. On the exterior, my little bungalow emits a whiff of Cape Cod charm, ever so slight, but a surprise nonetheless. In the middle of an unkempt grassy lot surrounded by tall pine trees, it looks authentic, like the houses of the region are supposed to look—neat and simple, shingles weathered gray, colored accents. Here, red is the accent. Red shutters, red flower boxes, red geraniums. But once inside, Cape Cod charm yields to yard sale drab, to a ragtag assortment of sagging stuffed chairs, wobbling tables, and creaking beds distributed among four boxy rooms. About what you'd expect for the seasonal price tag, and just as I predicted, perfectly suited to my needs. From here, I will willingly absent myself from morning till night. No distractions outside, either, no views of oceans or inlets or gardens in bloom. Not even a porch or a deck. Entertainment is out of the question, and chatting over the fence looks improbable, too. After only a few days' occupancy, I can detect a perpetual hush in the air, a hint of a sunroom society peopled by those long past their child-rearing, sunbathing, and barbecuing years. Not until I take several walks down adjacent streets do I hear the signs of life in my universe, and discover that the neighborhood has a name. A woman I chance to meet on one of my meanderings tells me that I am living in the *Ocean Heights* district. The name is inapt, since the ocean is invisible from most of the "Heights'" low-lying residences. But no matter, for that is the way of all summer colonies: to take license with euphemism, as if feeling obliged to assure the vacationer that he is getting a short-term lease in paradise on "Blueberry Lane" (where there are no blueberries) or at "Seaview Gardens" (minus sea views and gardens).

So from lowland Ocean Heights, I go in search of Martha's Vineyard, real and unreal. It is hard to tell the difference in the summer. People lose sight of the dividing line, and nature conspires in the cover-up. The morning fog rolls in and blurs the boundaries. The afternoon sun burns off the fog and replaces it with a blinding glare. By dusk, all eyes peer skyward at the setting sun and don't descend again until after the moon crests and darkness falls. After dark on summer nights, under the spell of the moon and the caress of warm, salty breezes, no one pays heed to harsh realities. Romance is the order of the summer night, the time to look for love.

But, in the daylight hours, through the fog and glare, I think I see the island setting its summer stage. Now that I am free to roam for days at a time, I can revisit the places I've seen in spring, enjoy an extended sneak preview of the little season that supplies the life blood for all the other seasons. And best of all, perhaps I can revive the island summer child in me by looking for and listening to the Vineyard's summer children.

In the down-island towns of Edgartown and Vineyard Haven in the summertime, so old-timers say, you don't hear screen doors slamming anymore. Everyone has sliders. So quiet, you can't hear them opening or closing, but if you listen carefully when the air is still and the morning is young, before the traffic starts, you can hear children's voices on the decks by the sliding glass doors. Some of these children live here year-round in neighborhoods that look like neighborhoods anywhere else. Ranch-style enclaves with lawns and driveways, or older-style neighborhoods where the houses still have porches in front and you have to crane your neck to spot the add-ons on the sides and rears with their mandatory sliders and decks. In the town of Vineyard Haven, there are more year-rounders than anywhere else on the island: families, single people, couples, retired people who used to be summer people, retired people who have grown up year-round on the island, or retired people who came here later in life just to retire. Summer people inhabit the posh spots along the harborfront. Their imposing houses, whether perched on high or low terrain, afford commanding views of the harbor and the East Chop peninsula. Theirs is a strip of the choicest real estate in town. It's star-studded. Art Buchwald, the syndicated columnist, lives closest to the center of town; William Styron, the noted author, a stone's throw up from there, and Mike Wallace, the *60 Minutes* anchor, just a bit farther. And, if one is looking for a politician to round out the mix, what better clue that he lurks in their midst than the huge steel eagle on the hillock adjacent to New Jersey Senator Frank Lautenberg's glossy summer retreat? These are summer people of an older generation. The children's voices you hear in their neighborhood are the voices of their grandchildren.

If you take the Edgartown–Vineyard Haven Road from Vineyard Haven to its terminus in Edgartown village, you will come upon neighborhoods of such splendid, classic simplicity and obvious importance that there will be no recourse but to stop, look, and snap the shot, to reactivate your memory to conjure never-learned or long-forgotten history lessons. In these houses, the first white settlers lived, and from their white facades, placed at angles facing the harbor, the men departed for their whaling expeditions (or made their fortunes as whaling merchants), as did their sons and grandsons, until finally America had no further need of whales and whalers. Today, some of their descendants still reside in the ancestral manses, mostly in the summertime. In this neighborhood, too, there are children, but hardly seen, as if to serve notice that it is now, and will be forever more, the pristine province of adults. Most likely, the young ones are at the yacht club for their sailing lessons, at the tennis courts for their tennis lessons, or attending a summer camp somewhere on the island or in the mountains of Vermont (for a change of scene).

More of Martha's Vineyard's summer children are on the island for vacations from other places; the majority from the East Coast cities and suburbs but some from as far away as Texas and California; a few from Europe and South America. There are those who come for the entire summer season, and those who come for a week or two to reside in rented quarters in other kinds of neighborhoods. In and around Edgartown, there are condominium neighborhoods erected on swaths of land that lucky developers could buy and build on in the boom years of the seventies and early eighties when environmental regulations were looser and banks less parsimonious. The upscale developments boast gleaming glass and shingled single-family houses with multiple decks and floors stretching skyward, affording grand views of the sea for moms and dads from their master decks, or peeps of the sea for the whole family from lower-perched decks. The children, of course, don't care much for sea-viewing. They have come to play. And they have brought all manner of equipment to play with: balls and buckets and bikes and bright-colored plastic things in canvas pouches that they will ask their dads to inflate into seafaring conveyances right now. Not later, not when Dad is through gazing at the water or turning his dog-eared pages of Tom Clancy or Stephen King, because Dad may never be done. The vacationing child's call to play is an urgent call, one that cannot wait until the sailboat slips out of sight or the chapter is finished. A certain number among this paternal delegation will fail to answer the call, and who can blame them? August's deck potato Dad is, in the other seasons, a fast-track, overworked Dad. So on the lawns in these neighborhoods, one sees the young nannies transplanted from Sweden or Ireland or Iowa surrounded by their juvenile charges, blowing up water wings and rafts, pumping air into bicycle tires, throwing balls into small, outstretched arms.

Oak Bluffs, the rollicking, frolicking down-island town that borders the harbor, is different. Not a deck town but a front-porch town. In the gingerbread-cottage neighborhoods close to and spreading out from the Methodist campgrounds, many of the houses are so close together that their occupants can touch each other across their porch railings. In the summertime, screen doors slam from early morning until well past sunset. When these Oak Bluffs children come out to play, they have only to call one another from porch to porch to begin the day's activities. And the grown-ups watch from their rocking chairs, and they, too, call out to one another and to each other's children. Oak Bluffs is a studio that plays to its audiences—a series of sets where action takes place, where you gawk while you walk. It is *Our Town* live, enacted all day every summer day, on location, all for the price of a boat ticket. The children who are old enough to go out on their own spill out en masse from the porches onto the streets and down to the waterfront and the beach, or to the parks, or the start of the main drag—Circuit Avenue—where the honky-tonk, the quaint, and the tasteful collide like cymbals opening an overture. At the foot of the street sits the crude, antique carousel building—the oldest working carousel in America, the one with the coveted brass rings. If you catch one as you ride by, you can ride free the next time. The Muzak from the carousel wafts up Circuit Avenue until it is drowned out by the din from the foot and vehicle traffic en route to the ice cream parlors, the take-out food stands, the bars and restaurants, the stationer and the grocer, the upscale clothing stores, the galleries and gift shops with their wares from every corner of the globe, and finally to the Oyster Bar Restaurant at the top of Circuit Avenue, where you need advance reservations for dinner on any summer night no matter who you are, but maybe not if you're the president of the United States.

Neighborhoods look less like neighborhoods the farther up-island you go, which is the chief reason that up-islanders consider themselves a superior breed to down-islanders. The up-island towns tuck their neighborhoods away into crannies nestled between its three main arteries: North Road, South Road, and Middle Road. Its neighborhoods are surrounded and separated by open fields, ponds, and forests. There are towns up-island with wonderful names: West Tisbury, Chilmark, Gay Head. Its streets have sweet-sounding names: Pinkletink Road, Blueberry Ridge Lane. There is a corner named Beetlebung, a fishing village called Menemsha. Each little hamlet has its special, rarefied charm and its landmarks: Alley's General Store and the Agricultural Hall in West Tisbury, Beetlebung corner and Menemsha harborfront in Chilmark, the Moshup Trail and the multicolored Gay Head cliffs. In Gay Head live most of the last remaining descendants of Martha's Vineyard's earliest inhabitants, the Wampanoag tribe of Native Americans, whose arrival on the island predates the first white settlers by many hundreds of years.

The farther up-island one goes, the more likely it is that the children one sees are summertime children, but because their houses are farther apart and often hidden from view, it is harder to see them at play. I imagine that they do all of the things that down-island kids do, and hope (because I am older than they) that their distance from the more citified, down-island amusements means that their pastimes reflect it. Maybe they create their own amusements, or do more of the country things—berry picking, horseback riding, tree climbing, and fair-going—the things of which childhoods are made.

Down-Island

Five Corners

Having chosen a peripatetic existence for myself, I have converted my car into a private caravan. It carries my lunches, beach equipment, walking shoes, bicycle, and notebooks. Often I begin and end my day at Five Corners in Vineyard Haven, at Bruce Eliot's Holmes Hole Car Rental office, always on the lookout for Johnny Seaview. I figure that I have the best chance of finding him there because it's a favorite haunt for both of us. But, while my appearances there are fairly predictable, Johnny's are not. He comes at different times each day, and some days not at all. We are the proverbial ships passing in the night. Bruce's location across the street from the Black Dog Bakery is ideal. With a cup of coffee and a Black Dog muffin, I can sit on his wooden chair looking out at the vehicular and pedestrian traffic on Beach Street, listen to him communing with tourists, or chat with him when there is a break in the action. Bruce's endless repertoire of pitches for renting his cars never ceases to amuse me, and they go well with his Wonder Boy looks, smooth talk, and savviness.

"Take *that* car, Lucy, it matches your hair," or "Listen, you've come all the way from Chicago. For a few dollars more you and the Mrs. can see the island in style. Come on, when was the last time you took her for a spin in a convertible? Think about it, she's not in Chicago; she's on vacation in Martha's Vineyard."

All summer long, Bruce operates on overdrive—waiting on customers, washing and waxing his fleet, running around with a phone at his ear. He can see dollar signs in front of his eyes, and he doesn't care who knows it. Bruce, a Connecticut-born transplant, is the *new* Martha's Vineyard, the go-get-'em entrepreneur unconcerned about the traffic problems and the preservation of old island ways—a good-time guy with an eye for a girl and a car.

Bruce is always adding oo-la-la cars to his fleet: souped-up convertibles, old "woody" wagons, and flashy, bright-colored Danish electric cars that look like toys. "We give our customers what they want," he boasts. The electric ones rent for ninety-nine dollars for three hours' use. (As compared to a standard, no-frills automobile, which can be had for forty-five dollars a day). Despite Bruce's warning not to take the electric models on bumpy roads, his customers don't always follow his rules, like the couple barely out the door one day when their car went dead.

"They didn't do what I said," rails Bruce. "I told them to stick to the main roads, but they were those crunchy types who think it's environmentally correct to cruise around in an electric car."

One of the first things I've done as soon as I moved to the island is to arrange with the management to spend some time at the Black Dog General Store, a small, unimposing wood-framed building set back from the street around the corner from Bruce's place. I feel an urgency to get a firsthand look at the business. I've read all about the store and its black dog logo. It has contributed as much in its canine way as celebrities have in their human way to putting Martha's Vineyard on the map. The image of the black labrador emblazoned on T-shirts, sweatshirts, and coffee mugs has leapt onto the pages of national newspapers and magazines, where prominent people in Black Dog attire are pictured prominently. Islanders say that on most days from May through October, the line in front of the store winds, snakelike, around the block, compelling management to hire friendly greeters (a.k.a. bouncers) to guard the entrance, control the number of active customers inside, and prevent mayhem among the waiting customers outside. Everyone in the world, so it seems, now covets something bearing the Black Dog emblem. And, sure enough, by nine o'clock on this drizzly July morning, a long line has already formed. Enthusiastically I take up my post next to Paul, today's friendly greeter.

"Move to your left, please. Keep to your left, please. Sir, can *you* move to *your* left, please? Madam, can *you* do the same?" Paul repeats in broken-record rhythm to his captive audience outside the door. "The line's like this all day long every day, rain or shine. My job is to keep the waiting people entertained and make sure they're not blocking the exit. It can get stressful. People just can't fathom why they have to stay in a line." The words are barely out of his mouth when two women in a hurry approach him attempting to bypass the line. "Listen, I have to catch a boat. Can you let me in for just a minute? I only want a few things," says the first one. "Look, I just wanna look around. Can't you see that I've got children with me?" says the second.

"Sorry, wish I could, but . . ." and then the old standard, "If I do it for you . . ." Then a litany of sorries. "Sorry, Ma'am, but you've got to stay back. You can't step over this line." "Sorry, you have to wait in line. Sorry," he repeats to the now-indignant women, one of whom shouts in parting that Paul is the rudest person she's met on the island. Paul's stress level is rising. "See what I mean. They just don't get it. And then we've got the people in there." He points to the T-shirt counter. "Look at them. Some of them have been browsing for half an hour. They know they can get the *necessities* next door at the bakery."

What necessities? Every item in the store bears the famous Black Dog emblem—mugs, plates, umbrellas, dog bowls, bandannas, pogo sticks, tote bags, caps, bags of granola, sweatshirts, and T-shirts in every size and color—but how did any of these things qualify as *necessities*? "Is a tote bag more or less necessary than a T-shirt?" I inquire of Paul. "There's nothing here that anybody *needs*."

"I can't believe that you don't know that these tees, sweats, and caps are *absolute* necessities." He explains, "Everyone has to have them. No one would leave the island without them. There's an express-line counter just for those things next door at the bakery. We've already run out of sweats over here. On damp days like this, we sell a ton of them."

Soon Paul and I are joined in conversation by the line's front flank. A chubby couple from western Massachusetts announce that they've been waiting a long time to outfit their labrador, "just like the one on the emblem," says the wife. They *need* Black Dog shirts for the dog, their friends, and most of their relatives. She explains, "We had to come here to get them because every time we tried ordering by phone from the catalogue, the line was busy." A man behind them *needs* something for his dog, too. As the line moves, new voices chime in. "I'm an *emblem* sort of guy," says a young man with an older woman by his side. "I'm trying to explain to my mother what all of the fuss is about. She's never heard of this place." An *emblem* sort of woman, an avowed collector of logos, is buying Black Dog products for all her friends, except her boyfriend. He wouldn't wear one if you paid him. Neither would Paul, but he has to make sure there are no managers within earshot before admitting that it's de-classé to wear them on the island.

Before long, it's apparent that customers cluster into categories. There is the marketing theorist type. This type is well represented. A middle-aged gentleman: "It doesn't help the lines that Brooke Shields and André Agassi wear these products. They showed them decked out in Black Dog apparel in *People* magazine. Those photos are what make these T-shirts necessities. If Brooke and Andre and the president of the United States have them, then everyone else has to. It's crazy when you think about it, but it makes you feel like you gotta have one, too. That must be why I'm here," he says with a self-deprecating chuckle. A gray-haired lady from Boston, her husband/entrepreneurial partner beside her, has been plumbing the Black Dog phenomenon for lessons to apply to their business in Boston. "We know why it's successful. It says Martha's Vineyard without saying Martha's Vineyard," she declares, and immediately attracts another kindred spirit. A young, very pregnant woman from California: She takes the beliefs of the marketing theorists to new heights. "The Black Dog management has demonstrated brilliance in turning their products into status symbols. It's all psychological. Unconscious. You're being duped, but you go for it anyway. Imagine attaching your self-esteem to a T-shirt, to a symbol. It won't do your self-esteem any good to wear one here on the island, but if you come from some distant community, you can feel really special in a Black Dog tee." Her own baby-to-be and her mother-in-law, thanks to this woman's thoughtfulness and stamina, will soon be feeling special in L.A.

But the marketing theorists are not the only group in attendance. A woman with a southern accent is of the Proud to Be Here variety. "I only came here for the Black Dog," she declares. So did a male Texan. "My vacation would be spoiled without a Black Dog tee." By contrast, a sleek-looking New York brunette belongs to the Ashamed to Be Here school. "I'm only here because my house guests want these T-shirts, and . . ." She is interrupted suddenly by a female voice, from farther down the line, hollering to Paul. "Do you know if Jackie has ever been here?"

"I don't know," he answers, then whispers to me that if a celebrity were to appear now, he'd move him/her to the head of the line and through the store posthaste.

A mother with several young children in tow who has been listening and looking increasingly frustrated finds an opening and signs in as Disdainful of Everything Black Dog. (There are many like her on the island.) "This is sickening. These lines here. It's one of the main reasons we're leaving. I've lived here most of my life, first in the summers, then year-round after I was married. We loved it here, the quietness and the serenity, but that's all gone. Now it's one continuous traffic jam. The Vineyard used to be funky and fun, but now it's a two-class society. The almighty dollar has ruined it." Then, giving up her place in the line, she pulls me aside. "The Black Dog is a big part of the island's ruin. It has created a subculture. Turned this place into a resort instead of a nice place to live and raise a family. These tourists don't see that they're bringing the traffic with them; that they *are* the traffic that they complain about. So, we're leaving, just packing up the family and heading for another remote location where we can raise our family in peace. Our kids are sad about saying good-bye." There is bitterness in her voice as she speaks. "The only reason I'm here today is to get T-shirts for the kids because they want them as mementos of the island."

A few hours of observing and listening, and my mission is accomplished. I thank Paul, and bid him and my informants from the line farewell. Over lunch, I ponder why Black Dog T-shirts are the only suitable island mementos for the kids. Why not seashells or books? Paul is right: No one can leave the island without one. Not even me. I have a faded Black Dog T-shirt I bought in 1991. I have never thought of it as a necessity, nor do I feel special when I wear it. On my morning walks in Boston, I pass countless people wearing them. (I must remember, though, to wear it the next time I'm in L.A.) After a morning in the Black Dog line, I understand (because my informal customer survey has yielded the answers) why the T-shirts are necessities, and have seen and heard with my own eyes and ears how the demand for them draws people to the island.

Since that day, I have also learned that the blame for the fallout from the Black Dog bonanza follows a circular course, falling first and longest on the tourists, then on the merchants, then on the college students, then the day-trippers, then the renters and back around again. The locals are exempt. Blame is their reusable, recyclable commodity, ever so friendly to their insular environment. Besides, they buy and wear their *necessities* in the off-season.

When the blame lands on the Black Dog owners and managers, they respond the way everyone does when forced to look their own dazzling success in the face. First, they tell you about the good things they do (all of which are true). They talk about the way they support the island by hiring its residents year-round even in the dead of winter, when it isn't cost effective. How they have a local silkscreen business, Marianne's, do all the Black Dog emblems on the apparel items with the help of resident employees. How the Black Dog contributes generously to island social causes (true). How Robert Douglas, the owner of the Black Dog enterprises, loves the sea and takes people out sailing every summer on his magnificent schooner, the *Shenandoah* (true). Then they give you a brief lesson on envy. Tell you about their unscrupulous imitators who are marketing Dead Dog tees and Bad Dog tees—the one with the black dog lying prostrate on the shirt's front emblem, the other with the dog sitting in shitting position. They tell you about their unsuccessful attempts to sue these aspiring T-shirt parodists. They describe the extremes to which the parody has gone, such as the store in Edgartown that sprang A Year of the Dog Campaign and displayed every dog item in its window *except* the Black Dog. Then there was the Vineyard woman, long ago departed to New York, who had designed the original logo way back when, and has now surfaced in court to extract a share of the profits.

After I hear it all, I think maybe it is possible that nothing hurts quite so much as success.

Oak Bluffs

From my starting point at Bruce's Five Corners location (known in bygone days as Holmes Hole), it is easy to get anywhere on the island because the main roads from there lead directly or connect to others heading to all the most popular island destinations. Despite the crush of traffic, there is no traffic light there, nor anywhere else on the island, with the exception of a blinking light on the Edgartown Road. Oak Bluffs is easily accessible, a few miles east down Beach Street, and by summer's end, it will become my favorite place on the island, but in these early days, the town and I are in the get-acquainted stage. Right away, though, I feel a chemistry, a subliminal tap at the core of myself. It seems to have its source in memories of things past, memories that have been lying in wait for a jolt.

Oak Bluffs is my jolt. It pulls me back to my own island summers, to laughing children slamming screen doors, to grown-ups in rocking chairs gossiping about everyone who passes by their porches. There is one difference, though. I grew up in a white summer community, and here is one of the largest African-American summer colonies anywhere in America. Still, it feels familiar, connected to another part of my life that left me mistrustful of white elites.

In the quasi-southern environment of Washington, D.C., in the mid-1950s, people of color were everywhere except my suburban neighborhood or the swanky, all-white, distinctly Protestant private high school that I attended. There I was a member of a minority group of girls with Jewish surnames. Our classmates were southern belles and D.C. debutantes. We were not invited to their balls. It was my first brush with overt ethnic prejudice. I got the bigger picture quickly: There was a hierarchy—a white elite on top and a black populus on the bottom, and me and my kind somewhere in the middle.

Ever since, I have been suspicious that the mightiest among us are often, with some notable exceptions, the unkindest. I've been to summer colonies where upper crusts look thicker than most anywhere else. All white: white for tennis and for golf, white sails, white houses, white people. Martha's Vineyard has its share of this ambience too, up-island and down, but not in Oak Bluffs. That's what I like about it. In Oak Bluffs, the circle bordering the Methodist campground is (and has always been) a white enclave, but move out beyond it to the adjacent neighborhoods, and the population darkens.

And Oak Bluffs' history has something to do with my preference for it.

Oak Bluffs was Cottage City until 1907, so called for its famous gingerbread cottages, with their decorative cornices and porches, pastel facades, and A-frame structure (mimicking the shape of the first Methodists' tents). First built in the mid-1800s in the circle around the Methodist campground, and later in circles farther out (some were moved from the original campground site to other locations), these cottages stand today as the best-preserved examples anywhere in the world of the carpenter's Gothic architectural style. But aside from its architectural significance, Cottage City had another distinction. It was developed for summer people whose origins were decidedly humbler than those of their wealthier neighbors in Edgartown and elsewhere on the island. Although mostly settled by white people from various Massachusetts cities and towns, Cottage City was home to Cape Verdeans and other Azoreans who had come there before, during, and after the whaling days. At the beginning of the twentieth century, the area began to become a summer haven for African-Americans.

* * *

Charles Shearer was one of the first black homeowners on Martha's Vineyard. The journey from his birth into slavery on a Virginia plantation to home ownership on Martha's Vineyard was long. He had grown up in Appomattox, the infamous town where Lee surrendered to Grant in 1865. After the war, Charles was admitted to Hampton Institute, and after he graduated he remained there as a teacher for more than a decade. While at Hampton, he met and married a fellow student who was a Blackfoot Indian. It was a natural liaison for him. On the plantation in Virginia, he had known Native Americans. They had taught him crafts.

Eventually, Charles and his wife decided to move north. They came to Boston, where he found employment as a head waiter in a hotel restaurant. He was overqualified for the job, but the pay was good, good enough for him to buy a house on the outskirts of town.

"Grandpa was a dapper man," his grandaughter, Doris Jackson, tells me when we meet at her house in suburban Boston. "He dressed in shirts and ties and a panama, and he was going places. For him to buy property at that time, the early 1900s, was an amazing achievement. He was a very religious man, too, and he'd heard about these Methodist campground meetings that were happening on Martha's Vineyard, where people came for the summer and lived in tents. He wasn't interested in the tent part, only in buying some property on the island. He joined a group, the Odd Fellows, who were brought together by their interest in buying property. Well, with a lot of effort and negotiating, he was finally able to get what he wanted—a house on the Vineyard at the bottom of a hill in Oak Bluffs. He was a pioneer. He sold that first house when he found one at the top of the hill, and that's where he lived every summer until he died in 1934. That house is still in the family. We own nine houses now. He paved our way."

Doris's appearance is deceiving. From the information she gives, I guess that she is in her late seventies, but she has the figure and litheness of a much younger woman. She is so light-skinned that had I not known that she was Shearer's grandaughter, I might have taken her for white. Whenever Doris speaks of her grandfather, her face brightens. She remembers his kindnesses to all of his grandchildren, the many Sundays when he took all five of them to the Tabernacle for church. While she talks about him, she moves around the house opening desk drawers, looking in bookcases to find photographs, check on dates, make sure she is telling it right. "Now, let's be sure to look that up," she keeps saying whenever she is unsure of her facts.

In between her checking and cross-checking, some of it successful, some not, Doris continues with the story of her grandfather. "Grandpa's friends from New York and Boston kept coming to visit us in the summer." By the early twenties, the family decided to turn the home into a boarding house. The Shearer daughters took over. "We only had nine tiny rooms, and not many bathrooms, but once we opened Shearer Cottage officially, prosperous, well-educated blacks came to stay with us, people like Adam Clayton Powell, Paul Robeson, Harry Burleigh. Some of them stayed all summer. They couldn't get rentals in those days. With us, they had room and board. Islanders came to Shearer Cottage, too. Our dining room was famous, and so was the entertainment we offered after dinner. On one very special occasion, the Commodores performed there. We had charity benefits. My sister started a summer theater and bought another property called Twin Cottages, which became another of our boarding houses. Those were heady days, full of excitement and energy. We're going strong today, renting rooms for short stays and houses for longer ones, but we don't have our dining room anymore, nor any theater since my sister Liz passed away. Those special times are gone."

By the mid-to-late thirties, blacks could rent and buy houses. Grandpa Shearer had started something. Today the Shearer descendants—six generations of them—own island property.

If Oak Bluffs is my kinda town, Royal Bolling's is my kinda house. It sits at the far end of Narragansett Avenue (my kinda street), just up from Sea View Avenue along the beachfront, facing the street with a good side view of the water. His is not a gingerbread cottage, though there are several on the street, but a big house fitting snugly between the abutting houses in the style of its gingerbread neighbors. On Bolling's front porch sits a series of the most inviting rocking chairs I've ever seen (and I've seen rocking chairs!), caned chairs with long, ornate spindles. Passing by, I have admired them often enough. This morning, because I am slightly acquainted with Mr. Bolling, I have the opportunity to sit in one. I tell him how much I admire his chairs. "They look antique, but they're not. They're made in the Dominican Republic," he tells me.

Royal Bolling is still a handsome man despite his advancing years. In his working days, he was one of the first black state representatives in the Massachusetts legislature, and the owner of a real-estate business in Boston.

"What brought you to Martha's Vineyard?" I ask him as we rock.

"I knew that property near the water was valuable, and besides, I was in the market for a summer place for my twelve kids. A friend of mine already had a place and called me one day to say 'Royal, I've got just the place for you.' But the place was part of an estate whose heirs were spread around the country. The title wouldn't clear until back taxes were paid, so I rented for two summers. Three years after the negotiations began, the house was mine. It was one of the best experiences of my life, bringing the kids down here for that first time. We had a VW station wagon with an open roof. They loved the ride down and the trip over on the boat."

And he has had his own thrills while living in the house.

"One morning I heard children's voices in the next yard, and I looked over and there was Martin Luther King, Jr., and his kids playing in my next-door neighbor's yard. He was my hero. I couldn't believe my eyes. I had known him a long time back before he was famous, when we were fraternity brothers. I'm the one who paddled his rear end to initiate him, but seeing him like that in the yard, that was something."

Royal and I talk for a while about the black presence in Oak Bluffs. From him, I get another slice of history. "By the nineteen thirties, a substantial community of black people had formed. A lot of the buyers were former servants of wealthy white summer residents. Some had houses willed to them by their employers. The word spread up and down the East Coast. An island where you wouldn't be discriminated against and where people of modest means could own property! Once the word was out, everyone came. In the nineteen fifties, with as little as forty-five hundred dollars in your pocket, you could get a ten-room house like mine."

Now that he has retired, he comes down to the island from May through October, then returns to Boston for the winter. From his point of view, the racial climate is better on the island than in the city, with more mixing between blacks and whites.

"Oh, I think the Realtors here steer blacks to Oak Bluffs more than to other parts of the island, even if the prospective buyers have a lot of money, but then, too, there's a natural tendency for people to flock to their own kind. The new people who are coming are higher income. They like to be where the action is, and the action is here," he said with a chuckle.

It is now midmorning and the street resounds with voices. "Morning, Royal," the women on the opposite front porch call out. "Morning, Ruth, morning, Mildred." And passersby stop, too. "Howya doin', Royal?" And children pour out of houses and convene on the street, waving at the porch-sitters as they move, hollering their greetings. No sooner have I vacated my rocker than a neighbor is sitting in it, and I've found another one across the street on the Dowdelles' front porch.

Mildred, Ruth, Catherine, and their widowed mother, Ozella, share the big house opposite Royal's. The three daughters, now middle-aged, are retired teachers with grown children who, along with their husbands and parents, had been able to pool enough money to buy the house in 1956. They put up 50 percent of the cost and took out a ten-year mortgage on the remainder.

"Everything was done to discourage us from getting this place, from the amount of the down payment to the choice of the bank. The previous owner was white, but we came at a time when other houses on the street were 'turning,'" Mildred explains, pointing to four houses nearby. "They all turned at the same time. None of us knew each other then. When black people started moving in here, the white people ran, and more blacks bought homes. And the funny thing was, in the nineteen-eighties, when this place was really on the map, a lot of those white sellers came back begging to buy. Right after Chappaquidick the property values started going sky high. We bought at the right time. If we had waited, we wouldn't have been able to afford this place. But, as I was saying, back in the fifties, the atmosphere was cold. When we moved in, the white man next door moved right out. That's all changed. Now there's a lot of interracial camaraderie on Narragansett Avenue."

The Dowdelles enjoy reminiscing about the good old days before the onslaught of visitors, the days when they could walk into town without being overrun by a crowd. For a while in the eighties during the housing bust, it looked as if they might get their island back, but then in the nineties, President Clinton came and everybody who had stopped coming returned, followed by more. It was spoiling their way of life, but the Steamship Authority kept encouraging the influx by adding more boats and ferrying more cars. Property taxes went up, and prices for food and other necessities rose so much in the summer that the island was becoming much less affordable. Although the Dowdelles feel the island is still a safe place, they no longer think it prudent to leave their doors unlocked at night. Those days are gone. The days when the police were your friends, when they knew you and cared about you.

The talk reminds Catherine of an incident a few years ago when her son didn't come home on time, and the police kept her calm. "They drove around checking on all the parties. When they found him, they called me to tell me he was on his way home."

And Ruth recalls how the postmen knew them. "It was a secure little island then. One of my friends came to the island. She'd forgotten our address, so she went to the post office and got it. Best of all, though, was the time a friend wrote a letter to the three of us. She addressed it THE THREE SISTERS, OAK BLUFFS, MASSACHUSETTS, and the postman delivered it."

Summers have always been busy for the Dowdelles. Porch-sitting and hopping take up a lot of their time. Because their porch is located so close to the water, it is a popular gathering place. Sometimes they'll return home from their errands, like Mama and Papa Bear, to find lots of neighbor bears rocking in their chairs, enjoying the breeze! And, when the Dowdelles aren't on their own porch, they're on others', or at church or meetings of their women's club, The Cottagers.

"It started out in the nineteen fifties when thirty-five women met for tea, five times a summer. Now there are eighty-three dues-paying members. We own our clubhouse. We raise money for island causes and sponsor classes for our members. Our meetings are held every other Wednesday morning throughout the season," says Mildred.

Every October, the Dowdelles move to Florida, and return to the island with the warm weather in May. It amuses them to know people who are so devoted to the island that they never leave, like one of their male friends who brags about it to everyone. "I've been to America once," he boasts. "I went to Providence."

Royal Bolling and the Dowdelles make me promise to call on Ruth Hatton up the street. "She'll tell you a lot about this place," they assure me.

As I approach Ruth's big white corner house farther up the block, people of all ages are gathered on the sidewalk, facing the porch. And there sits the high priestess of Narragansett on her rocking-chair throne, conducting her audiences. She is a heavyset, light-skinned black woman who looks younger than she is reputed to be.

"Howya doin', Jimmy? You're late getting around to see me this summer. Is that the new baby? Oh, bring him on up here and let Auntie Ruth hold him. My, my, he looks just like you did when you were his age. Hi, there, Sadie, come on up and see the new baby. Isn't he sweet? Spittin' image of his father, wouldn't you say?"

And on she goes until she has greeted everyone assembled there. Finally, when there is a lull in the action, and I have had a chance to explain my presence, she invites me onto the porch, but our conversation is instantly interrupted by a young woman just then passing by. Ruth talks to her briefly and, when we are alone again, confides to me, "She's a lovely young woman. Just got married. She consulted me before she did it. They all do. I've watched them all grow up."

As I have already told her what her neighbors have said about her, she has little choice but to do her best to live up to her reputation. First, she takes me on a house tour, and talks to me about the town as she's ushering me through the rooms.

"Now, don't let anyone tell you that there isn't prejudice right here in Oak Bluffs. Look at those houses around the campgrounds. They're all white, maybe one or two black families, but that's it. I go to the Episcopal church in Vineyard Haven. Those parishioners know me, but they still snub me, talk right over my head to the person next to me. They're very obvious about it. The priest isn't that way, though. See, when blacks first came here, they lived over there in the Highlands. They owned hand laundries that catered to white folks. When I came with one of my girlfriends in 1957, we stayed in a rooming house. We'd go down to the beach in Edgartown, but we didn't feel comfortable there. If it weren't for Adam Clayton Powell making a fuss, we blacks wouldn't have gotten a golf course and a relaxing place to swim. My husband and I bought this house in nineteen-sixty-five, but it was a stretch for us so we rented rooms until nineteen-eighty-two. Then we sold our house on Long Island and moved here year-round."

The house tour ends in her kitchen. "This is Ruth Hatton's kitchen," she says proudly. "Before my husband died, there was many a party right here. All of our friends came. We couldn't have children, you see, and my husband didn't want to adopt, so our friends and their families meant a lot to me."

My morning on Narragansett Avenue gives me an appreciation for what life was like in the old days for black people in

Oak Bluffs. I want to know more about what it's like now for a younger generation, so I invite my friend Candi to lunch one day when I'm in Boston. She likes talking about the Vineyard.

"I've been coming to Oak Bluffs for a part of every summer since I was a kid. It's the place in the world where I feel most comfortable, because it's a black community where no one questions who you are or whether you're OK. There's no other place in America where such a large collection of black folks vacation. White folks use the island for isolation, to get away from it all. Not us. In the winter, we live and work in the white world, and no matter who you are or how far you have come, you're not equal in a white society. It's a constant proving ground. For African-Americans, the Vineyard isn't only a place to relax and let down your hair. It's a big cultural and educational network, a launching pad for careers. Our kids can get professional mentoring there and develop connections for jobs all over the country. National political campaigns for black candidates are sprung from there. Now West Coast black folks come because there's nothing comparable where they are. The rents keep going up, and the people keep coming."

Candi's friends, a handsome, middle-aged couple named Ronni and Bill Lytle, loved the place so much that they bought a summer house before they owned a winter house in Connecticut. Bill had visited the island off and on through college. He came at the end of the Inkwell era, the years when the Inkwell beach was the "black" beach (while all the others were "white") and the hangout for a group of prominent black men who called themselves The Houndogs. The movie *Inkwell* was based on the scene on the beach during that time.

After military duty, marriage to Ronni, and a stint in Vietnam, Bill returned to visit friends who owned houses there. In 1968, the Lytles bought theirs on the outermost perimeter of the Highlands, the area of Oak Bluffs where the black community originated. Their house overlooks Oak Bluffs harbor.

"We felt like we belonged here, like we were around people like ourselves. Look, we just arrived last night, and one of our California friends has already been over to greet us. And it's not just the social life," explains Ronni.

"That's right," adds Bill, "I've made a lot of valuable business connections here. It's not the main reason we came here, but the network is here, and people use it aggressively. Our kids benefit from it, too. I'm the owner of a manufacturing business. In the winter, I'm around white people. I feel like I have to be 'on,' because most of the time I'm the lone black person in the crowd. I feel like I'm being judged and examined, so I'm not relaxed. We prepare our kids for that, because it's a fact of their lives—the endless scrutiny by white society. This is the best and biggest black summer colony anywhere. It's a letdown when you go home, though."

"So you don't feel any racism here?" I ask Bill.

"If it's here, it's not obvious. We're not confronted with it. There are very clear areas, though. We're isolated from other groups. We've never tried to go to the Edgartown Yacht Club. We don't give a damn about it, nor do we have negative feelings about day-trippers and tourists. Everybody should be able to come here, but we don't want it to be overrun. We do care about preserving the island environment and the natural resources, so we're against overdevelopment, and we've done whatever we can to help prevent it."

"Do you ever have your white friends down for a visit?"

"Oh, yeah," answers Ronni, laughing while she goes to find a photograph to show me. "See, here they are. We invite them down one weekend every summer. We call it our *white weekend.*"

When the Lytles introduce newcoming friends from California to the "scene" on Circuit Avenue on summer evenings, their friends are invariably stunned. "They can't believe that the town is so accepting of two thousand kids, white and black, just 'hanging out' on Circuit Avenue. It blows them away that parents aren't worried and don't think it is dangerous," says Ronni.

Even for one as familiar with it as I, the "scene" is spectacular every time. On Saturday nights, it's at its best—an adolescent takeover, youth on parade, a hybrid of fancy and funky. Sidewalks jammed, street traffic stalled. The Circuit Avenue kids fit every description: bejeweled, body-pierced white kids; dreadlocked blacks; clean-cut collegiates, black and white. White couples, black couples, interracial couples, hands entwined. Girls in form-fitting minidresses. BMWs and Volvos, four-wheelers and jeeps, radios blaring rap music and rock. Guys on motorcycles with girls clinging tight to their waists. Drugged-out kids and ice-cream-cone kids. And cops on the beat, just watching it all, trying in vain to move traffic along.

"Who are all these kids? They don't all live here, do they?" are the questions I put one Saturday night to a black cop whom I've met once before.

He replies, "There's the kids who live here year-round, then there's the summer kids, and then there's this whole subculture of kids who are kinda like nomads. Officially, they're homeless. They live anyplace they can find on the island until the cold weather sets in. Then they move on. They can give us trouble when the season ends. Breaking and entering, stuff like that."

"What are the summer problems?"

"Drugs, drugs, and more drugs," he explains while trying to get a convertible full of young black men to move along. In response, the men were neither rude nor especially polite, but they annoy the cop. "These are the ones who get to me, these rich black kids. I don't know what it is about them. They seem condescending to me. I have an easier time with the rich white kids. Maybe it's because I'm used to them. They've been around longer."

All over Oak Bluffs on most any summer night, there are side-shows of one sort or another, out of range of the Circuit Avenue "scene." There are dances, concerts, and lectures in the Methodist tabernacle, and band concerts in Ocean Park, but if these activities don't suit your fancy, you can stroll along the beach or the harbor front.

The L-shaped harbor front is a haven for tourists. On both arms of the L, there is a boardwalk complex of restaurants, souvenir shops, and ice cream parlors. Alongside the long arm, yachts are moored with their sterns facing the old Wesley Hotel and the gingerbread cottages on Lake Avenue.

There is no show like the tourist show. And for the ultimate in people-watching, the evening boat people take the prize. They remind me of a wish I clung to throughout childhood. I wanted my father to buy us a Chris-Craft. What was a summer in Maine without one? I'd insist. To me, a cabin cruiser was an obvious necessity when one lived on an island, and I could not understand why Dad didn't see it. "Look at what fun those people are having, sitting up there on the bow in their bathing suits, smiling and waving to us marooned here on shore."

"Too expensive and boring besides," he'd say and leave it at that. Expensive, perhaps, but boring, never, I thought back then.

But now that I've made an exhaustive study of the Oak Bluffs flotilla, I'm relenting. Whether it is the *Skip-to-My-Lou* from Wilmington or the *Lucky Lady* from Boston or any of the others (mostly from Wilmington, where, I am told, there is a tax advantage for boat owners), each boat houses a pink-skinned man and a matching woman swiveling in matching white Naugahyde seats, sipping matching cocktails from matching glasses, wearing matching frowns on their faces. Nope, they are not having fun, and yup (I hesitate before admitting it), they definitely look bored.

"OK, you win," I acknowledge silently to my father.

On other nights I watch the pedestrian tourists from the picnic tables at one or another of the outdoor clam bars along the boardwalk. I like eating my steamers and gazing at the endless stream of T-shirted, camera-laden, shopping-bag-toting people parading past or lolling on benches inhaling cigarettes and breath. Once while there, I make eye contact with an overweight woman clad in the standard tourist outfit: T-shirt and shorts. She smokes while doing exercises to straighten her posture. When she catches my eye, she explains, "I'm trying to sit up straight and not slouch. I don't want to get that osteoporosis."

Another time when I am seated at a table alone, I am soon joined by a man on my right, and across from him, his female companion. She asks the waitress how to pronounce the name of the clams she's been eating. "Are they *kwogs*? I'm not used to eating them with tails on them like this."

"I don't know, but I'll ask the manager."

The waitress returns.

"No, they're not *kwogs*," she says and leaves abruptly.

Now the woman is annoyed and calls the waitress back. "Well, then what are the kinds with the tails?"

"Cherrystones, those are the kind you're thinking of," the waitress reports after another consultation with the manager.

With the woman satisfied at last, the man is free to turn his attention to me. He has a series of questions.

"How's your corn? Your clams? Your chowder? Your salad?"

Before long, the three of us are communicating. The couple are lovers and business colleagues who specialize in the sale of parts for pinball machines. They love the Vineyard, and come every year for a week. This year they're staying at Westwood, which they enunciate rather proudly, as if it is a place of some status that surely I must know about. (I don't, but from their description, it sounds as if it is Ocean Heights.) Eventually, they get around to asking me what I'm doing on the island.

"I'm writing a book about the Vineyard," I tell them, "and I've already decided that you're going to be in it because of the way you pronounced *kwogs*."

"Well, how do you say it, then?" the man asks. "Is it *kwahogs*?"

I laugh. "No it's *Quohogs*," I say, sounding out *Quo*-hog like a know-it-all native, and learning a few days later from some genuine natives that I, too, have gotten it wrong. It's spelled *Quahog* and it's pronounced *Co*-hog.

Impressed with my knowledge of clams, the couple ask me to recommend restaurants. I reel off a few names and mention one that celebrities are reputed to frequent.

"Oh, no, we don't want that. We're anti-status people. We're shorts-and-bathing-suit types," he says, expressing surprise that the Vineyard has a reputation for celebrity chic.

Thereafter, our conversation is devoted to pinball machines, and by the end of it, I am as well versed on that subject as on clams, having discovered the following: (1) There is an annual pinball machine convention in Chicago. (2) The typical machine costs $35,000, but has a very short life because new high-tech, computerized models with a huge array of games are continuously invented. (3) The machines are all made in America, but are sold widely throughout the world. (4) The old machines become obsolete so fast that the factories forget about them, and lose track of the parts, too. (5) The factories refer all inquiries for parts to this couple at The Pinball Resource, who also have a worldwide clientele. (6) Selling pinball parts is a wonderful life, far more enjoyable than working for IBM, their former employer.

"We're anti-corporate people, too," the man says, nudged

into concluding our conversation by his girlfriend, who is eager to move along.

A few weeks into July, and I'm still head over heels in love with Oak Bluffs, but my affection goes unrequited. I give the town my undivided attention. It barely notices me. I am only one of its countless admirers, another outsider looking in, one with a right of passage but no citizenship. My circumstances make me wish momentarily for celebrity. Color me famous, and (so the fantasy goes) I will be instantly embraced, ushered upon arrival into a welcoming coterie. Lacking that, the best I can do is to be friendly and do as the natives do. In summertime, Oak Bluffs natives go to events. My husband and I join them one night at the Portuguese Festival of the Holy Ghost. When we arrive, a bluegrass band is performing in the center of the fairground. Throngs of people are milling about, grouped in clusters, eating, talking, drinking. There are game booths along the sidelines like those at every American fair and carnival. No sign of the Holy Ghost or anything Portuguese, except the *sopa* being served indoors—a thick potato soup mixed with sausage—heavy fare for a hot night. Disappointed by the mismatch between our expectations and the reality, we leave our half-full bowls of *sopa* on the table, take one more turn around the grounds (just in case we missed something), and depart. We hope that the festival's concluding parade down Circuit Avenue the following day will be truer to its ethnic billing. The next morning we join the bystanders along the parade route waiting for the action to begin. Alas, when the "parade" finally passes by, it looks more like a cordon of vehicles than a parade. Spit-and-polished fire trucks, police cars, motorcycles driven in formation by muscular, swarthy men, their midriffs encircled in the arms of halter-topped women. Nothing that says Portuguese here, either.

"Maybe we were supposed to assume that the drivers and passengers were Portuguese," my husband says as we're leaving.

And I'm unlucky again. I have to be off-island for the biggest, most legendary Oak Bluffs summer event—Illumination Night—an annual summer occasion that has been happening for as long as the oldest Vineyarder can remember. It is the night when all the cottages around the Methodist Campground are illuminated with decorative lamps, and everyone on the island comes to see the sight. This is supposed to be one celebration that never disappoints, so I am sorely disappointed to be missing it.

The International Festival is my partial compensation. Held in Waban Park, an open green space alongside the shoreline, this festival is a gem, a true multiethnic celebration apropos of its Oak Bluffs setting. It offers an afternoon and evening of storytelling, drama, and music from around the world, performed by people of African, Latin American, and European stock. Here I mingle easily in the crowd for hours, luxuriating in the ambience, inhaling the salty air. I am welcomed onto strangers' blankets. I make new friends and find some old ones. For as long as the festivities last, I feel a part of a community, a foreigner among fellow foreigners.

When I start playing late-afternoon tennis twice a week at the Island Tennis Club in Oak Bluffs, I notice that I'm beginning to take on a pleasing kind of "insider" status there. I wave to familiar faces on neighboring courts, and when my games are over, I fall into a routine of chatting with the pro. He is a friendly, middle-aged man named Tom Rabbit and he tells a good story. Tom is a Daggett on his mother's side. On Martha's Vineyard being a Daggett has cachet. There's a Daggett Avenue and a Daggett House Inn, so even if I'd never met Tom, I would have known that somebody named Daggett did something significant for Martha's Vineyard. Tom's grandfather, Silas

Daggett, did. In 1872, he built the East Chop Lighthouse. After he built it, he manned its semaphore station, which was one of several on the shipping lane to New York. When he spotted a ship, he'd teletype its location to the home station. Old Silas Daggett was a man of means, too, having made a fortune as a whaling captain. He had other vocations as well. He was the first island water commissioner, and later, when he gave up whaling, he ran a ship store (in addition to his signaling duties). He owned two houses on the island, one a summer place on West Chop, the other a winter residence barely a mile away in Vineyard Haven. He moved there in the winter so that his five children would be close to their school. At the time of his death, he was seventy-two, and his forty-two-year-old wife was six months pregnant. Tom never knew his illustrious grandfather. Silas died when Tom's mother was nine years old.

Only a few Daggets remain on-island—one from the second generation and three from the third. From May to mid-October, Tom resides in the old family homestead, located, conveniently enough, on Daggett Avenue in Vineyard Haven.

The more I talk to Tom, the more I appreciate that his Vineyard biography is noteworthy in its own right. Raised on the island, he stayed there year-round until his teens, when he went to school off-island. Every summer since then, he's lived on-island. For a few years, he lived there year-round. His story goes like this: When he was growing up, his father owned and operated a Vineyard hotel, The Tashmoo Inn, and when he was old enough, Tom was one of the summer help. Long before that, though, before his father was a hotelier, he had been a struggling attorney who resided in the largely Jewish residential area of Brookline, just outside of Boston. Once he opened the inn, one of his Brookline Jewish friends frequented it, and passed the word to all her friends. In those days, Jews weren't warmly welcomed on the Vineyard. The Tashmoo Inn became known for a time as the *Jewish* hotel. When his father retired, Tom came home again, bought the hotel, converted it to a restaurant and racquet club, and ran it for a few years. Then, he embarked on a fairly typical northeastern American's progression: marriage, children, divorce, sale of the business, relocation to Florida. Now he runs tennis clubs in Florida in the winter and this one on the Vineyard in the summer. A point of pride for Tom is the nondiscrimination policy he maintains at the island club. "One of the first things I say to new members is, if you're prejudiced this isn't the place for you. And you want to know something? Even to this day, there are plenty of island clubs where blacks and Jews aren't welcome."

After my talks with Tom, I often wonder about Silas Daggett looking down upon his grandson and his island. Is he grousing in his grave or resting peacefully? Is he sending signals of fair weather or of small-craft warnings?

It takes me most of the summer, but finally, thanks to the kindness of Bob Tankard, I'm a hair's breadth away from feeling like my love for Oak Bluffs is reciprocated. After attending two very intimate events—his family reunion and his high school reunion—I'm what you might call an outside-insider. And I like it.

The Tankard family reunion at the Hibernian Hall is a major event in its own right. Not every family has enough members to fill a hall, and even when they do, they don't usually live in the same place. Most Tankards are year-round island residents.

When I arrive at the party, it has been under way for some time. Music is coming from the bandstand. Tankards are dancing with Tankards: children with their siblings and cousins, adults with their spouses and next of kin. In the far corner of the room, smiling and watching the festivities, sits Mrs. Tankard, like a queen, surrounded by a fawning retinue of relatives.

Food and drink are in plentiful supply even as the evening is drawing to a close. I make my way to Mrs. Tankard. In her seventies now, she can look back over her thirty-three years on the island with pride and pleasure. She recounts for me how the family's Vineyard odyssey began. "It was in the late fifties. I liked listening to Patti Page sing 'Old Cape Cod' on the radio in New Jersey. Every time I heard it, I'd tell myself I had to go there. Finally, one day I did it. 'Let's go to Cape Cod,' I said to my husband out of the blue. A few days later, we piled the kids into the family car and came. It was a muggy, typical Newark summer day, and we were glad to be getting out of town. Well, while we were on the Cape, we took a day trip to Martha's Vineyard. We fell in love with the place, and the following summer we rented a house for five hundred dollars for the season, and brought seven of our ten children with us." She laughs thinking about the low rent and the crazy way the family just "up and left" Newark. "Well, eventually, we had to go back to Newark, but it wasn't for long. My sights were set on relocating the family to Martha's Vineyard permanently. Things were turning sour in Newark. I wrote to a newspaper in New York, called *The Age*, to find out more about the island. They said that it was a good place for black people to live. That clinched it. I knew it would be better for my kids. A year or so later, we bought a house in Oak Bluffs and turned our backs on Newark forever."

As I talk to her, I think I am seeing what she is seeing as she gazes at the activity in front of her. Her daring experiment has worked, and here, right before her eyes, is the pudding and the proof: children grown and prospering, grandchildren growing with every possibility for prosperity. No wonder she looks proud. It is a remarkable achievement, this rerouting of a family's destiny at the urgings of a song, the sweet rendition of its singer:

If you're fond of sand dunes and salt sea air
Quaint little villages here and there
You're sure to fall in love with old Cape Cod.

I find myself at the center of the action once again at the Martha's Vineyard High School class of 1964 reunion. It's a steamy Saturday night at the Portuguese-American Club in Oak Bluffs (the site of the Holy Ghost Festival). The class members eye me suspiciously at first. I know my presence is confusing them. They can't place me. Was I a wallflower thirty years ago? Where was I? Why can't they remember me? I hear them asking themselves these questions silently. I let them stew awhile, then offer my particulars. To good effect. The word spreads around the room. "Yes," I say. "It's true. I am here because I'm writing a book about Martha's Vineyard." People seek me out, eager to tell their own stories and those of their class's eighty-four graduates. Forty-seven still live on the island, about half the class. Amazing to me, considering the scarcity of jobs here. Rosemary is one such. She's been married for thirty years to a home health aide. "But, of course, he does other jobs besides. You have to be a jack of all trades and master of none to live on the Vineyard," she says. Birdie has stayed put, too, and is a nurse at the island hospital. Judy and Nancy have left the island but maintain their bond. After graduation, they lived together in Boston, and eventually married off-islanders, but come regularly to visit at their parents' homes. "The island stays with you even though nowadays it's too crowded," explains Judy. When they were kids they could walk anywhere, go anywhere unchaperoned. There wasn't much to do in the winter, though. That's the good news about the Vineyard now. There's more to do. It puzzles them that this generation of Vineyard kids complains about boredom. "My God, they have cars, roller and ice-skating rinks. All we could do was borrow our parents' cars, drive around, and smoke.

The boys had sports, and we girls put on talent shows. We wore crepe-paper skirts," Judy exclaims. Chris and Barbara join us. He is a conch fisherman with definite opinions about the island's population. "The only people who count here are summer people and winter people. The rest are tourists. They come to look, not to buy, but the Chamber of Commerce works overtime to keep them coming anyway."

Hugging and chatting continues throughout the stand-up cocktail hour, then we line up for the buffet and take our seats at two long tables. Bob Tankard comes to the dais and opens the ceremonies with a moment of silence for their deceased classmates. Then he addresses the gathering by nicknames: Thomas Sheraton Benton as "Mr. Hollywood," someone else as "Mr. Clambake," and a woman named Carol as "The Legs." After the roll call of nicknames, Bob coaxes the senior prom queen to the dais to relive her time of glory, but she appears more embarrassed than delighted by her recoronation, as if she feels that this time around, the queen's mantle doesn't fit.

At the tables, the professionals form one cluster, the workers (and me) another. Seated across from me is Ellen, who confides that she's known about this reunion for two years and hasn't had any "real" food since. She's been at the health club every day slimming down for it. From what I can see of her (a waist-up view) her regimen has worked. Bob continues with class highlighting and jokes. Some of their old teachers are in attendance, and Bob jokes about their classes, which draws big laughs. At conclusion time, he reminds the assembled that they have been a class of "firsts": the first to hold a function outside the school building, the first to put on a talent show. He could have also said, but doesn't, that he was neither the first nor the last, but the only black person in their class.

Ellen, so it appears, is not receiving the attention she has worked so hard to attract. A woman named Sandy is the evening's standout, its prom queen-come-lately. There is a buzzing undercurrent swirling around her. She is glamorous, a femme fatale; the kind of woman one can't visualize as a girl going through an awkward stage. She is dressed in a long, tight-fitting, bare-shouldered, purple-sequined gown with a big slit down one side, revealing a lanky, shapely leg; a study in sexiness. On one of her smooth, bare shoulders, she sports a decorative tattoo which has become the *numero uno* subject of the buzz. The story goes like this: Sandy once stood for a long time near the end of a very long line to see the Steve Allen show. She was afraid she wouldn't be admitted, but she was saved in the nick of time by a tattoo artist. He was scheduled to go on the show and do a demonstration. He needed a volunteer. Sandy accepted.

Wanting to verify the story, I approach her and ask. She smiles pleasantly and answers affirmatively. Then, with a little prodding from me, she tells me a little about her life. She has only recently returned to the island to live, having spent twenty-six miserable years as a married woman in the Midwest. For most of those years, she knew that she'd return to the island permanently one day. But back when she was young, what else would a fourth-generation islander of marriageable age have done? Especially if one lived with a status-conscious divorced mother on the wrong side of the Vineyard tracks. Of course, she'd wed a man reputed to have means and manners. On the Vineyard, that meant one kind of man—a summer man. Sandy followed the script and discovered too late that her hand-picked husband was a man of neither means nor manners. Yankee pride kept her married to him until her only child was through with college. Finally, she was free to come back, and solvent enough to build herself a house.

By the end of this oral biography, I have Sandy pegged as a boutique manager or owner, probably of some shop in Edgartown or Vineyard Haven. I am wrong.

Sandy, the razzle-dazzle girl by night, is a town librarian by day.

Tisbury Township—Vineyard Haven and West Chop

I don't spend all my time in Oak Bluffs. In my mind, the Vineyard has become a trope for the East Coast. Oak Bluffs is Manhattan, Vineyard Haven is Washington, Edgartown is Boston, and Chappaquidick and the up-island towns are the horsey, exurban communities along the Connecticut shore. Vineyard Haven, the biggest town in the township of Tisbury, is a nice second-best to me. Lucky for me that my good friends the Goodmans live there, seemingly among a minority of summer residents who are not from Washington.

The Goodmans use their house year-round; in the off-season as a family retreat; in the summer as a place to be shared with their many friends and relatives. Every week at the Goodmans in the summer is a full-to-the-rafters week. There is hardly a night when Sally or Roger Goodman don't go to the Oak Bluffs or Vineyard Haven boat terminals to greet a new batch of guests. Knowing that I am on-island and living in quarters ill-suited to entertaining, they welcome me warmly into their midst. Almost every weekend throughout the summer, I join them for lively Saturday night dinners. I am grateful for these invitations. Besides the companionship they afford, it is a joy to walk into their warm, old-fashioned kitchen, pick up a drink, and move through their spacious, comfortable rooms out to their huge new deck overlooking the water.

Unfortunately, athough I find the view stunning, the Goodmans feel, based on the terms of the documents they signed upon assuming ownership of the property, they are entitled to a finer view. They regret adding themselves as parties to the long list of property disputes that have become a sine qua non of island life. Nonetheless, a battle with their neighbor has been waging for two years over his refusal to cut those of his trees which spoil their panorama, and the Goodmans are disappointed that all this time has passed without a friendly agreement. The offending neighbor, a man of some prominence, and (judging by the expanse of his property) a man of some means, refuses to give in. Short of baking casseroles and passing them over the hedge, the Goodmans have tried everything to appeal to his good graces. They've taken the neighborly tack, the last-resort legal tack, and combinations of both. Recently, Roger has proposed a mediated solution which would afford both parties a savings that could be rolled over to the benefit of an island cause. Sally has exchanged pleasantries (over the hedge). She has offered to pay for arborists and treecutters, and to seek second opinions. Their neighbor admires her new deck. And around it goes. Now all the Goodmans can do is laugh at the absurdity of it, and recycle it as humorous dinner-table fodder for the incoming guests, all of whom register amusing opinions on what should be done. The lawyers propose improbable legal strategies, the businesspeople and physicians, farfetched financial incentives, and the psychotherapists offer an assortment of zany behavior-modification techniques.

I admire Sally's hostessing savvy. She has it down to a science. By placing fresh folded sheets and towels at the feet of their beds, she signals Sunday's departing guests to make ready for Monday's arrivals. Like the dutiful children in the Madeleine stories, the Sunday people place their used linens in the washing machine and remake their beds, making the preparations for the next shift that much easier for Sally, a Vineyard version of Miss Clavell.

When my next influx of guests is due, I am going to try it myself.

Even if Oak Bluffs is my favorite island location, I have a foothold in Vineyard Haven. The Goodmans' house is my home base on the island. I can stop in unannounced whenever an urge (or a call of nature) strikes. I'm downright sentimental about the privilege. I remember fondly those bygone summers when I could do as I do now at the Goodmans': Walk through the unlocked back door of a familiar cottage, holler out a greeting, hear it echo through unpeopled rooms, and feel secure knowing that it is all right to be alone there, all right to use the bathroom or pluck a snack from the refrigerator. Sometimes I come and go without leaving any evidence of my entry. More often, I write the same note I've written since I learned to write, the one I now leave cheerfully on the Goodmans' kitchen counter. HI, I CAME BY BUT YOU WEREN'T HOME. TOOK AN APPLE AND WENT TO THE BATHROOM. THANKS. TALK TO YOU LATER. LOVE, JANE.

If Vineyard Haven summer houses are known for their elegance, so are those of their near neighbors on Tisbury's West Chop peninsula, but West Chop's elegance has a different flavor. I am familiar with it only because I lived there for a week one summer while attending a women's essay-writing seminar. We would-be writers were housed in a grand old "cottage" on the West Chop beach. Its careless ambience reminded me of my family's smaller, but still substantial, summer house in Maine. This house, like mine, was a study in eclectics, a few valuable but many more worthless paintings, conch shell ashtrays, a few nice antiques, many rickety chairs, vintage appliances, old kitchenware, tattered Orientals, peeling paint, and comfortable, goose-down sofas. It was a Yankee house, sure of itself and convinced of its charm. It spoke to its occupants: "If you touch me up, fix me up, streamline me, you'll spoil my character," and it sparked controversy in our after-dinner conversations in the oceanfront living room. One or two of my classmates volunteered that they found the place charming. They were roundly challenged by a vocal majority who held the opinion that it was not charming, but rather in urgent need of major renovations which, if they were the owners, would begin *IMMEDIATELY*.

Not far from the "seminar" house is a similar one on the beachfront that I've admired many times. It is as gray and immense as its neighbor. By coincidence I have met one of its young occupants, Isabel Smith. She works at the Scottish Bakehouse in West Tisbury, and because I stop there often for their delicious shortbread, we've become acquainted. Her grandparents, the Dennisons, have been renting the big gray West Chop house for fourteen years, and she and her parents, siblings, cousins, aunts, and uncles have been spending all or part of their summers there ever since.

The day Isabel arranges for me to visit the Dennison clan is as gray as the house, and, although it is August, as windy and chilly as a late autumn day. The elder Mr. and Mrs. Dennison, dressed in sweaters and slacks, welcome me into their living room in front of the fireplace. They have been forewarned that I am there in order to hear their accounts of life on "The Chop" (the term of endearment for West Chop). We start slowly, working our way through introductory formalities until we are joined by Isabel, her aunt and uncle, and an assortment of Isabel's cousins. Soon we are off and running down Memory Lane.

They begin with an infamous cocktail party of many summers ago, attended by the West Chop summer folk. Women in chiffon dresses, men in fine summer suits, drank and socialized on the porch, unaware that the floor underneath them was sagging precipitously. The hostess detected the problem, but, not wishing to disrupt the merriment, she absented herself unobtrusively in order to prop up the floor with some old shutters she found in the basement. Meanwhile, though, a hula-hoop contest among the children was under way on one end of the lawn, which drew the entire adult assemblage to one corner of the porch. The rest you can guess—the porchful of dresses and suits, canapés and cocktails, crashed to the ground in an undignified heap!

And we mustn't forget the time, back in the sixties, that the Dennisons' sons dared to invite a winter person, the electrician's daughter, to one of their teenage "makeout" parties. "One of our neighbors let it be known that she had an objection to the girl's presence. We could have been drummed off The Chop," volunteers the senior Mr. Dennison. "Imagine how amused we were. Here was one stuffy lady from West Chop threatening my boys with a dishonorable discharge from this little bastion of snobbery. It happened during the Vietnam era, when they and their peers had begun elevating adolescent unruliness to new heights in order to be discharged, honorably or not, from military duty to the United States Government. But, you see, West Chop has always had a distinct culture with its own rules, and its own pecking order. For example, West Chop people have always regarded the Edgartown people as Old Guard New Yorkers, the type whose days begin with pitchers of bloody Marys. We considered ourselves a superior breed. We climbed out of bed (early) and onto the courts for brisk games of tennis. But not everyone conformed. We've had our eccentrics, too, like my own three-hundred-pound mother who dressed in a black cape whenever she played badminton. She taught her children and grandchildren to tell stories. 'Any story that's worth telling is worth improving,' she'd say in defense of her penchant for playing free and easy with facts."

The elder Mrs. Dennison has been patiently waiting her turn to enter the conversation. She strikes a contemporary note. "Every Sunday morning we all go to church in the casino. We have no preacher, no denominations. Some members are Jewish, but there aren't any blacks, although there are many very distinguished blacks in Oak Bluffs. We sing hymns, and people speak up. Someone tells about the boat he's building. Someone else conveys his thoughts. There are announcements of upcoming secular events and reminders about paying our dues (to the West Chop Association). We all go to church in our tennis whites. No one can be on the courts while the service is in progress, but as soon as it ends, there's a mad dash for the courts. These are the things you just do. You're supposed to be in good taste, and yes, let's face it, in the old days, the West Chop summer daughter was not supposed to date the winter tradesman. Now we're just glad if she's not a lesbian."

"I was always getting in trouble for climbing on the tennis club roof, and sometimes for being on the courts when adults wanted to use them. That was big no-no," recalls the Dennisons' son, Allen, who is now a father, husband, and Providence physician. "Oh, and my father forgot to tell you that our grandmother played the part of a gorilla at a birthday party for my father. Granny dressed in a gorilla suit, and before the festivities began, the gardener hoisted her up in a tree. My grandfather greeted all the arriving children and informed them that the party couldn't begin until a very dangerous gorilla was located and killed. Well, the children hiked all over the property until they were frustrated and exhausted. Finally, menacing sounds and grunts were heard from the tree. Then, to heighten the drama, Grandpa fired a few blanks from a shotgun, and the gorilla slumped into the crotch of the tree. When Granny finally descended wearing a stocking mask and making weird sounds, all the kids shouted, 'That's not a gorilla, it's Mrs. Dennison.' And the funniest thing was that subsequently, Dr. Rainsford, our family doctor and one of our neighbors, came over and chewed out Granny. 'Ever since my son saw your gorilla performance, he's been wetting his bed and having terrible nightmares about gorillas,' he shouted."

All the Dennisons get into the act on the subject of Hurricane

Bob, and how he'd unleashed his wrath the day after the Dennisons' fiftieth wedding anniversary party. The harbormaster had called to warn "Your boat is going out to sea." Then another call came from someone else. "Your boat is dragging. It's about to come through our living-room window. You better get down here." Hurriedly, driving through fierce wind and rain, the Dennison men and the adolescent boys scoured the shoreline looking for the boat. Finally, they found it on a sandbar. They couldn't dislodge it, so they slept on it until two high tides and the harbormaster's launch enabled them to extricate it. It had been a thrilling adventure, and what's more, the boat had emerged undamaged.

Before I have a chance to ask them another question, they ask me one. Do I know, they ask, that *shabby* is *in* in West Chop? By way of an answer, I tell them the story of my brief residency in their neighbor's house, but they tell me one better, about the time Bianca Jagger visited that same house. "She'd sunbathe topless on the West Chop dock, spreading her creams and her lotions all over the place. One of the local grand dames reprimanded her indignantly, 'We don't sunbathe topless in West Chop.'"

"Well, why not?" responded Bianca.

When the word got around that Bianca was there, people who never went swimming went down for a dip. All of West Chop turned out.

"Yeah, even Grandpop went down. He took his camera," said one of Mr. Dennison's adolescent grandchildren. "But he came back disappointed. 'Nothing to see, just a lot of bee stings for my trouble,' he told us."

We come back to *shabby*. "In West Chop, you don't complain to landlords about falling plaster, lumpy beds, and such. That just isn't done. It's supposed to be a privilege to spend many thousands of dollars to rent these wrecks. Come on in the kitchen so you can see what we mean. Look at this fan. It's supposed to clear out the smoke and the fumes." The fan is a tiny, rusty ancient model from which a racket as loud as a motorcycle engine emanates. "See, we put our milk in these chamber-pot pitchers, because they're the only containers in the house. And take a look at this old stove over here. That's where we cook. We have to remember to light the oven whenever we bake or we'll gas ourselves out."

And wanting to make sure that I really and truly understand *shabby* before I take leave, they inform me that it is a West Chop custom to offer vignettes about the summer's high points in church at the end of the season. On one such final occasion, a five-year-old boy rose and announced, "I'll never forget this summer. The best time was the night the whole ceiling fell in."

Other magnets of a personal nature keep drawing me to Vineyard Haven. The Vineyard Studio Gallery, for instance. My husband has been invited by the gallery's owner to exhibit his sculpture there. At the opening, the usual wine and cheese is served, on an outside deck where attractive, well-dressed people are gathered. I linger there long enough to overhear a funny story that an older woman is relating to her younger friend. "I went to a party in Gay Head one evening, and there was this stunning woman there who looked familiar. I introduced myself. 'How do you do?' I inquired, and added, 'I'm sorry, I think we've met before, but your name escapes me.' The woman looked at me with a bemused smile on her face. 'I'm Jackie Onassis,' she said."

Inside the gallery, the conversation centers on people less exalted, closer to my sphere of influence. Four male island artists are talking to my husband, complimenting him on his work. When I enter the room, my husband introduces me and my mission on the island. The talk turns to the local art scene.

How it's a staple of Vineyard life. It's there for the buying and the selling, supplying bread and butter for a lucky few and pure enjoyment (and no cash) for many more. There are plenty of buyers, but not at openings like this. "These people are here to see and be seen. If any of them are going to buy, they'll do it discreetly," explains an artist in the group whose comments are embellished by one of his more garrulous cohorts. "Yup. We've got plenty for everyone right here on the island. Fine art, schlock art, safe art, artists, galleries. And guess what, safe art sells the best. It's summer art. You know, vases, landscapes, portraits of summer houses, children in the sand. But, all that aside, there are some very good artists here, like your present company, for example!"

Barney Zeitz is among them. He, like my husband, is a sculptor who works in steel. According to the grapevine, he is one of the lucky island artists who is commercially successful. When he invites me to visit his home studio in Vineyard Haven, I gladly accept. His modern wood-frame house, which he designed and built, is near the gallery, set on a knoll in a wooded area off the street. Outside and in, I see pieces of his artwork: sculptures, lamps, chandeliers. On the far side of his house, he has a spacious, well-equipped studio, and adjacent to it, outside and under cover, is an area for his welding equipment. Once I've had a good look around the premises, we seat ourselves in his backyard, and I ask him if the rumors of his success are true.

"Yes and no. Yes, if you include my off-island commissions. No, if you mean making a living solely from Vineyard sales. I have an agent in New York, and I go there several times a year. At heart, I'm a city person, but New York is too dirty and unsafe. I make valuable connections on the Vineyard, and I do sell some work here." He recently received a big on-island commission. "Even with all that, though, financial struggle is interminable and tiring. Here, people come right to my studio. I do stained glass and metal work. People here can afford to pay twenty-five thousand dollars for a stained-glass piece. But I don't want to cater exclusively to the wealthy. I'm not into decorating. I have higher aspirations. I want my work to have spiritual meaning."

Can't get more spiritual than one of Zeitz's prize commissions: a metal sculpture he designed for the Holocaust Memorial Museum in Providence. The piece is a twelve-foot tower of steel with the mournful reminder of a Star of David at its base, and as a symbol of hope a flowerlike crown rests at its pinnacle. At first the base was too small, but after consulting with a structural engineer, Barney widened it so that when the sculpture was bolted to the ground it had enough strength and width to support the sculpture in all kinds of weather. The task of getting it to its destination was formidable. "I had fifteen friends, a flatbed, and a hydraulic lift," he notes.

Zeitz has a brooding, searching quality which shows when he speaks about his life on the Vineyard: "I used to visit the island a lot in the sixties. I liked the interracial atmosphere, the beauty and safety, but once I moved here, things weren't so perfect. There wasn't much racial mixing. There was more poverty than I expected. It's the brutality of winter here, the paucity of jobs, and the brutality of summer, inflated rents forcing people to relocate for the season, and alongside that, the sudden reappearance of the big-money crowd. A frenzy of energy and consumption, always in your face. For a while, I got seduced by it. I'd find myself making lamps instead of art. Finally, I just said the hell with it, and went back to making art."

Whenever I'm in Vineyard Haven, I always stop in at the Holmes Hole Car Rental. Or I go across the street to the Wintertide Coffee House, managed by my new good friend, Tony Lombardi. I go there at all times of day to talk to Tony, and I spend many an evening there in the audience for its musical and dramatic performances. The Wintertide has good food, good entertainment, and is dedicated to a good cause. The proceeds from the Wintertide's performances go toward the benefit of island children. Its virtues are not of the righteous kind, but of the wholesome kind: no smoke, no alcohol, almost no fat. Put me there long enough, and I begin to feel myself losing all the remaining traces of insalubriousness that I've been carrying.

These ties I have to Vineyard Haven make me less inclined to attend public events there as a way to feel the pulse of the place. I go to only one, the Tisbury street fair on Main Street in Vineyard Haven. Unfortunately, it seems to be just like its counterparts in Boston and New York, except that here the pedestrians and prams crowd into a shorter, narrower corridor. I am hemmed in by the same sidewalks of trinkets and T-shirts, food stalls reeking with the pungent unctuousness of curbside cookery, lemonade and ice-cream stands, miniature rides for the kiddies. A pregnant pedestrian catches my eye. She's wearing a bumper sticker on her belly. SLOW DOWN, YOU'RE ON AN ISLAND NOW, it reads, and I consider myself lucky to have found at least one distinctive thing about this fair.

It is his uniqueness, the agitprop that accompanies the mere mention of his name—"You won't meet anybody else like him"—that provides the impetus to continue my search for Johnny Seaview, though by midsummer I feel less urgency about it than before. There are other Vineyard curiosities to distract me, and I've grown more confident that, sooner or later, Johnny and I will cross paths. On the advice of those familiar with Johnny's comings and goings, I've even narrowed the hunting ground. Now I limit myself to the Five Corners area in Vineyard Haven, and more specifically to three establishments: Bruce Eliot's storefront, the Cumberland Farms convenience store, and The Artcliff Diner, all within walking distance of one another.

All for nought. I miss every time, sometimes by a hair. It's become a joke between the proprietors and me. The more Johnny eludes me (he knows I'm looking for him), the better I like him, the more mysterious he becomes, and the more persuaded I am that he's a nonpareil. He's a "real character," everyone says, as if there's no one else on earth who holds that honor. As often as I ask how he comes by it, I am disappointed by the answers I receive. Typically it's "Well (followed by a long pause), I can't explain it exactly. He's just a character." Or, "He talks funny," or "He's an oddball." Some people point to the way he once was—reputedly a drinker and carouser, rather on the randy side. Only a few voices are specific. "He recites poetry," or "He picks flowers for the ladies," or "He studies the racing forms every day," or "He might be crazy, you know, mentally ill." From these snippets (always laughingly delivered), I glean that Johnny has the quintessential qualities of a true character—the ability to keep 'em guessing and laughing simultaneously.

I chuckle thinking that if I were giving out the prizes for the most intriguing Vineyarders, they'd go to Tony Lombardi and Johnny Seaview, each at his opposite end of the spectrum. The former looks like a character, but isn't, the latter (so they say) doesn't look like one, but is. Tony is a big, bald, corpulent man who wears an earring in his right ear and bright shirts on his torso. Johnny is reportedly slight and slender, with a full head of hair under his signature red baseball cap and tool belt clasped around his waist. You can pick Tony out of a crowd. The security people did during one of Clinton's island visits. Tony swore that they nabbed him because he looked different. They said it was his wearing of a jacket on a warm day and having his hands in his pockets. Johnny is less conspicuous. Tony leads a selfless life totally dedicated to children's causes. Johnny is his own cause, a cause célèbre.

And I suppose I'd have to say that Princess Di was intriguing, too. Ohmigod! When she came to the Vineyard for a vacation, not even the most jaded of Vineyarders could ignore it. It's one thing to see Mike Wallace, Spike Lee, Diane Sawyer, Goldie Hawn, or the president of the United States walking down the street, but to see Princess Di—now that's unique. The atmosphere was charged with secrecy and anticipation. Was she here? Where was she staying? When did she get here? Where and when would we see her? Who would be invited to meet her?

Well, I have to confess (like any mortal) that I wanted to see her, too. Just a glimpse. Although I wondered *why* I did, and why everybody else did, too. After all, we knew exactly how she looked and every detail of her life. We knew that she was thin, blond, unhappy, and beautifully dressed. I pondered the question for a while and concluded that we wanted to see her, not because we wanted to *be* her, but because we yearned for the kind of attention she received. We feel *unrecognized* and *insignificant* in the increasingly impersonal society we inhabit. Witness the widespread use of the term "ordinary citizen" to describe the majority of us, and think of the subliminal message it sends. Perhaps we fantasize that if we get close enough to Di, some of her *extraordinariness* will rub off on us. (At the very least, we might garner a sound bite of attention on national TV, talking about seeing her.)

Curious though I may have been about whatever a fleeting glance at Diana might reveal, I was ill-prepared for the extremes that curiosity could take until I accidentally encountered the paparazzi. They were gathered a dozen strong by a boat slip in Vineyard Haven on one of the mornings when Where-is-she? was the most pressing question of the moment, and the most fashionable rumor was that she would be coming to this behemoth of a yacht moored alongside the boat slip. Now of course I knew that there were photographers who followed Diana, but what astounded me were the lengths they'd go to to snap her picture, to record every detail of her every move. Soon I found my curiosity shifting its allegiance from Diana to these predators who were being paid (some very handsomely) to be curious about her. When I approached them, they were working their cell phones frenetically. An excited few among them announced that this time, if luck was with them, they would be getting their first sighting of her. Their eagerness was matched by a group of middle-aged women from New Jersey who apparently had been keeping watch for some time from benches on the tiny beach alongside the boat slip. One photographer who looked unexcited and extremely frustrated was standing alone next to me.

"What's the matter?" I asked the young man.

The answer came back in a crisp English accent. "I'm here for Windsor Pictures. This boat could be here for Goldie Hawn or someone like that. Then we could pack up and leave. I don't think Di would ride on a boat like this with an unfamiliar American crew, but you can't be sure. My job is to photograph the Royal Family. If anybody can get a shot of her, it ought to be us, but we've only seen her four times this year. There's something wrong with a lady who keeps hiding her face and her children's faces behind anything she can find—tennis rackets, you name it."

His words struck me as harsh. "Don't you ever feel sorry for her?" I asked somewhat abashedly.

Clearly, I'd made matters worse. His face reddened, and his voice rose. "Of course not. She's one of the richest, most beautiful ladies in the world, the mother of a future king. Publicity makes her who she is. She expects to be photographed. Let me tell you, if she was doing something charitable here, she'd be asking us to shoot her. When she's being generous, she comes out. When she's not, she hides. Worse than Jackie. And Jackie was *bad*."

Having rid himself of some of his venom, the photographer grew mellower and explained that in the old days before the sorrows and scandals, Di was easy to photograph.

Meanwhile, his fellow photographers were edgy and restless and still on their phones. One of them, another Englishman, approached us.

"Here's a guy who rides ski lifts with Di," my new friend told me.

"Listen, if anyone here has good connections, it's me," boasted the newcomer. "Ninety percent of my work is Di. London's on amber low right now. Di is away. So is Charles, but no one cares about him. It's costing my boss a fortune to have me here," our new companion boasts, and goes on. "This isn't the rich. It's the special rich. This is *celebrity* celebrity. Not the Goldie Hawn kind of celebrity. It's bloody embarrassing what you'll do to get a shot of the special rich, celebrity celebrity. Once I stuck my camera inside a taxi window for a shot of Di. I got an exclusive. That night I went out and bought myself a car, with *cash*."

Suddenly, a call came through to one of the American photographers. He shouted to everyone present, "She's at Seth's Pond, wherever the hell that is." Within seconds, the beach was vacated.

Needless to say, I never saw Di, nor did the paparazzi. One island photographer got the exclusive shot but, as far as I know, did not purchase a car with the spoils.

Later that same day, Isabella White, the owner of the Scottish Bakehouse, told me that only a few days earlier (before it was widely known that Diana was on the island), one of her clerks had an odd experience which she related to Isabella at closing time. "A young, very beautiful woman came in today for a loaf of bread. I could swear it was Princess Diana."

"You must have been seeing things," Isabella had replied.

Edgartown

In early July, I go frequently to Edgartown. I want to love it, I'm prepared to love it, but alas, I can't. After a few weeks' time, I grow ever more disenchanted. I keep wishing that I had seen it long ago when surely it must have been a (if not *the*) premier New England village. How could the town fathers have allowed it to fall into this refractory state, I wonder. If it had not been so distinguished in the first place, merely a pleasant resort town, the damage done to it might be forgiveable. But now, though its beautiful white mansions and its old public buildings still stand as architectural marvels, everywhere else there are imitations of imitations. The battle between the quaint and the commonplace, the old and the new, has been fought and won. Suburbia has come to Edgartown, bringing its usual smorgasbord for shoppers—the trademark "this-place-is-prosperous" boutiques and galleries clustered at the center, the humdrum "we-cater-to-your-daily-needs" mini malls reserved for the outskirts. For dwellers it is the usual smorgasbord: the old mansions still gracing the harborfront, newer mansions and upscale tracthouse developments by the sea, low-scale tract developments in less desirable locations.

But I don't give in to dismissiveness without a try. I visit and admire the old landmarks. I peruse the shops. I walk along the harborfront, but always I see Edgartown in an older time frame. As a last-ditch effort to resurrect some contemporary admiration for the place, I spend some time talking to a town father, sharing my sentiments with him, asking him how the transformation happened. If I can no longer be an admirer, at least I can feel more forgiving after I've heard his rueful words. "We were naive. We didn't know what we were doing until it was too late. When the boom came, we weren't prepared for it, didn't know how to put a finger in the dike. We had no idea how to deal with all the big-money people who kept coming in here with their teams of high-priced lawyers. They intimidated us," he confesses, and quickly adds, "We're much braver and wiser now. We can preserve what we have left, and make sure we don't overbuild again, but that's all that we can do."

There's one not-to-be-missed annual event in Edgartown, the Possible Dreams Auction, an annual fund-raising event for the island's community service agency. For the price of admittance, it delivers a close-up look at Vineyard glitz and glamour, generosity and vanity, its special hybrid of tawdriness and taste. The auction is a signature event, and Art Buchwald is its signature auctioneer.

The first rows of chairs in front of him on the oceanfront lawn of the Harborside Hotel in Edgartown are reserved for a pantheon of island notables who have sponsored and/or donated larger-than-life, bigger-than-big-ticket items to the auction. Behind them are rows of chairs for just plain folks: bidders and gawkers, tourists and residents, renters and day-trippers, each of whom has paid fifteen dollars for the privilege of being there. Longtime resident Carly Simon is not there this year, nor is her famous ex-husband, James Taylor, but Alan Dershowitz, Patricia Neal, and Rose and William Styron are here, along with a host of other reputedly illustrious names, many of whose faces I cannot identify (in part because I'm not a TV buff), unlike many of the people around me, who intermittently exclaim loudly when they spot people approaching the front rows. "Look, there's X." "See, way up there, she's the one on..."

Buchwald is "on" for this event. The rumor mill has it that he is often "off," but I'm not sure what "off" means. I speculate it has something to do with depression, because a number of Vineyard luminaries, including Buchwald, have described their personal bouts with it in books they've written. But depression, of either the psychiatric or economic type, is not in evidence here.

"There are supposed to be celebrities here," begins Buchwald. "Every year the reporters mention the same ten people. We made Carly Simon famous at this auction. She's gone on to be a big star in New York, and now Barbra Streisand won't speak to her." A little more light stuff for the audience, and he opens the proceedings.

"Here's a guided tour of the Big Dig tunnel project in Boston for four people. Don't ask me why four people would want to do this, but they can go into the tunnel, get a tour, and be guaranteed that they won't see the sun. If you don't want to go, you can send four of your best friends or your children." For this bleak experience, the winning bid is well into the thousands. And so it is for a sail with Walter Cronkite, a studio tour with Mike Wallace. "Maybe he'll take you to prison," Buchwald quips. "He's always going to prisons." A low bid of $600 earns its winner a jumble of items: a weekend pass for four to Lucy Vincent Beach with a picnic lunch from the Chilmark store as well as steamers, lobster, and swordfish from Poole's fish market and four Lucy Vincent T-shirts from Marianne's silkscreening shop. "What they don't tell you is you don't wear clothes," adds Buchwald once the sale is clinched. For $5,500, twenty people can be the high bidder's guests for the screening of a new movie with Jack Valenti. "You can invite the whole Whitewater Congressional Investigating Committee," Buchwald suggests. "And look here, we have a tour of the ABC news bureau. Meet Brinkley, Roberts, Donaldson, and Will. Now, this is very serious for people who are very serious. I know Brinkley. He doesn't ever talk to anyone." This serious item goes for a serious price— $5,300. There's a tour of *The New York Times* with Mitchell Levitas, the op-ed page editor. A chubby husband-and-wife team in front of me start bidding on it. He keeps his hand up until the $6,000 mark, after which she pulls it down. Someone sitting farther up front gets it for $7,500. Afterward, Buchwald muses, "I think for that you can get your kid a job on *The New York Times*." When the next item comes up, he announces that he is trembling because Alan Dershowitz is the donor. It is an autographed basketball, a pregame buffet in the Celtics' front office, and a chance to see the game as the Dershowitzes' guests. As the bidding climbs to $4,500, Buchwald cajoles his audience, "Come on, you can't get him for an hour at that price." It hits $5,000 before the bidding closes.

On it goes for several more hours and thousands of dollars: a round of golf with Vernon Jordan, two house seats and backstage passes for a James Taylor concert, a tour of Disney Studios in California. If you are the Possible Dreams neophyte that I am, you start out gasping for air from the shock of hearing the colossal sums people spend for proximity to celebrity (and for a worthy cause), but by the end of the whole extravaganza, you're inured to the economics of it. Thousands seem like ones, fives, and tens. The sociology of it is the confounding thing. Why would people empty their wallets for a basketball game with Alan Dershowitz or for a sail with Walter Cronkite? Familiar images, total strangers. What does one say on such occasions? Isn't it like paying for awkwardness to happen? My mind wanders off into imaginary conversations.

Another not-to-be-missed Edgartown offering is its section of the State Beach which stretches all the way to Oak Bluffs. Surely, it is as marvelous now as it was in the good old days, the same pure white ribbon of sand adorning the same aqua shore. As it's a short bike ride from my house, I go there a few times a week in the late afternoon. It is my favorite island beach, infinitely swimmable, with a smooth, sandy bottom, gentle waves, warm water, and no menacing undertow. But before I take you there, a word about me and a few more about Vineyard beaches.

I am an unrecovered beach addict, and have only a few requirements to satisfy my habit. The beach, wherever it is in the world, must be: oceanside, not lakeside (the Italian lakes might be an exception); scenic from every lookout (What beach isn't? you might ask. Answer: One that is a garbage dump, as in Bombay, or one that is otherwise unsightly, like the grimy, gritty Revere Beach on the outskirts of Boston); preferably, at the edge of warm, clean, swimmer-friendly salt water (though the cold waters of Maine are tolerable). Martha's Vineyard beaches meet all of my specifications and then some. Unfortunately, they meet everybody's—thousands of seminude addicts, lathered in sunscreen with number 8, for whom a solar fix is more compelling than the probability of an ozone-hole death. We clog the public beaches and the parking lots. One of the most beautiful island beaches, the Lucy Vincent, spectacularly situated on the south side and studded with giant, glacier-formed moraines—is closed to the public but not to the lucky residents of Chilmark. Hundreds of acres of beach all over the island are privately owned. In the final analysis, though, these are only minor impediments. With the right exertion of will and the endurance to stretch inconvenience to its outermost limits, one can still get to a desirable public beach.

Thankfully, my residence is close to State Beach, eliminating most impediments.

Appearances suggest that "my" beach (I've grown proprietary) is frequented by hardcore addicts like me. Many are reading *Midnight in the Garden of Good and Evil* or novels by Tom Clancy in the full glare of the sun. I watch their children make dozens of round trips from sea to shore, their small bodies leaning sideways against the weight of sea-filled pails whose contents will soon be poured over emerging sandcastles and into deepening wading pools. Whenever I am there, I share the Edgartown end of the white sand ribbon with a full panoply of Vineyard residents and visitors. We swim together in the calm, soothing water and recline towel to towel or chair to chair, eavesdropping on each other's conversations, striking up new ones across our artificial boundaries (with the certain knowledge that we will never meet again). State Beachers look like they come for the day, not for snatches of it. People of all ages, races, and sizes—the white skins dappled with poignant pinks, multitonal bronzes, white lines—alone and in groups. They move there, like refugees to a camp, inadequately clothed and with all manner of portable furnishings and supplies: mini markets in coolers, seats and bedding, amusements, lotions and potions, changes of clothes, canvas shelters.

I do some of my best people-watching here. I see middle-aged white men, standing awkwardly knee deep in water, talking. On the beach, as in restaurants, the guy talk is mostly about money, but here the men are unprotected by their business suits. In their bathing trunks, they reveal hairy legs, the outlines of undershirts emblazoned on pink chests. They wrap their arms around their torsos in futile attempts to hide the moles and folds, the sundry disfigurements of age. This in contrast to their peers among the women, who make no such attempts, but rather take their malformations in stride, claiming their bodies as themselves, unselfconsciously. This is not the way it is supposed to be, certainly not the way the media says it is. The women pictured on glossy magazine pages are ageless, trim, and fit, and if not, why not, where have they gone wrong? But the State Beach women, sizes 14 and 16, defy Madison Avenue, appearing in every way more at ease than the men. Collectively they represent their own advertisement—the skirted bathing suit with padded breast cups is back again. One woman of advanced age, a regular at my end of the beach, wears a black and white polka-dot suit that I admire, especially for its daring décolletage. It plunges deeply into sharply pointed cups shaped like those inserted into plastic coffee holders. Trouble is, the cups aren't equal to their task. Great mounds of bosom overflow their containers. And, down below, the suit is oddly oversized. It falls formlessly over her flat posterior and balloons around her spindly thighs. She doesn't care, shows not even a hint of awkwardness. She tops off her fashion statement with a white tennis visor, sunglasses, and an extra-long cigarette. Never moving from her chair except for an occasional walk to dowse herself with water, she stares straight ahead through rings of smoke at the great blue expanse.

The power boat people like to anchor off State Beach using their boats for swimming or transporting paraphernalia to the beach. One afternoon, I watch a man jump off his boat, retrieve a giant cooler from its deck, and place it on his shoulder. As he wades toward his waving family on shore, he shouts what sounds to my ear like a thinly veiled racial slur. "I'm Bandu, the manservant," he screams, his words audible to the multiracial beachside congregation. And his three children, sensing that his burden is too great, rush voluntarily to his aid with a Styrofoam floatboard.

There are precious moments on this beach. Full-figured grandmothers photographing and rephotographing sun-bonneted grandchildren who giggle and lift their tiny chins above the sprays as they ride inflated dragons and ducks over gentle waves while their slim parents look on. Reunions of friends. Reunions of families. Reunions of generations, arm in arm, hand in hand, brought together again by the accidents of leisure, but soon to be parted by the exigencies of labor. These moments beg to be recorded on film and enshrined in albums because they are the rarer ones, the ones that ask to be remembered, and, at the same time, those that are easiest to forget,

"Q.T." Bowles, 1990.

All photographs are reprinted courtesy of Betsy Corsiglia.

Chris Murphy, conch fishing, 1996.

Ross Gannon, 1997.

Tony Lombardi at home, 1997.

The Dowdell Sisters: Ruthie, Meredith, and Catherine, 1994.

Ron Rappaport, 1990.

Dorothy West being publicly honored in Oak Bluffs, 1997.

Oliver "Johnny Seaview" Perry, 1994.

unraveling along the stretched seams of people's lives. But if these images can be captured, to sit framed on the coffee tables of the eldest generation, in Manhattan (with the youngest family members far away in Los Angeles, or some similarly distant place between Boston and Boise), maybe, just maybe, the memories they record can be saved on a hard drive in the mind, reachable and almost touchable—the next best thing to being there—*together*.

South Beach is a different experience. It, too, is a long swath of beach, browner and sandier, but only parts of it are open to the public. If I could follow it up-island, over the private beaches the Clintons enjoyed, and go farther along, I would eventually come onto the majestic Lucy Vincent Beach. South Beach, with its sand dunes and warm, pounding sea, is more a body-surfing beach than a swimming beach. When I bicycle toward it on the Katama path from Edgartown center, I can hear the waves charging toward shore long before the beach comes into view. South Beach has its share of families and old folks, but mainly it is favored by the undaunted, unsinkable young, who fling their perfect bodies astride its high-rolling waves and ride, porpoise-like, into shore, repeating the ride time and again, until, water-logged and weary, they make for the crevices and caverns of the dunes, and lie tangled in lovers' knots on blazing sand.

On the South Beach perimeter, four-wheel-drive vehicles line up side by side as in a trailer park, their interiors chock full of beach gear. The cars serve as way stations for their owners, friends, and families who, like squatters, erect temporary patios along the beach near their vehicles. The furnishings: blankets, pillows, chairs, radios, and sometimes television sets. And, though I enjoy whiling away a day like this, I wonder how much longer the delicate environment can withstand these intrusions. Can the dunes coexist with tire tracks and gas-powered engines into the next millennium? Already, most of the island's other dune-bordered beaches are closed to cars. They have been banished to lots often at considerable walking distance from the beach entrances, as at Cape Pogue beach on Edgartown's Chappaquidick island, and Long Point Wildlife Refuge beach in West Tisbury, and in some places even foot access to certain beach areas is limited or restricted altogether. One doesn't ride roughshod over the Gay Head dunes. She pays fifteen dollars to park in a lot if she arrives early enough to find a space.

I cannot leave summertime Edgartown without mentioning that 1994 is another banner year for the town and for Martha's Vineyard. President Clinton and his family are spending their second consecutive summer vacation in Edgartown. This year, the Clintons are staying, for the first time, at the home of Richard Friedman, a Boston developer. As in 1993, when the first family came to the Vineyard, the whole island is agog with anticipation. Everyone, including those islanders least inclined to fawn over celebrities, is eager to get a look at, or shake the hand of, the president of the United States. And, unlike Princess Di and other island celebrities, Bill Clinton likes to see people and be seen. He enjoys mingling with folks on the street, shaking hands in a crowd, and popping into restaurants and stores. He's fantastic for business. Shopkeepers put up signs announcing that he drank a cup of coffee here, bought a T-shirt there, and had a sandwich (which now bears his name on the menu) someplace else. After it's all over and the Clintons have left, negative-opinion makers seem to come out of the woodwork. Poor Bill Clinton gets blamed for everything; for increased traffic and for attracting more curiosity seekers to the island even than *Jaws*. On his coattails, so it is said, more people fly in, yacht in, move in just long enough to get a good look at this watering place where the leader of the free world vacations—and maybe, with a little luck, at the man himself.

One person who is unequivocally positive about having the

Clintons vacation on the island is their host, Richard Friedman. Thanks to the kindness of his attorney, whom I chanced to meet at a dinner party, I am able to meet Mr. Friedman a few months after the Clintons' visit. We meet in his high-rise office overlooking Boston and the harbor. He is on the phone when I arrive, thus affording my gaze a leisurely sweep of the surroundings: the cityscape below, the decor of the office. It is comfortable, understated, and casual. There are the personal touches, photographs of the Clintons alone and others of Mr. Friedman and the Clintons, attractively arranged along walls and on tabletops. From my seat at the opposite end of the room, I can see that Mr. Friedman is casually dressed and short in stature. I guess that he is in his mid-forties.

Whatever he lacks in height, however, he amply compensates for in authority. On the telephone at that moment, he appears to be in the process of selling and buying houses for himself. A call from a realtor in one state is followed by a call from another in his home state of Massachusetts, and to both he gives clear, fast-paced instructions on how business will be conducted. "I'll FedEx a check to you for twenty-five grand or so," he says, completing the last transaction with the dispatch of a buyer of Boardwalk and Park Place, and then joins me at the table. He owns several houses already, and is about to buy another on the Vineyard adjacent to the property where the Clintons stayed. That way, he can make a compound out of the two properties.

In the relaxed, self-confident manner that seems to come effortlessly to men of power, he talks about how he knows Clinton, and how the president happens to be spending his vacation at his house. Friedman has been involved in Democratic fundraising locally and nationally. He first met Clinton at the 1988 Democratic Convention. Thereafter, he saw him on and off in Washington and Boston. They met again in 1993, when Clinton was staying at Robert McNamara's Edgartown home. Friedman and McNamara own interests in abutting beaches. Clinton and Friedman spent some time together one afternoon during the president's first island visit. Later, Friedman suggested to a key presidential staffer that Clinton stay at his house the next time he visited. The following April, the invitation was formally extended and accepted. The security people came and checked out the property. By mid-July, all systems were go. The chief staff person told Friedman that he wouldn't have to change a thing.

"I did a lot of stuff anyway, some just cosmetic, but a whole lot of planting and painting and then bigger things, too, like putting power lines underground. I could have stayed on the property while he was there, but I didn't want to. I figured he was entitled to all the privacy he could get for a family vacation."

Another phone call comes in, which sounds as if it has some connection to renting one of his Vineyard homes. "It's going to be very expensive," he reminds the agent before he terminates the call.

"So when the big day came, my son and I went to the island airport to meet the Clintons. After greeting them we left them alone."

I am eager to learn about the security procedures.

"They were mind-boggling, unbelievable," he says, sitting up in his chair. Clinton arrived a day ahead of schedule. There had been a lot of last-minute hurrying and scurrying to get the place ready. The president, after all, was not just another tenant. "It's much more complicated than that. They have to install all these high-tech electronics. The day before he got there, they had to secure the property. That means checking every nook and cranny, starting from the inside and working out. Even the telephone systems had to be changed. After that was done, you had to be sure all the accommodations for dozens of security agents were ready. My caretaker's house was the command post. We had to have additional places to stay for the national security advisor and for the nurse and doctor who are present, along with an ambulance, in every motorcade. We got all that done, and wouldn't you know that the very first morning when I was settled in at a friend's house on the opposite side of the island, the fire alarm went off in the main house where Chelsea, her friend, and some senior staff people were staying. Would I come down? the security people asked. They didn't want the local police or an alarm company disconnecting it. By the time my son and I got there, they had already shut it off. They were all very relaxed."

I find myself appreciating Friedman's vitality. Others I have met who are accustomed to hobnobbing with the royals of the realm (the celebrity celebrities) have lost the capacity to be excited about experiences that deserve excitement. Friedman, though, appears still to get a kick out of things that call for a kick—subtle things that one as removed as I could not have anticipated.

"When I got to the house, I saw Mrs. Clinton serving coffee in my kitchen," he says. "It was really something for me, an unforgettable moment. I stayed for almost half a day, and we had a great time relaxing and talking about people and policies."

Friedman was grateful to all the islanders who pitched in to help make the president's stay enjoyable. People donated extra horses for the presidential party, and two island women came over in advance of their arrival to train the horses. The boat builders, Gannon and Benjamin, sent over a sailboat for Clinton to sail on the pond. A neighbor, Allen Norton, worked hard patching up the road leading into the property. All the neighbors helped spiff things up along the road, and were gracious about having to go through checkpoints to enter and exit their homes. To show their thanks, the Clintons decided to throw a small reception on the dock for the neighbors. All twelve families came. A photographer was on hand to take their pictures with the Clintons.

"I came down for that event and for a couple of other occasions, but I stayed with friends. You wouldn't believe the number of calls and letters that came in from all over the country, and the invitations from islanders for the president to attend every conceivable event. I turned all the correspondence over to the Secret Service."

This prompts me to ask Friedman about Clinton's social life on the island, how he decides which invitations to accept, and how his presence affects the people around him.

"Clinton went to high-profile and smallish parties. In the small gatherings, he talked about serious things, a lot about policies. He's very good at crossing class lines, much more comfortable than a man like Bush would be, I think. When he is with unknown people, he listens to their hopes and fears. He didn't want to meet only celebrities. He had his own ideas about whom he wanted to meet. Wherever he is, though, there's an atmosphere of high tension around him, from what I can see. Vibrations and electricity. I think it's all the security people who make it that way. They're all over the place. I felt the tension around me when I talked to him alone. It's not him, because he's not pretentious. He's a funny, regular guy who is also happy and energetic and does not appear to require a lot of sleep. He was up early the next morning after a late party at Vernon Jordan's. Another striking thing about him is that he can do a lot at once—like rise from the dinner table to take a call from a head of state, then come back and pick up the conversation where he left it. He can have a serious policy discussion with me and do a Sunday *Times* crossword puzzle at the same time."

"Will you do the same thing all over again if the opportunity arises?" I ask Friedman at the end of our time together. As it happens, the opportunity came again in 1997, and the Clintons spent their second vacation in Friedman's house.

"Oh, sure. Having the president there does make for some household disruption, though, little things you don't expect like the staff moving your lamps or your objets d'art to make room for fax machines. Because they were surrounded by staff people and for security reasons as well, the Clintons needed more privacy than I do when I'm there. That meant that they had to install some window shades and drapes so that it would be harder to see them, and to see where they were housed. For me, that was really funny to see because these houses of mine are designed right down to the soap dishes."

Up-Island

Chilmark, West Tisbury

It is my interest in art that first pulls me up-island. I want to spend some time at the Field Gallery in West Tisbury, where Tom Maley's larger-than-life sculptures adorn the lawn. Besides, what would a summer colony be without art?

One evening before sunset, I stop in the Field Gallery. A Jules Feiffer exhibit inside the gallery has drawn a large crowd to the grounds. There, over the heads of all the people, Tom Maley's alluring, oversize, whimsical human forms are visible. The largest among them are done in fiberglass, the smaller ones in epoxy, but large or small, they're white like plaster, their whiteness all the more stunning juxtaposed against the blue and green of their surroundings. One wants to touch them, be near them, dance with them as if to declare that life is a festival after all. And indeed, a Field Gallery event is a festival—a festival of the gentry, a gathering of beautiful people, willowy women in skirts, men in their sartorial summer best, all smiling their summer smiles, mingling around and among the inanimate forms. I recognize some faces from my suburban past. Years have gone by, but we slide back facilely into mother tongue. Yes, all of our children have made spectacular ascensions from the nursery school where they first met to their various colleges. Isn't it amazing? Some of the "children" are right there, full grown, standing by, looking awkward and embarrassed while their mothers describe their successes at Brown or Oberlin, and revealing through a myriad of bodily contortions the fervent wish that they would just shut up for Christ's sake, showing relief when we part company passing through the gallery. And, since many in the slow-moving line summer alongside Mr. Feiffer on the island, they hasten past his drawings onto the lawn hoping for a word with the great man who is now imprisoned in the center of a circle of fawning admirers. Suddenly I want to escape and return on another day for a private seance with the sculptures.

One late afternoon, I venture further up-island to Open Studio Day, an occasion when artists' studios are open to the public. For fifteen dollars, I can visit all the open studios and contribute to the Martha's Vineyard Community Services at the same time, but something detains me, and I get to see only two Chilmark studios near closing time. First, Heather Sussman's. She exhibits ceramic pieces that have humorous, dreamy Vineyard themes. One is a couch with bathers sitting on it, and on the back side, the Gay Head Cliffs in bas-relief. All bright and cheerful, like Heather and Heather's high-perched, seaview house, but I can't linger long here because she is closing up. So I hasten across the street to Betty Martin-Wlodyka's dark, wood-framed modern house and studio, low-lying, burrowed organically into a woodland, as if it has always been here. Here there is still action at closing time. People move through the rooms admiring her work, while a woman, acting as an official greeter, continues to admit new arrivals in the foyer. Betty's work is the Vineyard depicted in oils—landscapes, seascapes, fog, sheep—good art, subdued and soothing, popular on the island, exhibited in galleries here and hanging in many Vineyard homes. I sense that she is "making it" as an artist, and I am glad for her, because she seems deserving of good fortune—she's a hard worker and a straight talker, devoid of any trace of the easy-to-acquire Vineyard aura of self-importance.

I like her even more when she tells me that she's suspicious of writers and reporters ever since *New York* magazine did a profile on her husband, an island exterminator whose specialty is skunk removal.

"They made him look like a profiteer," she says with an attitude of high dudgeon. "Of course they didn't write about all the times he goes to houses, finds no skunks, and doesn't charge for his time. Would that happen in New York? No way. They'd charge just to come and take a look."

Still, there he is in *New York* magazine, and now everybody knows about him. Like love, fame comes when and where it's least expected. Betty leaves me thinking more about skunks than art. I wonder about the size of their population in Manhattan and the reasons for their prevalence on Martha's Vineyard. That night at a café I ask a friend about Vineyard skunks. He says there are thousands of them, but they're not indigenous to the island. Somebody had to bring them over, but he doesn't know whodunit or how to find out. An amused woman at a neighboring table overhears our conversation, and leans toward us. "I want you to know that skunks are the only living things on this island I'm afraid of," she volunteers. "Sometimes when I'm walking up my street at night in Vineyard Haven, in an unlit area, one suddenly appears in my path and lets me have it."

My Open Studio Day ends at the Field Gallery as the sun is setting, throwing a pinkish cast on the white statues. No one else is there. I have my seance and my festival watching the statues change color as the descending sun plays with them, dressing and redressing them in pastel costumes until the sky is blue-black and they've turned white again.

Even though she doesn't live in Chilmark or restrict her camera to its boundaries, I associate Alison Shaw's name with the town because the first photograph of hers I ever saw was a Chilmark beach scene. The image is a permanent fixture in my mind. Alison Shaw is one of the vaunted artists of Martha's Vineyard, and for good reason. On almost every coffee table on the island sits her most recent compilation of Vineyard photographs, *Vineyard Summer*, as vital to a Vineyard household as its furniture, like a Bible in a pew. Her images are engraved in people's minds like hymns and prayers, a celebration of place no Vineyarder can forget, a reminder, a call to the good-hearted sides of all her readers. Each sunset, flower display, field, or porch through her lens seems to be saying: "Keep it this way. Don't let it be lost." *Vineyard Summer* doesn't languish the way so many coffee table books do, dust-covered and unread. In whatever Vineyard home I visit for a day or more, someone, be it host or guest, opens the book and instantly commits or recommits its contents to memory. It is neither small praise nor exaggeration to say that Alison Shaw touches every islander and island-lover like no other Vineyard artist, across all the dividers of race, class, and celebrity. Her work is so transcendent that I am willing to wager that her book sits also on the tables of those *least* friendly to the island's protection, those who see money still to be made on a piece of shoreline or parcel of meadow made hallow by her camera.

✳   ✳   ✳

In a chance conversation with a friend about a weekend he is due to spend with a friend of his, I learn that his hostess-to-be lives in Chilmark, and has been going there for many summers. I ask him to arrange for me to meet her so that I can finally make the acquaintance of a bona fide up-islander! Within a few days of my friend's visit with her, Vicki Hayes invites me to her spacious modern house on Abel's Hill in Chilmark, promising that she'll take me on a tour during our time together. She spent her childhood summers in another house in Chilmark, which she wants me to see, was married to and later divorced from a summer neighbor, and is now living alone in the house they built before they separated, the place where they raised their own children in the summertime. "I was a second-generation summer person, and my husband had just the right summer credentials for a suitor in my mother's eyes. In her day, the women sat on the beach with their kids. The younger women called them The First Line of Defense. And they were strong-willed. They would throw rocks at nudists, and feud among themselves." Vicki and her family were part of the WASP enclave that was Chilmark then. Today her friends on the island are the adult children of her mother's crowd. "We're still kind of like our mothers. We talk about who our kids are dating, the kinds of jobs they have, the values that they adhere to, their achievements. We never talk about money, nary a word about trust funds and inheritances. Now that I'm divorced, I know that I'm a favorite topic of beach gossip. Not long ago I asked one of my friends what the scuttlebutt was. 'You are,' she answered."

Vicki's generation of women have a history together. They share it at their Friday-night cocktail party they call The Ladies' Friendly, dubbed by the men The Ladies' Frenzy. The gathering itself has a history dating back many years. "It's been a place for us to unload, but now that I'm divorced, it's not as comfortable for me. We all stay here in July. All their husbands come on weekends. My friends try to be protective of me. They give me advice on gussying up my house so I can get a higher rent in August. I think that they regard my place as a little under par, a bit too casual."

Vicki likes talking about the island. Seen through her eyes, the Vineyard is a composite of self-contained groups. "Remember, you have to cross a boundary to get here. We're more insulated up here than they are down-island. There are all these different clusters of people, each saying 'We're here now, but let's not let *them* in.' Look at that Methodist Campground area in Oak Bluffs. It's still a closed community of descendants. Vineyard Haven has changed the most because it's the commerce center, but Edgartown is still haughty if not quite as exclusive as it once was. In the very old days, Chilmark was a fishing community, then a summer WASP community, then it subdivided into fishing families, year-round residents, Jewish and WASP summer communities. Now it's more varied than that, a potpourri of people, all belonging to self-contained units. Gay Head is another place altogether— home to those descended from the original Native American settlers. The whites who summer there are a different breed, less conscious of appearances or obedience to social strictures, but they're nervous about the Native Americans encroaching on their land. It's kind of like they're saying, 'We want you to stay just the way you were.' And the funny thing is that with all the white people's breast-beating about ecology, the Native Americans have been the best ecologists of all, the least invasive and money-grubbing. They haven't dammed up anything. We summer people feel so entitled. We're all for protecting the environment, as long as we have what we want. When I was growing up, I knew some of the Native Americans because they were caretakers on the estate surrounding our house. We owned our house and a small portion of the land around it. Those caretakers would take my sister and I for rides in their oxen carts.

We'd go to collect seaweed, then help them dry and pile it before spreading it on the fields. They'd take us to see the sheep in the barn and the horse named Chief."

For several summers before they owned their house, the Hayes family would come for a few weeks' stay at an up-island inn, but in the 1940s when Vicki's sister became ill, they decided to buy. "My mother thought that the fresh air would be good for my sister. We had no electricity or running water, just kerosene and a hand pump. We were isolated until we learned how to get around. There was hardly any traffic in those days, so we hitchhiked and walked to our friends' houses. Our mothers certainly didn't drive us around, the way we do now for our kids. Once a week there was a square dance—the big event—and we'd get there by hook or crook, and on Sunday afternoons, there was baseball—only for up-islanders, of course, and mostly for summer people. There was always a conscious separation between summer folk and winter folk. You weren't supposed to socialize with the year-rounders."

Vicki broke that rule, as did (and do) many a summer person up and down the eastern seaboard. If ever there is a rule begging to be broken, this is it, and the more parents reiterate it, the more it is broken. Some, like Vicki, sustain lifetime friendships as a result, other turncoats wed the objects of their rebellious affections. For the majority, though, the rule-breaking is temporary, like a fad or a first visit to a foreign country. Alluring, promising something new and different, a taste of the exotic, but then inevitably, one comes home again. And after it all, what does one learn? That winter teens aren't much different from their summer counterparts. They all like suntans, substances, and sex.

After an hour or more of living-room conversation, the time is right to move on to the old Hayes house and the estate on which it sits, a mile or so up-island from where Vicki now lives.

As we turn off the main road onto a long, winding dirt road that climbs uphill to a barn (the barn of her childhood memories), she admonishes me. "We have permission to look around, but don't bring your notebook, and whatever you do don't say who owns this estate or to whom they sold any of their land," she says, pointing from inside her car to one secret house on secret land off in the distance.

Having taken the vows of secrecy, I am freed to follow Vicki around the barn and up another hill overlooking acres of green fields, Vineyard Sound, and Lucy Vincent Beach. The estate is so vast that I can't see the main house or any other buildings on the property, but I know they are there—somewhere. We climb a short distance to a knoll from which finally the old house is visible. It is a small, modest, gray-shingled structure with spectacular views of the fields and the water. In today's market, it would fetch a hefty price. We walk around the premises, and Vicki proudly shows me the places where she once played and gardened. Our return to the old homestead brings back memories of the hurricane of 1952 when Vicki and her family had been marooned for a week, surrounded by water. Her sister, whose boyfriend was visiting at the time, had by then recovered from her illness. Smitten as she was with the boyfriend, her father nonetheless felt an intense dislike for him, and wanted him to leave. Still surrounded by water, Mr. Hayes, in desperation, borrowed a rowboat and rowed the young man away. It worked. That was the last that was seen of him.

Our tour of the estate concluded, we thank its handsome owner (whose name I remember well, but my lips are forever sealed), working alongside the barn, and head out to the main road, taking a detour to see the Chilmark cemetery where Vicki's father is buried (as is John Belushi, whose gravesite, Vicki says, is always littered with bottle caps and assorted junk left by his admirers). From the cemetery, we go to Menemsha, the fishing village in Chilmark where the docks are lined with big fishing vessels because fishing still happens; where fish markets beckon (and boutiques, too); where families romp in and around high-rent, quaint little houses adjacent to the waterfront; where in the hills above, other families romp around bigger, more glamorous, higher-rent houses hidden from view, or sequester themselves on private beaches. We have lunch on the deck of a harborfront eatery, seated elbow to elbow with tourists chewing, clicking their cameras, marveling at the wonder of it all. And it is wondrous in a way. Despite the encroachment of trendy enterprises, the little port has managed to retain its charm and color, its old-world ambience. Unlike any of the more populated areas on Martha's Vineyard, Menemsha still conveys the illusion of innocence, as if yesterday and today are all of a piece and joined by a purpose. Men fished then and men fish now, out to the same sea and back again, hauling their catches and unloading them in front of wide-eyed shorebound gawkers. This daily repetitive activity has a comforting, seemingly unbreakable and eternal rhythm that even the very real threat of overfished waters can't dispel. Still, I've read enough by then to realize that fishing probably won't go on here forever, and that without it, Menemsha surely (and rapidly) will go the way of most of the Vineyard—toward the fulfillment of an ever-changing, insatiable appetite for the accoutrements of pleasure.

Vicki's thoughts must have been similar to mine because she tells me the story of a man she knows of who had been happy with his little fishing house for many summers, but he had grown prosperous over the years and wanted to build another house nearby for his adult children. The town was at first reluctant, but finally accommodating. "They had to dredge a pond for it," she explains. Not long after that was done, the man decided that two wouldn't do. He applied for a permit to build a third house. "No, no," the townspeople and their elected officials screamed. Every foot went down. The project was eco-logically insupportable by any standard. Somehow, though, whether through bribery, a phalanx of fancy lawyers, neither or both, the man prevailed and erected his third house.

In just these mysterious ways do humble fishing shacks convert to luxurious family compounds, and open fields to mini malls.

Not from a humble fishing shack, but from scratch—from the ground up—David Marston, an island contractor, has almost finished building a Chilmark summer house, and an acquaintance of mine, a member of his crew, has arranged for me to see it. When I catch up with David in mid-July, he is on the home stretch, preparing for the owner to take occupancy in August. What I see before my eyes is three thousand square feet of splendor on a hill overlooking Squibnocket Pond, the ocean and Nantucket in the distance—an idyllic summer getaway. Although the house looks finished to me, David says that there are many loose ends still to be tied. He and his crew are working hard and fast to meet the August deadline. If David is stressed, it doesn't show on his face nor in his manner. The only hint of anxiety beneath the surface calm is the occasional smoking of a cigarette. The house would have been ready sooner, but for the inevitable delays: waiting for infrastructure setups, subcontractors, supplies from the mainland—all the usual glitches one confronts when building an island house, but now the end of the punch list (a builder's things-to-do list near the end of a project) is nearing. For David, this has been a plum job, one he's gotten without waiting on tenterhooks to prevail in a bidding competition with the many other island contractors. From the outset, the owner wanted David to build it. If a dream house is one that has everything, then this is it: a massive cedar deck, granite counters and custom-built cabinetry, a huge oceanside glass-fronted living room with extra-high ceilings, bedrooms spread throughout the house's different levels and wings, each with built-in drawers and closets and adjacent luxury bathrooms. Many more conveniences than convenience requires.

"Look at these mouldings," says David proudly. "Here's one around the door. It's made of nine pieces of wood, each cut to fit, then glued and nailed. It takes a lot more time to make, but see, it changes the whole appearance of the room. In a ranch house, it would be one piece of wood all around the frame."

I admit that it's a nice touch, but one that I would never have noticed if it hadn't been pointed out.

"How much time will the owners be spending here?" I ask.

"Oh, for weekends and a few consecutive weeks in the summer."

And the price?

"It's standard for a summer house—around half a million. Not an extravagant place or price," he says matter-of-factly as he seats himself on the empty living-room floor to take a coffee break with the crew. The crew nods affirmatively at David, expressionless.

"Not extravagant?" I repeat, so dismayed that I almost choke on my coffee.

"That's right," says David. "It's in good taste, this house. No swimming pool, central air-conditioning, blow-testing [a way of making sure a house is tight]."

I am dumbfounded, unable to let the matter of extravagance rest. "What do you mean it's not extravagant? How can you say that? This is a very extravagant house, especially as a second residence. Most of the time it will sit here unused and unadmired. Whether it's half a million dollars' worth of gaudiness or of good taste doesn't matter. Either way it's extravagant," I blurt out like a true spoiler.

Not a rise out of David, only a pensive stare. A hush in the room until one member of the four-man crew, a gray-haired guy who looks like he's done more heavy living than David and the others, finally breaks the silence. "You know now that I think about it, yeah, I'd have to agree with you. The cost of the lumber for that deck out there is the same as for my whole house, and when you add the cost of the flooring inside, you've outpriced my house. There is something offensive about that, but I can't put my finger on it."

But the finger finds the blind spot when David says, "Look at what a guy like this [the owner] is doing for us. Without him, we don't have a life. He's providing jobs for a lot of people, most of them islanders. The money gets distributed, and that's good for everyone."

That said, the lone detractor is silenced. David has other peeves as a builder. On the top of his list are people who are fussy just for the sake of being fussy. He's seen a lot of that on the Vineyard—the kind of people who keep adding to the punch list and holding out the money until every additional item is checked off. Among his peeves, he offers one that even he sees as an example of the confluence of extravagance and good taste—a house he's built and then painted with hard-to-apply paint imported from Europe at $130 a gallon (versus $32 a gallon for high-quality, easy-application American paint). Not only the paint, but also the labor had been unduly expensive.

David and his crew have deep ties to the Vineyard. Only one of them is a transplant. The others have lived elsewhere for a time and have then returned, called back by their emotional attachment to the place. They are college graduates who give living on the island priority over education-based career paths. They don't mingle much with their seasonal customers, but now and then, there is an occasional invitation to a cocktail party or to dinner. "I think the unspoken reason for these invitations, when they come, is to give the party a lift by including a winter person or two, make it a success by adding something a little different to the usual mix. But all we really have in common is the customer's house, and when that's done, there's nothing to keep us connected," says one crew member.

While David has been building the new house, Ted Delaney has been helping to restore an old one in Edgartown for a wealthy New York executive.

Ted, whom my husband has met previously at a North Carolina art colony, lives with his wife in a house he built for them in Chilmark on land they obtained through a bank foreclosure. The house is set back from the road in a clearing surrounded by trees. It is modern, spacious, and charming, filled with whimsical, high-art furniture that Ted has designed and built. Furniture making, in fact, is his first love, the job he would have liked to spend most of his time at if he could, but island living is too expensive. Most of his income came from subcontracting.

"The woodworkers on this island are great people. Very honest, but all of us are in the same boat. We can't live on what we like to do. Even the basics here are expensive. It's a do-it-yourself economy in the winter. The tradespeople are so expensive that we can't afford to hire each other. Look at half the contractors and carpenters you see; they're in costume. They're really shirt-and-tie people. Their prices are high, but most of them aren't rich either. So, a lot of us winter people get together in groups and buy what we need in bulk off-island. A livable income here for an average-sized family is forty- to fifty-thousand dollars. That's not so easy to come by."

Ted is a fairly recent transplant to the Vineyard, and is refreshingly opinionated about island life. "The old-money summer people respect this island, but not the new rich. They don't care that much about protecting the environment, nor for that matter do they care a whole lot about craftsmanship. Tradespeople don't get good vibes from most of them. I do some catering in the summertime at these big summer houses, and let me tell you I've had people dig their fingernails into my skin to get their hands on the hors d'oeuvres. That doesn't go over well. Right here in this neighborhood, we're surrounded by summer people. They are definitely not friendly. Chilmark is a hoity-toity, unembracing community. But then, we don't have to deal with the nervosas that our summer neighbors confront back home—the crime and grime. Maybe they just need to chill out when they come here. I can understand that. We year-rounders are pretty reclusive in the summer, but boy, as soon as those people leave, we come out in droves—like locusts. We whoop it up at each other's houses. Good food, good wine, singing and dancing."

Ted's description of the summer afterlife reminds me of fairs and festivals I've seen or read about in foreign countries—celebrations of the coming of the rains or the washing away of sins. If Ted is right, the Vineyard has one, too—an autumnal celebration extending through the winter, a rebirth festival, during which the celebrants can finally shed their summertime costumes and recognize themselves again.

Every summer at the Agricultural Hall in West Tisbury, there is an authentic Vineyard fair—the Agricultural Fair. If the International Festival is a celebration of the diversity of island people, then the Agricultural Fair celebrates the diversity of the peoples' produce. Inside the hall, I find a spectacular display, like a luscious still life of island agriculture. Huge, plump potatoes in variegated earth-colored skins, lush red cabbages, and giant, multishaped pumpkins. The prize ribbons alongside each individual display show the exceptional caliber of the competition—in the youth and adult categories—and the same for fruits and flowers. Art and crafts are on display, too. Photography, paintings, furniture, and needlecraft—the work of islanders, the majority of whom are not renowned. One photograph of a serene, happy-faced Bill Clinton holding a Vineyard child in his arms remains in my memory. It reveals his innate charm to greater advantage than more famous ones I've seen.

Sword dancers parade through the hall, and from a neighboring field, contra dance music sounds through the open windows. Children giggle as they go around on merry-go-rounds and bump each other's miniature moving cars. Old folks sit on benches on the hall's front porch, watching and listening. People cluster around the outdoor stalls, where homemade food is on sale—jams and jellies, pies, sandwiches, and fresh lemonade.

I fall in love with this event because it lends so much to pride of place. To me, it seems to epitomize a Martha's Vineyard of yesteryear and this year. The fair is simple yet elegant, a potpourri of beautiful colors and creations, aesthetic, heartwarming, soul-settling. Once I've seen it, I think the island's naysayers (myself included) can't be right. Nothing in the name of progress can take this away. It cannot be imitated.

Gay Head

Like Chappaquidick, the Gay Head community feels inaccessible to me, its houses far from the roadways and concealed by rolling topography and thick woodlands. And even if its residents are out and about in the summertime, one can't see them for the tourists. They come by the busloads (and by cars, mopeds, and bicycles) to view the famous Gay Head Cliffs, enjoy the surrounding beaches, eat at the clifftop restaurant, and buy trinkets at the stalls that flank the entryway into the viewing area.

Faced with such formidable obstacles, I decide to leave most of my explorations of Gay Head for the off-season, but I do wind up there on a hot August day that I devote exclusively to beach-hopping. It begins in Menemsha at its pretty little harborfront beach. Since beginning my rounds of public beaches, I have discovered that each has a distinctive character and culture. Menemsha beach is intimate and cozy, with a rocky shoreline and a jetty alongside which boats enter and exit the harbor. The water here is choppier, less inviting than at State Beach, but on a day like this, I'm not choosy. Drying off on the beach, I look around at my neighbors. They seem to be families, literate Moms and Dads who intersperse the reading of good books with the making of creative sandcastles with their children. This is a solid sunscreen number 20, pale, under-the-umbrella assemblage, whose literary tastes seem not to favor Mr. Clancy.

Across the bay from Menemsha, I can see the Lobsterville Beach in Gay Head. Amazingly, considering the heat of the day, it looks empty. Although I could get there by a little ferry which runs between the two places, I decide to pick up a carry-out lunch in Menemsha and eat it on the Lobsterville Beach. Up close, the beach is long, gentle, and quiet, barren of humanity but for a lone walker off in the distance and a family swimming together in front of their beachside house a few yards from where I sit with a book and my picnic lunch. I read, eat, swim, and sunbathe in solitude for two hours and grudgingly return to my car. Next to me in the roadside parking area is a newly arrived middle-aged couple who have spread the makings of their lunch on a towel in the rear of their station wagon. We chat while I am brushing the sand off my feet. They are Canadians.

"We're here on a two-week vacation," the wife volunteers. "We don't go to the restaurants. They're too expensive. Lunch is at least twenty dollars, but it's not Canadian dollars. It's American dollars, and for us that's forty cents more for every dollar."

"Where do you stay?" I ask.

"At a camping ground," the husband answers. "It's nice there. We bring our tent and our car, and just travel around the island. Can't afford to stay in one of these hotels. Even with the bad exchange rate, their prices are still way out of line."

"What's it like spending a vacation in a tent?"

"It's great," says the wife. "Ours isn't just any tent. It has rooms, even has a porch, and, of course, a stove and a refrigerator. Really keeps out the rain, though there hasn't been any since we've been here. Ours is the biggest tent in the campground. I guess you'd say it's a luxury tent. We feel we deserve it at our age. We don't use it for all our trips though, not when we go to Europe or travel around Canada, just when we come to the U.S."

With that, our conversation has run its course, and I have wrapped myself from head to toe in clothes to protect against the sun. I am preparing for my next activity—a walk along the oceanside beach in Gay Head. Meanwhile, my new friends have unpacked their sandwiches and closed themselves into their car's makeshift dining area. "If you want to see our tent, come on by the campground," the wife offers cheerfully through the passenger-side window as we exchange good-byes.

One could travel the world and never find a beach as breathtaking or as dazzling as Gay Head, with its gigantic, multicolored clay cliffs. The rawness of the place—the sea-carved cliffs, the tidal pools, the shifts of sand and rock patterns—pulls one into a timeless zone. Gay Head demands respect and reverence; the people visit it more as they would a shrine than a playground. And, to lend further credence to the shrine concept, a justice of the peace I chance to meet in my travels around the island has told me about a wedding he conducted on the beach alongside the cliffs. He was asked to meet the groom in the parking lot before making their way to the wedding site.

"You'll recognize me," said the groom. "I have a mohawk and a braid."

The justice met the groom at the appointed hour, 7:00 P.M. The bride and the mohawked groom were dressed in kimonos. As he and the couple made their way to the site, the justice noticed five Japanese men in business suits and ties, laden with cameras, walking nearby along the beach. The wedding party consisted of the bride and groom and two witnesses. As the party continued farther down the beach, the bride announced that she and the groom were naked under the kimonos and would be disrobing for the ceremony.

"I was a nervous wreck," says the justice, laughing at the memory of the experience. "I told myself that I could only look into their eyes, nowhere else. Well, the ceremony began, and I kept my vow until a twinkling coming from somewhere lower on the bride's body blinded me. Up to that point, I'd been perfect, but that twinkle caused my eye to wander to her breast, and there, implanted in her nipple, was a gleaming diamond stud. I caught myself in the nick of time, and brought my eyes back up to where they belonged. But let me tell you, it was all I could do to maintain my composure. Well, after the ceremony was over and the couple was still nude, they asked me to take a picture of them and their friends, which I did obligingly. As I moved out to take the shot, I saw the Japanese tourists out of the corner of my eye. They had been hiding behind the curve of a cliff photographing the whole thing. They were bent over with laughter. I came really close to losing it then, but somehow I held myself together, and kept their presence secret from the couple."

Of all the weddings he'd performed—and they were countless, Martha's Vineyard being by his reckoning the wedding capital of the world—this one was truly unique, the one he'd never forget.

"When the bride kissed me in gratitidue and farewell, all I could manage to say was, 'God, do I feel overdressed.'"

Five Corners and Home Again

I remember the dread I felt as a child at summer's end, leaving Maine and our home on Little Diamond Island. Summertime was unrestricted, creative playtime, a time when we loved ourselves more, our parents loved us better, and our friends were better friends. It didn't seem like a dream world then. In fact, I think we experienced our summer world as real and that of the other seasons as artificial. It was as if, during the long interregnum between summers, we were cast as unwilling performers, and incessantly directed to strive for favorable reviews. If we experienced ourselves as inauthentic, then we experienced those seasons that way, too. Come summer, though, things returned to the way they were supposed to be, the way God intended them to be. The cast and the directors were set free, the great winter burden of role-playing was lifted, and we, adults and children alike, could at last succumb to relaxation, to being ourselves.

Of course, we had it all wrong. Soon enough, we children discovered that it was the other way around. The real world *was* a stage. The unreal world was Little Diamond.

But childhood images are powerful, even after they undergo correction. I know I have brought them with me to Martha's Vineyard this summer. I have come divided in two—one-half filled with childlike expectation that the island summer colony will be the real world, the other half bearing adult resignation to accept however it turns out to be, real or unreal.

And, by summer's end, to my disappointment, my adult half-expectation that this island will be more like the real world has become whole: I cannot find on Martha's Vineyard that vital sense of *innocence*, that carefree timelessness, and that easy nonchalance about profits and products that was characteristic of Little Diamonders. Money has changed the summer face of Martha's Vineyard, not just Edgartown, and made it look more like the rest of the world. So much so that islanders no longer can be certain that signature T-shirts are not necessities, that a half-million-dollar summer house in good taste is superextravagant, as is five thousand dollars for an evening with Alan Dershowitz (on behalf of charity or not). To my ears, the voices of the Vineyard sound more and more like those in the mainstream culture.

There's still one that is unique, though, and it is persistent and audible. "Look," it admonishes, "there is no crime here. We don't even lock our doors at night."

Ted Delaney doesn't lock his, and thanks to him, I can hold on for a little longer to my childhood interpretation of a "real" island world. The Vineyard, so he says, drops its artifice in September and lives happily and naturally until May. Just think, my old seasons of dread will be, thanks to Martha's Vineyard, my new seasons of joy. I can hardly wait to leave so I can turn right around and come back in the fall.

On my last summer day, I sit for a while with Bruce at Five Corners. He's counting his cash and ruing the day, just around the corner, when the till won't be as full. We go through our usual routine of jibe and counterjibe until it's time for me and my car to line up for the ferry. I tell him he needn't mourn my absence. I'll be back soon enough. "Please," I say. "Deliver me Johnny Seaview when I get back."

"OK, Mrs. Garcia, I'll do my best," he promises, and while I'm heading for my car, he's renting another one of his. "It'll only cost you forty-five dollars and a tank of gas," I hear him tell the customer.

6

Autumn

*I*n October, Martha's Vineyard grows quiet. The action slows. There are human voices, but now their hum is subdued. The dialogue is different, too. This season's talk is all about the absence of people and their traffic, and the relief islanders feel to have the place to themselves again. Indeed, the summertime automotive din has vanished, the incessant idling of engines, the beeping of horns and blaring of radios. And the island's panoply of colors has changed. Green blends with orange, amber, and gold instead of with pink and blue, and surrounding the new calm and color, like a lovely gift wrap, is Indian summer. The first blush of autumn makes the island look as if it has regained its innocence.

The illusion is abruptly interrupted when I make my ritual stop at Holmes Hole Car Rental. There I watch commerce marching on, right into the "shoulder season." Across the street, the moped rental shop is doing a brisk business, and so is Bruce. His cars are still going out and coming in with off-season tourists driving at high-season prices. I overhear one customer balk at the rental price, and Bruce telling him in his inimitable, jocular manner, "Look, you're getting a bargain. You can go all over the island in this, and there won't be any traffic to slow you down. In July or August, you'd be lucky if you made it to the beach with all the traffic." After the perplexed customer drives away, Bruce seats me on the bench to tell me about his latest plans. He's going to buy an antique business down the street. While he's renting cars up here, he'll have someone else stationed there selling bric-a-brac. By next summer, two cash registers will be clinking and clanking joyously—and simultaneously.

For this fall visit, I have the Goodmans' house to myself. Since I am used to being there when it is overflowing with people, it seems eerily silent at first. But soon I find advantages to the emptiness. The solitude, combined with the unseasonably warm weather, allows me the privilege of sitting on the deck seminude and unobserved (to the best of my knowledge). Even better, through a window in the neighbor's trees created by newly fallen leaves, I am given a more expansive view of the boats approaching and departing Vineyard Haven harbor than I could have had in summer.

When I am not lolling in this blissful condition, I am wandering around Vineyard Haven, keeping my eye out for Johnny Seaview (whom Bruce has not managed to deliver to me yet). Most of my days begin with breakfast at The Artcliff Diner (too late for Johnny's predawn rise). I like to sit there with a homemade muffin, a glass of orange juice, and a cup of steaming coffee reading the Vineyard newspapers: the esteemed *Vineyard Gazette* and its folksier cousin *The Martha's Vineyard Times*. (Someone I once met described *The Martha's Vineyard Times* as the Vineyard version of the *New York Post*, and the *Gazette* as its *New York Times*.) My favorite articles are the profiles of year-round local personalities which frequently appear in both weeklies. Written in admiring, affectionate tones, these pieces have a cozy inclusive quality, inviting the reader to come right into their subjects' spaces. Into Poole's Menemsha Fish Market, for example, showing the way it was then and is now, and how Mr. Poole's pluck and ingenuity have turned a little market into a national fishmongering enterprise so that Mr. Poole can now afford to hang up his retailer's apron and go fishing just for the fun of it. Or into Ida Levine's Vineyard Dry Goods Store in Vineyard Haven, which in 1994 is about to close after sixty-four years of loyal service to its customers. Ida, about to turn eighty-seven, is retiring. She reminisces about a bygone era when personal service was commonplace and dry goods were all the rage. Those days have passed, but throughout the years she's had a loyal following of customers who haven't abandoned her. "I love them all. Knowing them has made mine a wonderful, wonderful life," she tells the reporter.

The "wonderful, wonderful" year-round life theme is played repeatedly in these newspaper stories, but the average islander steals some of the bloom from the journalistic rose. He points out the harsh side of year-round life—the perpetual catch-up game that everyone plays with the bill collector and the mortgage holder. As the man or woman on the street sees it, Martha's Vineyard offers a wonderful, wonderful life to only a small minority who can make enough money from the summer demand for their respective skills and crafts to enable them to ride out the lean times. For everybody else, it's a matter of job overload in the summer and scraping by the rest of the year. It is not unusual to hear of people who work three jobs in the summer to keep themselves afloat through the winter.

An article in the *Gazette* makes me intrigued about the weather vane maker Travis Tuck. According to the article's opening paragraph, "While some island artists see a slackening of work after Labor Day, this weather vane artist remains as busy as ever." The story goes on to detail the important people and organizations on-island and off who have purchased the weather vanes and copper sculptures made by Mr. Tuck: James Taylor, Beverly Sills, Dennis O'Connor, and recently President Clinton, to whom Tuck donated a plaque.

But it is not weather vanes that leads me to Travis Tuck, it is mopeds. A young man of my recent acquaintance has been complaining to me about mopeds, and mentions Travis. "If you want the lowdown on mopeds, the man to see is Travis Tuck. He'll tell you all you need to know. But, as far as I'm concerned, it's those goddamned day-trippers," the man says. "They come over here for the day, rent one of those things without the slightest idea about how to operate it, take to the road and cause all kinds of havoc. Hurt themselves and everyone in their path. There's so much demand for them that every summer a new moped entrepreneur opens a business."

As I'm ambling through Vineyard Haven on one of these September mornings, Travis Tuck is out of mind until I happen upon his studio. At that moment, I am not particularly inclined to socialize. I am pleased to have the pavement to myself, and startled to realize how quickly one catches the antitourist bug on Martha's Vineyard. It amuses me to recall that just a few months earlier, I'd been a tourist myself, marching up Main Street in stride with an infantry of tourists, uniformed in our emblem T-shirts and well-cushioned sneakers—browsing at store windows and standing in take-out lines for ten-dollar lobster rolls. But now I walk in a different guise, feeling smug, superior, proud of my familiarity with the place, as if the island and I share a secret pact. Full of these conceits, I step out of the warm air reluctantly and descend into Travis's studio, perched low in an alley off Main Street.

He and his teenage son are there when I enter the subterranean room full of machinery, weather vanes in progress, and scattered pieces of copper. Travis looks to be in his mid-forties, with a stocky, rugged frame and a full moustache under his nose—a kind of garnish for his smile. For someone of his esteemed reputation, he is disarmingly casual and friendly. My introduction accomplished, we have only to seat ourselves on stools by his drafting table before we are deep into a discussion about mopeds. He's been campaigning against them for years, ever since he completed the intensive training required to be an emergency medical technician and began a fourteen-year stint on the ambulance corps. "Serving as an EMT was one of my ways of paying back the island for the privilege of living here. I also served as a volunteer fireman," he tells me. During his summers as an EMT, he'd see five or six moped accidents a day. By the time he retired, he had handled two hundred moped accidents and made a thousand ambulance runs.

"Each of the six island towns had one ambulance. Moped accidents tied them up, and then when there were heart attacks or other emergencies, we'd have no ambulances available. It got so bad that I threatened to resign. It started a ruckus. A campaign began to banish mopeds. I wrote letters to the selectmen and to the island newspapers. We made some progress. Eventually, helmets were required and mopeds were excluded from the bicycle paths. Bike-path accidents stopped and head injuries declined, but we didn't succeed in our mission to eradicate the insidious vehicles. There are more of them now than ever before. Worse, they're not even classified as motor vehicles. You don't even have to have a license to operate one. Requiring licenses would hurt business, and the moped business is a cash cow. A lot of the owners live in Florida and don't even pay taxes in Massachusetts."

From mopeds, we segue into Travis's life and his weather vanes. I ask Travis how he got to Martha's Vineyard from his native New York. "Most year-round residents here are transplants," he explains. "Not natives [born there to year-round families], not former summer residents, but people who come here from somewhere else because they're drawn to the place." Like his fellow transplants, Tuck visited the island, decided that it would be a wonderful place to work and live, then moved here permanently. By then, he had four years of sculpting experience under his belt, having served as a three-dollar-an-hour apprentice to a Manhattan sculptor.

"America's premier weather vane maker," as Tuck is described in the October 1994 issue of *Condé-Nast Traveler*, is a self-made, self-taught sculptor. He is the only person he knows of who makes weather vanes from scratch; that is, without molds. His competitors produce the Betty Crocker variety, either stamped out in molds or copper hand-hammered into molds. Whereas their designs are mass-produced, each of his is unique and copyrightable. Every couple of years he goes to Boston to buy the copper sheets and brass tubing he needs. A glance at his order board shows that he needs a good supply to fill the forty-two commissions that are posted there. Some won't be completed for two years or more. The majority of orders are from summer residents on the island, the remainder from people in distant places: from Dennis O'Connor, the three-time winner of the America's Cup, who had commissioned a weather-vane replica of the *Stars and Stripes*, the boat he would be sailing in the next America's Cup race; from a German sea captain who wants a rendition of Neptune bearing a trident. Maker and buyers fax their design specifications across oceans and continents.

"How would I get one of these?" I ask Travis.

"I don't sell them off the floor. Typically, you'd come in here for two or three visits before you'd clinch the deal," he explains. "You'd have to decide on the design. Since you're a writer, you might want a typewriter weather vane, or if you play tennis, you might prefer a tennis racket. I did one of a bunch of bees for an apiarist. You might be someone who would want both your curricular and extracurricular interests reflected in yours."

"Let's say I just spring for the typewriter, what will it cost?"

"The typical weather vane is six thousand dollars, but they can go higher. I had a telephone executive who wanted a huge one for his winter house. He wanted me to play with the image of Mercury, maybe move his wings from his helmet to another part of his body, and put a cellular phone in his hand. All that costs more."

"So what your customers are really doing is putting their egos on their roofs," I say in my best sour-grapes manner, as my pocketbook will not permit such an extravagant adornment for my own roof.

"Yeah, it is art tailored to ego, and I'm profiting from the chic ambience of Martha's Vineyard, from the switch from the old picnic-table summer crowd to the new blue-blazer crowd. I bet you think that with all this success, I have it easy," he says, reading my mind, "but let me tell you it's tough paying the mortgage. Some months I can't make it. There's one or two artists or artisans here who are rich from their work. The majority of us are just getting by."

Struggling or not, Tuck gives every impression of having a wonderful life and having emerged, cheerful and unscathed, from mortgage difficulties and two divorces. (While at his studio, I met his second wife, the mother of his son, as well as his third and present wife, all of whom appeared to be on the friendliest of terms.) In his spare time, he mixes things up socially, sometimes cavorting with the locals, sometimes with the Fortune 500 types.

Like the others in his class of successful Vineyard artisans and tradespeople, Tuck has an easy, uncynical acceptance of the lifestyles of the lords and ladies of the summer manors on whose largesse he depends. I am certain that in the winter months when the lords and ladies are safely offshore, they are the butt of many a night's joshing in barrooms and living rooms, but by this time in my Vineyard odyssey, I do not expect such confidences to come to me. So I try to assume this accepting stance myself, to think of the summer nobility as job providers (they are), ecologists (some yes, some no), contributors to every aspect of the island economy from fish to fine art (true). But some contrarian sentiment always interferes. As soon as I feel affirmation building, the alarm goes off. Usually, it happens when I am driving around and notice an especially imposing dwelling I haven't seen before. I think how amazing it is that on twenty-three miles of ocean-locked land, there are as many different architectural ways of saying "I'm rich" as Hallmark has cards saying "Happy Birthday."

On another day, I drive up-island past a myriad of newly discovered, unoccupied villa-like edifices on little streets with adorable names such as Tea Lane and Kettle Cove. In my imagination, I devise a plan for opening the houses and moving the entire homeless population of Manhattan in for the winter. I picture the story on the nightly news: A close-up of me thanking the mayor of New York for donating buses and the director of the Steamship Authority for free passages to and from Woods Hole; a cutaway to me in my makeshift office in Chilmark administering the new halfway house community; and shots of Mr. Poole delivering free fish; the local grocer, Mr. Cronig, free produce; Mr. Douglas, owner of the The Black Dog Bakery and General Store, the bread and clothing; shots of the new residents at home, tools and brushes in hand, doing touch-ups and tasks for the absentee owners, and enjoying evening card games and spontaneous sing-alongs with James Taylor, Billy Joel, and lesser-known local entertainers. And, at the end of the winter, I'm on-air again for the wrap-up, the anchors brimming with praise for my efficiency at disbanding the community. I envision the penultimate shot: zooming in on the interiors of houses in their states of preoccupancy spotlessness—the antiques polished to a sparkling luster, the Steuben glass shimmering in winter sunlight. Then, the finale, the climactic moment: the departure hour. The island's young star photographer, Alison Shaw, will be shown taking a group shot on the pier (with an extra-wide-angle lens) for the front page of the *Gazette*. And in the last seconds of the sequence, a close-up of her instantly developed photo of the smiling New Yorkers in Black Dog T-shirts under the headline MANHATTANITES PLAN TO RETURN NEXT WINTER.

In this delusional state, I drive back down to Vineyard Haven, down the lonesome road to reality.

Travis has told me about the boat builders, Ross Gannon and Nat Benjamin, who are co-owners of a thriving boatyard in Vineyard Haven. "Go talk to one or both of them, if you can," he advises. "They're great people who have been successful as year-round artisans. They build beautiful wooden boats like the sailboat they built for James Taylor."

At this stage of my island tenancy, I see James Taylor as having become, unwittingly, the arbiter of island taste. Everywhere I go on the island, no matter to whom I talk (except in the black community, where Spike Lee reigns supreme), his name emerges unsolicited around various matters of no consequence. I'm told where he gets his fish and his produce. Farther up the price scale, in the big-ticket item category, I learn that he owns one of these and one of those. He lives here, he dines there. It isn't simply that he is famous and has been a lifelong island summer resident. There are plenty more who fit that description, but none perhaps as beloved and admired.

One day, not long after I've visited Tuck's studio, I wander over to the far side of the Vineyard Haven harborfront and stand on the beach fronting the Gannon and Benjamin boatyard. For several minutes, the air is still, unpunctuated by the sounds of machinery or human voices, only by the mewing of seagulls.

As far back as I can recall, I have loved the sound of seagulls and the sight of them dipping down to the water, then soaring into gliding formation overhead. In those parlor games in which players declare what animal they want to be in another life, I've always answered "Seagull." Now, calmed by the graceful performance of the gulls, I lean against the edge of a boat trolley admiring a huge, majestic wooden sailboat that is moored not far offshore, content to let time roll by, but a young man appears and diverts my attention. I guess that he is either Gannon or Benjamin because he looks the way a boat builder should: tanned, blond, and bearded, clad in the trade's telltale faded flannel shirt, worn dungarees, and weathered leather boots.

"I'm Ross Gannon."

"So you must know whose beautiful boat that is," I say.

The boat once belonged to General Patton. Awhile ago, a storm had cut it loose from its mooring in the seacoast town of Manchester, Massachusetts, hurling it onto the rocks and damaging it extensively. The accident happened as the boat was about to be sold to a private individual who planned to share it with the institution to which Patton's widow had donated it—The Landmark School. It was especially appropriate that it was given to a school for dyslexic and learning-disabled children, as Patton himself had been dyslexic. The school had used it for their sea-training program for almost twenty years. Patton, who had fittingly named the craft *When and If*, could not be sure when and if he'd ever return from battle to sit at its helm. He never did. His prophecy about his death was right except in the particulars.

For the prospective new owner, it must have indeed seemed that the boat was jinxed. Was it possible to fix it, the owner had inquired of Gannon and Benjamin over the phone, and if so, when could it be fixed and for how much? Ross went to Manchester to look at the boat, saw that it was reparable.

"The boat had been launched in nineteen thirty-nine, made

by John Alden, a great American designer. It was a work of art. For me, it was heartbreaking to see an old wooden boat so badly damaged. The new owner couldn't afford the repairs. We had to replace one-half of the boat. On one side, we did a complete restoration job. Finally, what we agreed to was doing the work at cost in return for part ownership in it."

Renowned for their ability to repair catastrophic damage to wooden boats and for building new boats, Gannon and Benjamin were the right men for *When and If* and have been equally right for many other devotees of wooden boats. Nowadays, there are several boat builders on Martha's Vineyard, but Gannon and Benjamin are the only wooden boat designers *and* builders. Benjamin designs. Gannon and Benjamin engineer and build.

"When we started this business fifteen years ago, there were no boatyards on the island where you could work on your boats yourself. When Nat and I met, he was already in the process of planning a career in boat repairing and building. He and I had seen do-it-yourself boatyards in other places. Both of us were avid sailors as well as fix-it men. We thought we could make a go of it."

No bank would lend them the money. "No one wants wooden boats anymore. They're dying out," the lenders told them. So they turned to Nat Benjamin's brother, who lent them the start-up money.

Curious about how the business operates, I ask Ross for a guided tour of the yard and the shop. By then, there is activity in the boatyard. Someone is hard at work on a boat in one of the cradles. "He owns that boat. We charge our customers twenty-five dollars for lay days [the time the boat is housed there], eight dollars per foot to haul the boat in, and a fee for the use of shop tools. [Only experienced people can operate the more dangerous equipment.] If the owner does all the work himself, that's what it costs him, but if he needs our help we charge him forty dollars per hour. When we're not repairing boats, we're building them. We don't do much on motorboats, but we do build some dinghies. It takes us about a year to build a forty-foot sailboat."

We move to the rear of the building into the shop—a long, rectangular room full of complicated, now-buzzing machinery, an assortment of tools, and cluttered workbenches all overseen by a young apprentice. "This is where the building process begins," Ross explains. "We start by developing a working relationship with our customers, building trust. It's like commissioning a painting. They see boats we've built and get a feel for our work."

Customers come slowly until the word is out. Then things get easier. Gannon and Benjamin's location on the Vineyard Haven harborfront is ideal for drawing summer people. Additionally, they cater to a select group of year-round wooden-boat people, and have enough deep-pocket patrons to keep business on course.

Gannon is another island transplant. The seeds of his transplantation were sown in his high-school years when he sailed from his home in Connecticut into Edgartown harbor and spent a few nights there. Five years later, he was out of college and clear of the draft, and came back to visit the island. He stayed. For the next ten years, he earned his keep doing household carpentry and contracting. When he had earned enough, he bought one boat, then another, bigger boat, and spent as much time as he could working on them.

Gannon says that for all his twenty-five years on the Vineyard, the only unrewarding times have been the hectic summers when the roads are clogged and the moorings scarce. Every August he disappears for a few weeks to go sailing. But for the rest of the year, his life there is wonderful: a family, close friends, beautiful scenery, work he loves, a professional partnership he values greatly, a good day's pay, and a community that cares and showed it when the boatyard burned to the ground a few years ago.

"The outpouring was fantastic. Everyone helped us rebuild. They gave us money and time and as much of their labor as we needed. I don't know whether that would have happened anywhere else."

Before I leave the boatyard, I sneak one last look at Ross. He strikes me as a man at peace with himself, and why not? He and Benjamin are good friends and good partners. They build beautiful boats. Their work is highly acclaimed. On his vacations on the island, the president of the United States has sailed on one of their boats with James Taylor, and has been lent another for his personal use. The newspapers, national and local, have played it all up, putting the boat builders on a wider map than they've been on before. It is only a matter of time, I assume, before the next crop of buyers comes along, people who can't sleep at night until they have a Gannon and Benjamin boat—maybe one just like James Taylor's.

That morning, after I leave Gannon's boatyard, I make my way up Beach Street in Vineyard Haven toward Main Street, and come across Calico Sue's Country Studio a few yards up and across the street from the boatyard. It is a few minutes before noon, and the store is closed, but that doesn't matter. Closed or not, Calico Sue's screams to be noticed. Everything one would never need is jam-packed in the windows: wooden cows for lawn decoration, cow mugs, cow T-shirts; calico dolls, calico aprons and sweatshirts with MARTHA'S VINEYARD imprinted in calico; fabric items of every description known to tourists. For some reason, the contrast between Calico Sue's window and that of her storefront neighbor around the corner on Main Street amuses me. Where Sue's window is chock full, the neighbor's has only a few items: a hand-knit sweater for $899, a ceramic bowl for $400. Funniest of all, though, is the sign on Sue's door:

WE'RE NOW OFFICIALLY OFF SEASON. I HATE MORNINGS SO BE PATIENT. I'LL BE HERE BEFORE 11:00 A.M. DON'T MISS VISITING THE STORE. WE MAKE EVERYTHING HERE ON SIGHT. SUE.

I suspect I would like Sue, and oddly enough, during a later winter's stay on the island, she will be my next-door neighbor. I do like her then. She tells me how tough it is to make it through the winter on the Vineyard, and how mad she got one day in the supermarket when she heard Carly Simon's voice on a video talking about how easy it was to get renovations done on island properties. "Maybe for her, but not for most of us," exclaims Sue. But today, the sight of her store gets me thinking about the obsession with taste that is characteristic of the Vineyard. However it is defined, good taste (dare I say of the James Taylor variety) has assumed the status of a moral imperative, one of the benchmarks of island culture. Vineyarders talk about it incessantly. Off-island, weeks go by without its mention, so accustomed have we Americans become to the desultory placement of good taste next to bad. Bill Bryson, in his witty American travelogue, *The Lost Continent*, comments on the ugliness of strip malls he finds adjacent to a lovely old white church or nineteenth-century brick courthouse. Why are we Americans so tolerant of these juxtapositions? he asks. On the Vineyard, though, the matter of taste, besides having legitimate aesthetic and ecological underpinnings, seems elitist, as well. While I hear some railing against the number of high-priced clothing stores, the preponderance of T-shirt shops in the three big towns generates a real head of steam. "Will it never end?" many educated, middle-class islanders ask themselves repeatedly.

From the look of things, they have good reason for gloom. As soon as one upscale boutique closes (usually for lack of sufficient revenue to offset rent increases), a T-shirt establishment claims its space, and stays.

Moving on from Calico Sue's with taste on my mind, I determine that I can conduct a mini survey right then and there on Main Street. Since it's October, the idea of comparing the off-season sales between Shirt Tales and Song of the Reed appeals to me.

The clerk behind the counter at Shirt Tales is at that moment alone with her racks of T-shirts.

"How's business?" I ask cheerily.

"Really busy, especially for this time of year, and our Edgartown store is even busier. I guess it's because it's Saturday. The 'word' is out in town that people browse on Friday and buy on Saturday. I think it's true. Mario, the owner, should be happy when we close in December. He can go down to Florida with a light heart."

I thank her and move onto Song of the Reed farther down the block.

"How's business?" I repeat, a little more cheerily to a clerk I don't recognize from previous visits to the store (on sale days). She is also alone and behind her counter, looking out at an inventory of French-made shoes, hand-knit sweaters, few-of-a-kind dresses.

"Not so great lately, but we haven't had a bad fall. August was fantastic, though." She also has gotten the "word." Her word is that all the money people come in August. The power people come in July. In her opinion, though, the nicest people come in September. "After that you have to depend more on the locals. They buy at half price or not at all. People who live here don't have any money. We can't take a bite from the hand that feeds us. It's really a crazy place when you stop and think about it. Only the summer people can buy what most of us have to sell."

The results of my survey will not be heartening to the taste sensibilities of the anti-T-shirt brigade. I picture Mario sitting out the winter on a yacht in Florida and the other storeowner huddled by a woodstove in a drafty West Tisbury cottage. Come April, Mario will be back, ready and able to launch another Shirt Tales store in another prime island location. (Indeed by 1996, Mario had opened another store, and the Song of the Reed was out of business, though not replaced by T-shirt store.)

I like the way time slows down in autumn on the Vineyard. In spring, the pace is slightly faster because islanders are busy gearing up for the summer onslaught. But in the fall, artisans, merchants, islanders of every stripe have time to spare. In summer, I wouldn't dare engage people in expansive conversations, especially about their jobs, but now I do so unabashedly. They seem to welcome it. Take Paul, for example, the owner of Paul David's hair salon in Vineyard Haven, whose acquaintance I have made during the summer. His chair is right next to my stylist Melinda's, and I've enjoyed eavesdropping on his conversations with customers. He's a good storyteller. In the high season, he's too busy for rambling discourse, but not now. So, mostly as an excuse to talk to him, I go in for a coif. While Melinda is styling me, I'm working my way into a dialogue with Paul. The chairs on either side of me, including his, are occupied by ladies in curlers talking about the summer traffic jams.

One says to whomever is listening: "Weren't those crowds terrible?" "Yeah, yeah," comes a voice from underneath a set of curlers. "It sure is nice being able to drive into town again. But, then again, I guess we shouldn't be biting the hand that feeds us," her words, echoing the sales clerk's at Song of the Reed. "That's right, Elsie, you got it right."

When there's a pause, I get Paul going. "Tell me your favorite beauty parlor stories," I ask. He doesn't disappoint me. He launches into one about Lillian Hellman.

"I'll never forget it. She was sitting right over there in the front room, the waiting area, with some of the blue-haired ladies from West Chop. A black woman in a maid's uniform was there accompanying one who was about to have her nails done. At some point during the manicure, this woman raised her gold-braceleted arm and blew on a Tiffany whistle hanging from the bracelet. The black woman jumped up and came to her side. Well, you wouldn't believe what happened next. Lillian got out of her seat, approached the woman at the manicure table, and started screaming. 'Who the hell do you think you are treating her that way?' she asked indignantly, and before she got an answer tossed her coffee in the woman's lap. She was a character, that Lillian. Once during the McCarthy era in the fifties, Frank Sinatra came to the Vineyard with Claudette Colbert. Rose Styron was having a party for them, but she wasn't inviting Lillian because Lillian didn't like Frank. Guess what Lillian did? She sat for a while on her porch, watching the guests arrive at Rose's, then she put on her fur coat, tucked a bottle of wine inside it, and went to the nearest pay phone. She called the police and said that there was a bomb on Frank's yacht. Of course, he left the party immediately. She had it her way. She spoiled the party."

Melinda remembers her, too.

"I used to cut her hair. She liked a lot of attention, and boy, when she didn't get it she could be a real bitch."

On my previous visits to Paul's salon, he and I had had some brief conversations about the culture of beauty parlors. I'd tell him my theory about women confiding more in their hairdressers than in their therapists, certainly more than in their husbands, and usually without being asked. A simple "How are you?" would elicit a stream of self-revelation. He had agreed wholeheartedly. I reintroduce the subject now, and am even more delighted that Paul is in an expansive mood.

"You know why? Well, I'll tell you why. I've been at this for twenty-one years. People tell us everything because they're stripped down in here. Their husbands never see them the way we do, hair all over the place, all kinds of gadgets and goop in it. They look worse than they do naked. That's why they spill so much."

Over the years, Paul has done the hair of any woman who is anybody on the island, and contrary to the typical islander's pretense of nonchalance about celebrities, Paul is something of a celebrity buff. About Barbara Walters: "not very friendly, doesn't want people watching her. She asked me if I lived here all winter, and when I said I did, she asked what on earth I would be able to do in the winter. The same things everybody else does in the winter, I told her." He adds other notables to his list. He's done Beverly Sills and Lady Bird Johnson, and once even Jackie Onassis. Jackie's, he tells me today, is his favorite personal story.

"When I got the call to do her, I was in seventh heaven. A maid with a foreign accent called to arrange the appointment. She wanted me to come to Jackie's Gay Head house, and said someone would come around to get me. I was really excited. She wanted me to come at two P.M. Well, I looked in my appointment book to make sure I was free, and damned if I didn't have Lady Bird booked at that very hour. I couldn't believe it, two first ladies at the same time. It was unbelievable. I thought I'd lost my chance with Jackie, but I didn't. We made the appointment for the next day. When I got there, Jackie was reading *Madame Bovary* in French. Right there in the house, I did her hair and Caroline's. Jackie was friendly and warm, Caroline a bit shy. That very month, Jackie had been on the cover of almost every magazine. I said that I bet she was staying away from the newsstands, and told her also how much I admired her for protecting her kids from the fishbowl. She said the nicest thing in response. 'Oh, I haven't had to do much. They're wonderful kids. I didn't have to work at it.' Before I left I told her about how amazing it was for me to have had two first ladies wanting me at the same time. She laughed, but I didn't know how much of a kick she got out of it until she left the room for a minute, and I overheard her repeating the story to Caroline. They were both laughing their heads off. And that wasn't the only treat for me. Rosie, Caroline's daughter, came in with a Frisbee, and led me to Jackie and Caroline in the other room. All four of us played Frisbee in the hallway."

A year or so later, Paul will become a big winner in the state lottery. I read about it in the *Gazette* and in the *Boston Globe*, and after an unusually long lapse between visits to the island, I drop in to see if he is still behind his chair, to congratulate him. There he is, listening to the traffic stories, telling a few of his own, putting in curlers. Nothing has changed, and I take a certain comfort in that, as if Paul is a symbol of this island community standing hard and fast against the forces of change and emerging triumphant.

But I know that there are as many Vineyarders who welcome change as there are those who resist it. Change, with a positive spin, means money flowing into pockets, getting rich quick. Take that little parcel of land, that small business, that fishing shack on the waterfront and poof, it turns to gold. Horatio Algers are everywhere on Martha's Vineyard.

Trip Barnes is one of them. He has a moving and trucking business, and by the time I meet him, he's been at it long enough to have made a small fortune moving practically everybody on the Vineyard into or out of a house. Although he is officially in the trucking business, 90 percent of his business is moving. Clarence A. Barnes III is the name on the sign over the door of the ramshackle building where his office is housed, but everyone knows him by the nickname Trip.

Trip Barnes dresses like a trucker and has the rugged look of a trucker, but his roots are decidedly shirt-and-tie. He was born blue-blooded, a descendant of the founder of Barnes Publishing, later to become Barnes and Noble. His trade-in of a white-collar birthright for a frayed-collar Vineyard lifestyle is not unusual on the island. There are many others like him who have veered off their prescribed familial courses, taken up tools and stepped into pickup trucks instead of donning suits and inhabiting urban office suites in order to enjoy the good island life. He is what is known on the island as a "shifter."

The Barnes clan summered on Martha's Vineyard. In 1939, Trip's father bought a twenty-room Sanford White Victorian on Chappaquidick and added it to the Barnes' stronghold on the island.

"Dad was an ad man. He invented Sugar Crisp bears, the Maxwell House slogan, 'Good to the Last Drop,' and merchandised all kinds of cigarettes. In 1948, he authored a best-selling book called *White Collar Zoo* and followed it with sequels. He was a scrimshaw collector, and wrote a book about it which earned him, a lifelong Republican, the friendship of the most famous Democrat-collector—John F. Kennedy."

Trip and his sister grew up in Manhattan in the winter and the Vineyard in the summer. "My mother was tough. She didn't let us do anything. I went to St. Bernard's and Trinity in New York. In my junior year, I dropped out. I had this thing about cars. I spent time with my grandparents in Florida during the winter. I had a Florida driver's license when I was fifteen. By the time I was sixteen, I was living and working on the Vineyard. I'd bought myself an old car and fixed it up, but it was inconvenient to get across the channel from the family house in Chappaquidick to my job by four A.M. Half the time, I lived in my car."

He met a girl in Chilmark. She was twenty-four, divorced, and working as a cook on a fishing boat; he was sixteen, a milkman, and single. They moved into her place, married eventually, and had a son. "I was interested in trucks, and learned as much as I could about them. I bought my first one in nineteen forty-eight. My wife and I moved to New York for several years until we separated." There, he dispatched trucks for *Time* and *Life* and did some editing, too. "I was upstairs and downstairs." In 1962, he came back to the Vineyard and drove a sightseeing bus. This stint was followed by a short-term reconciliation with his wife, a temporary residency in Boston, a high-school diploma, a job with a car dealership where he sold mostly trucks, and then a chance meeting with his second wife-to-be on the ferry between Martha's Vineyard and Woods Hole. Both of them were commuting from the Vineyard to their Boston jobs. "Soon I was back again on the island full time, driving a truck for Cronig's market, building up my own trucking business on the side—hiring people, discovering that there were laws that helped get you around the laws. In a few years I was remarried, had two more children and twenty trucks. We were hauling scrap iron for cash during the Vietnam years. The workers were loyal and stayed until they burned out. We built houses for some of them, threw them up in three days, the tent houses like those in Oak Bluffs, but without the gingerbread."

As Trip is telling his story, we're driving around the island on his various errands. Every time he stops to do something, he's distracted, and I have to bring him back to the story. "So what happened next?" I ask after each stop.

"Well, eventually I got a partner. We trained our drivers really well, but we had a hard time getting good help in the winter so we did a lot of the driving ourselves. Still do. In the summer, we get kids from Ireland. They make good money. Our drivers have to be good mechanics, good drivers, and good navigators. They've got to know their routes and their way around in cities. We give our customers the personal touch, handle their stuff like it was ours. Well, I was on the road a lot, and after twenty-four years of marriage, I got divorced again. All my fault—wine, women, and song. The wine part was the worst. I checked into detox and stopped drinking altogether. That was nineteen eighty-nine. Later I met another woman down in Florida. Much younger than I, she was in her mid-thirties, a nurse from Canada. She'd been a Canadian body-building champion. I brought her here, and she loved it. We're living in the truck terminal now because all the houses I own here are uninhabitable."

No sooner has he finished this part of his monologue then we pull up to a house in Edgartown in a state of obvious vacancy. This is the most important "errand" of the day. I get out of the car with him to take a look around the house. On the way in, Trip points to several houses in the neighborhood. "I moved that one, and that one, and that one. This one we're going into was just sold by an old lady. I'm going in to see how much is left for me to clear out."

Inside, the house shows its age. Peeling wallpaper, fireplaces everywhere, old fixtures, second-story rooms under multishaped eaves, buckling floors. Lots of charm, even in this lonely condition. We aren't there long before the new owners appear, two middle-aged women, who, when Trip asks where they're from, reply, "the Main Line," and act surprised when he says, "Oh, Philadelphia," and more so when he adds that his daughter lives in Rittenhouse Square. The Main Liners bear no resemblance whatsoever to their Edgartown slacks-and-sneakers neighbors-to-be, some of whom have just then crossed the street to meet and welcome the newcomers. In contrast to their understated well-wishers, the two women are "done up" in urban chic: mascara, lipstick perfectly applied, styled hair, gold jewelry, stretch pants—like they're set for a day of shopping in Philadelphia instead of a morning excursion through falling plaster dust. Soon their new house will be "done over" from stem to stern by their island contractor, who has suddenly appeared, as if by magic, and joined our little congregation. The renovation talk begins in earnest. The contractor gets out his pad and pencil. Everything inside will be new, the walls will be painted in warm shades of plum and peach; and, once the women realize that the welcoming contingent includes the residents of the house opposite theirs with the beautiful columns in front, they determine that their facade will have a new look too. They implore the contractor to get them some columns for their entryway.

"Not just like yours, of course," one of the women says reassuringly to the couple.

Sooner or later, Trip will be moving these women into their house, but for now, his business there is finished, and no other pressing errands remain. He is free to show me one of his uninhabitable houses nearby, the one he and his third wife will eventually make into their home. It's a quaint little place in total disrepair on a side street in Edgartown. "Got it for a song," he says. We take a quick run-through, and get back in the car. There's a story behind the car: "I was out in Helena, Montana, on a moving job, and bought it for five hundred dollars. It was cheaper than flying home, and I've gotten a lot of use out of it since."

On the way back to his office in Vineyard Haven, we stop to look at the "tent" houses he'd built for his workers. Now they're part of the Sea Glen development off the Edgartown Road. The tent shapes are still there, but they have countless appendages, like so many tails pinned on the donkey: wings, decks, porches, enlarged windows, skylights. Nearby there is a trailer. It, too, has add-ons.

"We need more of these, out by the airport maybe. Places where you can flush the toilet and cook an egg for next to nothing," declares Trip.

Back in the car again. By now, it is apparent that vehicles are Trip's most comfortable habitat, his parlors. On his feet, he's witty and personable, but the words don't flow as easily. We are nearing the end of our time together, so he uses the last stretch of road to give me his thoughts about the island.

"I don't like the Chamber of Commerce encouraging all those day-trippers to come over here. They have no money to spend. They're not like the renters who will buy property eventually. I don't think it's so hard to make a living here, but to do it you have to have an island mentality, be a member of the club so to speak. Look, you've got eighty thousand people in the summer, fifteen thousand in the winter, a workforce of six thousand. Half of them are in the restaurant and hotel trades. Another one thousand in carpentry and two thousand for everything else, boats, plumbing and electric, retail. There's plenty of work, but you've got to play the 'people' game and be good at it. Personality is what it takes. I don't think much of the real estate brokers. There are two hundred of them, and only a handful who are smart. The smart ones know how to take people by the hand and show them what to do. Someone might not get his dream house at first, but with ten thousand dollars he can get a good start on the land and the lumber. And I'm sick of all the celebrity blather around here, the reporters running after Carly, Mike, Art, and Walter to fill up their columns. Celebrity is not what this place is about. It's about security, knowing that things will work out. Peace of mind. I've got a great business, and when I cash out, I'll be as well off as anyone else, a lot better off than I would have been if I'd stayed in New York and gone into advertising. I'm doing just fine, and I don't have to lock my doors at night. There's cross-fertilization here, too. Summer people with winter people, types of people with other types. Maybe Chilmark and Gay Head are the Golan Heights, East Chop and West Chop and some of Edgartown, staid little British colonies, and Oak Bluffs, the seat of the black aristocracy. But we all get along. I love it when I go off-island and people see my truck with MARTHA'S VINEYARD written on it. It's a happy association, makes me feel like the Good Humor man. The only thing that worries me at all about the Vineyard is that maybe we're killing the goose that lays the golden eggs."

Of all the people I talk to, Trip Barnes takes the prize as the provocateur, the person who goads me into contemplating a wonderful, wonderful life on Martha's Vineyard for myself. "Personality is all it takes. You've got to play the 'people' game and be good at it," he had said, making it sound easy. I fit that bill, I think to myself, and only later do I realize that there's something he's omitted. Alongside personality and people talent, one would need a service or product to sell or a generous trust fund in order to survive. From what I can see on my wanderings around the island, the goose is postmenopausal. She's already laid her cache of golden eggs. Every high-priced service and product imaginable is now available on Martha's Vineyard. Since I have neither product nor service, now is not my time. If I'm destined for the wonderful, wonderful island life, it must, of necessity, be in the twilight of my career, in the bloom of senior citizenship like the people I accidentally meet at the Woodside Village retirement community in Oak Bluffs.

Woodside is home to Johnny Seaview, and I'm hoping to get lucky by dropping in on him there at the end of a workday. Expectantly, I take a turn onto the dirt road adjacent to the big, green Woodside sign off the Edgartown Road. A short drive into the woods brings me into a parking lot in front of a long, rectangular apartment building. On my way into the building, I pass several residents sitting on benches outside the entranceway enjoying the warm October air. Thwarted again. Johnny doesn't respond to the buzzer, and I'm frustrated not only because this is not my first visit to Woodside, but because he's so damned elusive. I share my frustration with the assembly outside.

"He's never around when I come," I complain, seating myself in an empty space on one of the benches. "Does he really live here?"

"Oh, yeah, he lives here, but we never see him, either. He's always out. Don't know where he goes," says one woman who checks the accuracy of her remarks with her companions. They all nod in agreement.

I change the subject.

"How do all of you happen to be living here?" I wonder aloud.

"Excessive age and limited income," answers the same woman, who gradually emerges as the group spokesperson.

Her name is Virginia, and for someone of her "excessive" age, one can see, underneath her baggy Black Dog sweatshirt, that she has an extremely trim and shapely figure. It is capped off by a full head of faux blond hair. "Here's the way it usually works," she goes on. "You have an adult child who lives on the island, and he or she thinks it would be a good idea for Mom or Pop, or Mom and Pop, to be close by. Mostly, it's Moms because a lot of the Pops have died off, like my husband. There are a few couples, but it's a tight squeeze in one-bedroom apartments like these. Otherwise, it's people who've lived on the island year-round or in the summer." She points to Suzette and Barbara, both looking vibrant and healthy, as former summer people. Virginia is in the mother-of-the-adult-child category, but she wants to register how much

166

she hates the island. She is there only because Woodside is an affordable place to live. Everything else on the island is unaffordable. Worse still, there aren't any men.

I study my benchmates more carefully. They support Virginia's census by gender—eight women, seven white, one black.

"Did everyone get their flu shots?" asks one of the women, a raincoat pulled tightly around her thin, slightly hunched frame. "Yes," they reply to her as she draws hard on a cigarette. When I ask her what she has done with her life, she answers, to everyone's amusement, "I grew up."

The conversation turns to the upcoming events on their calendar: aerobics, a movie, an island gathering for seniors, and the various times the van will be arriving to transport them. The talk would probably have remained in this vein if Virginia hadn't spotted Herschel West approaching them from the parking lot. From that distance, he looks considerably older than most of them. He has stooped shoulders and a scruffy beard, and is dressed in a fisherman's cap and a plaid flannel shirt. Alongside him is a toy poodle on a leash.

"You oughta talk to him, that is if you can get him to talk. He and his dog, not the one he's got there, were in *Jaws*. He's lived on a boat most of his life, and his family has lived here for ten generations. They came over on the *Mayflower*. He's never been married," explains Virginia.

"Hey, Herschel," Virginia calls out to him. "This lady wants to talk to you. Tell her your story, you know, the *Jaws* story." Herschel eagerly obliges without pausing to be introduced to me or place himself comfortably on a bench. Closer up, he looks younger than he does from afar.

"Well, I was walking on shore one day, and these people came up to me and said, 'You know what? You're going to be an extra in our movie.' My dog was going to be in it, and I was going to have a speaking part. By the end of the movie shoot, they had me running a camera boat. I spent six days on the set, and I still get the royalties from it. I'm on screen for ten minutes. I'm in the court scene, way in the back, and then in another scene where I'm loading the boat. This dog here is Minnie. She wasn't in the movie. Tipper was the poodle in the movie." Herschel ends his story abruptly and sits down.

"Tell her about the rest of your life," coaxes Virginia, "about living on a boat and all that."

Haltingly and with less ardor, Herschel fills in the blanks of his life. He vouches that he has lived on a boat for most of his life, one that was moored in Menemsha. In his heyday his fishing expeditions took him as far north as Newfoundland and as far south as the Gulf of Mexico. He started fishing at five. In his teens, he was a dragger for bay scallops and later a swordfish harpooner on another man's boat. At sixteen, he quit school and went to sea until he retired to Woodside Village, the first land-based housing he'd occupied since childhood. Now he is seventy years old, by birthright a native, but by the yardstick of years, a transplant. I wonder if he takes the sea with him into his sleep, if he feels his bed rolling, hears the waves crashing against the walls, pulls the blankets up to protect him from the chill and the dampness.

"You see, I've always had poodles," he volunteers enthusiastically, moving forward in his seat as if suddenly struck by a bolt. "The reason is that they don't shed, so you don't have any hairs mixing in with the fish. That wouldn't be allowed. The poodles have kept me happy, so why be married? I never wanted to. I was having too much fun in the ports." The last comment was accompanied by a wry smile and a footnote. "I don't get lonely, and when I want company, I've got lots of cousins to visit on the island."

"Yeah, but they're not kissing cousins," says a portly woman named Meredith, clearly pleased with her own humor.

Herschel is a hard act to follow for the two neatly dressed men who come out of the building, Fred and Manny, but it is obvious that the women, especially Virginia, enjoy the male company.

"You oughta see Fred's cross-stitching. It's beautiful. He sells it all over the place, don't you, Fred?" She turns flirtatiously toward a blushing Fred.

"Hey, that's not fair," says Manny. "Fred has all the girlfriends."

A woman named Mickey comes to Manny's rescue. "He throws parties and puts mickeys in our drinks." Her audience laughs at Mickey talking about mickeys. "But the funny thing is, Manny doesn't drink a drop. Just the female guests."

"Now make sure you say something in your book about how Fred cooks a New England dinner every Saturday night. He always has hot dogs, but no beans or brown bread," says Virginia. Fred smiles and blushes some more, and the chatting continues until the air grows cooler and the shadows longer. Then, one by one, my companions file into the building, imploring me as they exit to come back for another visit.

All things considered, I think I'd prefer the retirement life of the mother of a friend of mine, Virginia Besse. She, like many Vineyard retirees, lives not in an age-segregated compound, but in the house she owns with her husband. She has a long summer memory and a long Vineyard lineage. My friend has paved the way for this conversation I'm having with Virginia in her light-filled living room.

"I never thought I'd adopt Vineyard Haven the way I have," she tells me as if recounting a dislocation akin to an immigrant's. "I'm from an old Edgartown family, and I was sure that Edgartown was forever, but it's livelier here in the wintertime. There are no lights on in those Edgartown houses once the cold weather sets in, but those houses are so beautiful. They set Edgartown apart from everywhere else. There's no other place like it. That's why I still go to church there. At least, I can stay connected," she says with a touch of nostalgia.

Virginia Besse is a descendant of an old Vineyard family, the Peases, of whom there still are a few on the island. Unlike her forbears, she began her life there as a summer person. In the winter she lived in suburban Boston. In the summers she had a thoroughly Edgartown kind of upbringing—a yacht-club childhood. "I wasn't anything like my daughter. She was the belle of the ball growing up here in the summers, but I was a serious child and a tomboy. I had my own sailboat, and I could beat the men in sailboat races. I was the first female sailing instructor at the Edgartown Yacht Club. It was just after the war. I learned a lot about male chauvinism in those days. I was an expert racer. I broke some gender barriers. The men didn't like it much, but they got used to it. That yacht club was very sophisticated, but when I grew up and married a Vineyard Haven man, my days there were numbered. My kids liked the Vineyard Haven Yacht Club better. It was casual and not so snobbish. There were Jewish members there, and now there's even a black commodore. At the Edgartown Yacht Club, you don't get that mix."

Virginia doesn't race anymore but still sails—right through the adult stages of her life. "I got tired of racing after the big-money people took over. They had the biggest, best class of boats with the finest sails. That ended the lure of racing for me." She turned to watercolor painting and community activity. Her Vineyard watercolors are exhibited all over the island and on some of the island ferries, and she is an active board member of the Martha's Vineyard Center for Visual Arts. "We have a dream of buying an estate that would house a gallery for shows for all the local artists and provide spaces for other community-service programs, as well. Until we get enough money for it, it remains a dream."

I admire Virginia's vibrancy and resilience, the way she has expanded her horizons and made the most of her island life. Once I've met her, it is easier for me to entertain pleasant visions of my golden years, to think that retirement could be fun. This Virginia is, from all appearances, another Vineyarder who is having a wonderful, wonderful life.

So far, my autumn time on the Vineyard is shaping up to be an expository, from the perspective of middle-aged and older folks, on the quality of year-round Vineyard life. I'm curious about the island kids. How do they see it? My friend Tony Lombardi doubles as the manager of the Winterside Coffeehouse and a faculty member at the Martha's Vineyard High School. Since he knows everyone on Martha's Vineyard under the age of eighteen, I ask him to gather a group of adolescent students for me to talk to. The kids he delivers are all involved in one way or another in his volunteer projects. About fifteen of us sit outside on the patio in front of the Wintertide and talk about island life.

"There's nothing to do in the winter," they all say in unison, and will repeat it many times during our conversation. Only two disagree. They are not the social kind. They like to walk in the woods, to paint and read. They can tolerate long periods of solitude, so the Vineyard in winter is ideal for them. The kids who complain of boredom can visualize themselves living on the Vineyard as mature adults, but not when they're young. That's a time for exploring the world, and they intend to take advantage of it. "This is a cool place to be a parent or a grandparent, but not to be a kid," says one pretty girl with long braided hair.

"Yeah, we're overprotected here from everything, from violence and traffic and the whirlwind of city life, but not from drugs. They're everywhere. You don't even have to look. In the eighties, it was all crack and coke. Lots of parents were doing it, too. Now it's a mix of drugs," says Jeff. "In the summer, it's worse."

These days, the parents of these kids work hard. Paul's parents own stores in Edgartown. Janet's mother works two jobs in other people's enterprises. Most of the parents, like Paul's, own businesses catering to tourists.

"Money, money, money. That's what's on our parents' minds all the time. Making a lot of it in three months so they can get by in the winter. It affects us. You don't want to, but you feel like you have to care a lot about money. It's so in your face here," says Curt.

"Yeah," adds Zoe. "I worked the register at Cronig's last summer. I can't believe how the tourists behave about the moneyed people who live here, the celebrities especially. One day Goldie Hawn came in and went through my line. After she left, the tourists behind her wanted to know how much she spent, what items she bought, brand names and all, and would I mind letting them take a peek at her checkout stub. Can you believe that? Everyday, they asked me if Princess Diana had been in. Most of us who live on the island pay no attention to the celebrities, but these tourists sure do. They want to be like them, to buy what they buy, eat what they eat. It seems crazy to us."

What does the world out there beyond their sheltered environment seem like to them? Of course, I know that their answer will be what it is: they will describe the world as violent, but I am surprised by how their thoughts about the world beyond the Vineyard contrast starkly with those I hear from their contemporaries in the inner city, who regard violence as inescapable and intrinsic to their lives. These Vineyard kids, they see it from afar. One boy wonders aloud why America is more violent than other countries. He supposes that it has to do with the commingling of so many cultures. Another thinks it is related to our historical habit of settling every major event with a war. A minority feel that it is due to poverty, overcrowding, and joblessness. Among the group, there is unanimity that free-flowing guns don't cause the problem, jails don't help it, and the government can't do anything about it.

"You sound turned off," I remark.

They agree that it is true. About half say they won't even vote when they're eligible. None of them wish to be politicians or work for the government. Adults generally can't be trusted. "They listen, but they don't hear. They don't even talk to each other anymore, let alone to us. It's all me, me, me."

To his embarrassment, I ask the group about Tony. Isn't he an adult who listens and hears?

"He's a rare bird. He cares about other people and the community," says one.

"Last year, the shopowners didn't want us hanging out on the street in front of their stores. There was no place for us to go. There are no malls here. Tony stuck up for us. He's trying to get us a youth center," says someone else.

"Nobody on Martha's Vineyard comes close to doing what he does," says another.

But there was a time in his life when Tony didn't stand as tall. At the age of eighteen, his family disowned him, having tolerated all they could of his unrelenting heroin habit. For the next six years, he languished on the streets. Thereafter, he could have qualified as Nancy Reagan's poster boy.

He tells me his story on another day when we are alone. "One day, when I was twenty-four, I just said no to drugs. I realized that I was still alive, that I could have a second chance. But before that, God, I worked hard to be dead. Well, I decided

I'd been too selfish for too long. I needed to be selfless. I vowed to become a service-oriented person, and that's what I've become. It's how I see myself."

After he kicked his heroin habit, Tony was living in a halfway house, in no mood for socializing, wanting only to keep to himself. Fortuitously for him, there were deaf kids there. They taught him sign language. He moved to Martha's Vineyard because he thought of it as "a healing place." In the beginning, he was a program coordinator for a halfway house treating deaf alcoholics. Later he was a teacher for deaf high-school students. But Tony was not one to wear a single hat. He became, in his off hours, the island's de facto adolescent substance-abuse therapist-crisis manager. Kids called him day and night, hung out at or crashed at his house. His was a one-man shelter operation and foster home. He mediated disputes between the kids and their parents. Parents trusted him because he was consistent and delivered on what he promised. All that was not enough for Tony. He started a camp program for children with AIDS, another program for volunteer high-school students in Boston shelters, was the driving force in converting the Wintertide Coffehouse from a Saturday-night establishment to a full-scale nonprofit community performing arts center, and worked tirelessly for the establishment of an island teen center. These were his unpaid activities. His only paycheck came from Martha's Vineyard High School, where he taught. (A year after I met him, he resigned from teaching to devote more time to his community work.)

Kids are honest. They haven't had the benefit of years of practice at creating complex mental plumbing systems for rerouting truth. They know who the real heroes are, and how high or low the quality of life around them is. So it is with these young Vineyarders. It is only after I have talked with them that I come down from the "wonderful, wonderful Vineyard life" cloud, back to terra firma. These kids, underexposed to the violent world offshore, are overexposed to capitalism on-island. "Money, money, money, that's all our parents think about," they say. They look at violence from a safe, theoretical distance and at capitalism from a personal, very proximate location. The latter gives them pause. "You don't want to, but you feel like you have to care a lot about money," as Curt has said. His sentiments are shared by his friends. None of them gives so much as a hint at a possible connection between the money and the violence. Worlds apart, they seem to think. I leave them wishing that I could think so, too.

7

Winter

I am not a lover of winter. So to ease into a Vineyard one, I
arrive on the island on a Friday afternoon in November to spend
a transitional weekend at an inn in Gay Head that a friend has
recommended. Even though it is not yet winter, the look of it
is there—the brown blanket of earth and the blue-black sea—
and the feel of it—the penetrating chill, the cold wind's sting.
As soon as I round the corner from the Vineyard Haven boat
terminal to Holmes Hole Car Rental, I see another sign of
winter. Bruce has pulled his sidewalk benches inside behind the
closed door, and outside his lot is full of unrented cars. The
place is shut so tight that I head immediately up-island. The
land looks still and barren in the dwindling afternoon light. I
drive faster than usual to keep pace with daylight. The only
vehicles I pass are pickup trucks—a seemingly endless parade
of them. Soon after I cross over the town line into Gay Head,
I see the small sign and the abrupt turnoff to The Duck Inn

to the left of the main road. The dirt road winds down for some distance until, out in the middle of nowhere in a wide, sloping field, it leads me into a driveway adjacent to a medium-sized house. The air is hushed outside the car. No sight or sound of life. Perhaps I'm in the wrong place, I think, until I am startled by a loud oink from a black pig who appears suddenly from a thicket near the rear door of the house. If this pig is a marketing gimmick for the inn, it's a gimmick that appeals to me. I'm laughing out loud as I come through the back-door entrance. I know I'm in the right place when I see a check-in desk (minus a clerk) inside the door. This inn does very well at serving up homeyness to its guests. Inside, the place is only slightly inn-like. A quick sweep of the first-floor living area reveals the prominence of the duck theme, which is suggestive, if not telltale, evidence of an inn, but otherwise the ambience is homelike—actually more cluttered, relaxed, and cozy than most real homes.

As an innkeeper, Elise Lebovit is a natural. She makes an appearance just to get me settled in, then disappears rapidly without chatting me up the way so many innkeepers do. I don't see her again until the next morning at breakfast, when I sit down with her and a visiting mother and daughter from New Hampshire. In place of the usual loosening up, hostess-to-guest questions, Elise and I reverse roles. I am the interrogator. As might be expected, the first question I ask Elise is how she has come to where she is.

A romance with an island man and a calm, inexpensive way of life were the lures that brought her here twenty years ago, and even though she is in her forties now, it's hard to believe that she is no longer young. She has a petite, toned frame and a youthful face. If one looks closely, though, a kind of plaintive expression is etched in it. Perhaps it hints at disappointment—not only for a lost romance, but for the shattering of the dream of an inexpensive life on Martha's Vineyard.

When Elise walked by this house several years ago, she knew at first glance that she had to have it. It took a lot of wrangling to get it, but finally she prevailed. "I bought it to have a roof over my head, not to fulfill a romantic notion of owning an inn. But even with a full house, five rooms, from May to October, I can't make ends meet. Taxes are always ways ahead of me. In the summer, I live in a tent on the property. To cut fuel costs, I have converted the house to solar."

"And the idea for the name and decor of the inn, and the pig as greeter. How did they happen?" I ask.

"Well, it's a low-lying place that you have to duck into, and I like ducks so that's what's behind the duck theme. That duck-decorated toilet paper you use, that's imported from Virginia because I can't get it anywhere else. I realized that playing with puns wouldn't hurt business, and might even help. You know, guests *ducking* in and *pigging* out."

Figuring that innkeepers, like hairdressers, have good stories to tell, I ask her if she has any. She doesn't have to think to answer the question.

"There was one Labor Day weekend when we had twenty people around this breakfast table. A young man in faded cut-off dungaree shorts and a scruffy T-shirt and one of his buddies came through the door without knocking. 'Hi, my name is John, and I live here in Gay Head. I'd like to rent out this place for a stag party I'm planning,' he said. Well, I was rather annoyed at the way he just popped in unexpectedly. I thought maybe he was a criminal. As I stood in the doorway explaining to him that I ordinarily don't do stag parties and that he'd have to come back at a more convenient time to discuss it, I turned around to see all my guests craning their necks and leaning over to get a look at the guy. After he left and I returned to the table, twenty faces were staring at me dumbfounded. 'Didn't you know that that was none other than John-John, John F. Kennedy, Jr., you were talking to?' they asked incredulously."

She hadn't known, and not because she was unaccustomed to celebrities. They were always ducking in, some as guests, some to have her rub their backs and shoulders. Massages are her second source of income (and selling real estate her third). Before she left Manhattan for the Vineyard, she had been a Broadway masseuse to the stars. Nowadays, on the Vineyard, she gives four or five massages a day. She's massaged Lady Bird and Lynda Bird and—I should have guessed—James Taylor.

The more we talk, I come to see a cloud of regret that hovers over Elise. For many years, she had enjoyed happy relationships with her Wampanoag Native American neighbors. The lover who had wooed her to the Vineyard was a tribe member. Ever since their breakup, he has lived next door to her, but they no longer speak. Elise lost favor with the entire tribe when, while serving as one of the majority whites on the town zoning board, she cast the deciding vote against the Wampanoag's proposed public-housing project. She says she did so after many attempts to compromise, and solely out of concern that the tribe's tax-free status combined with the influx of school-age children would break the town's bank account. It cost her dearly. Thereafter, she was ostracized, branded a racist. "It was kind of ironic, like I was the Native American, and they were the whites. In retrospect, I think I was the victim of their long-smoldering anger at white people whose population in recent years had ballooned. The newcomers were wealthier and more proprietary. Before the influx, the white population had been small, liberal, and unconcerned about Native Americans trespassing for any reason, including their visiting ancient holy sites, which were located on whites' private properties. It's really sad, but now Gay Head has become an 'us' and 'them' community."

The infamous symbol of this schism was the well-publicized

ten-year imbroglio between Jackie Onassis and a prominent Wampanoag family. Located in the midst of Jackie's multiacre estate was a small parcel of land that her disputants claimed as theirs because it was an ancient, sacred spot. Unfortunately, privacy was as sacred to Jackie as the land was to her adversaries. Finally, very long after it began, the dispute was settled. The Native American family was deeded a neighboring parcel of land considered to be equal in spiritual significance and given rights of easement to cross over an outer rim of the Onassis property en route to it.

For Elise, the "us" and "them" battles have passed, but the wounds haven't healed. By the end of my weekend stay, she has confided that she cries a little everyday. "I remember the hurts and all the bonds that I lost."

In the ensuing winter months, I think often of Elise and the contrast between her person and her inn: how her Vineyard life has not been wonderful, but rather bittersweet, and how one could never guess that fact by the playful, whimsical, happy stamp she has put on her little Duck Inn.

I spend the first of my two in-the-dead-of-winter stays on the Vineyard in the Vineyard Haven Inn, which is nowhere near as atmospheric as The Duck Inn but is more conveniently located. Most of the time while I am there the building is underoccupied, but on weekends high-school hockey teams fill the vacant rooms. Then it turns boisterous, and its old wooden innards creak and whine, straining under the siege of pounding feet. Otherwise the three weeks I spend in the inn are calm and peaceful, easy to get around in, typical Vineyard winter weather—mild and snowless. Later, when I move into a rental house in Oak Bluffs for a month, the island is snow-ravaged, with storm heaping upon storm. Shoveling, for no other purpose than opening the door of my house, is a daily activity. My house is next door to

Sue, of Calico Sue's, and at night our houses are the only lighted ones on the block. The rest stand like ghosts, dressed in full skirts of snow, waiting for summer.

Whether blanketed in brown or white, the Vineyard in winter is a study in starkness. Most stores are closed. "We'll open in April," the signs on their doors read. The supermarkets and the banks are open, and here and there, a clothing store. People, bundled up in outerwear, straggle in and out of the open doorways. Parking spaces abound, and the roads are clear of foreign travelers. "This place belongs to us" is the message that winter sends to chance invaders.

I have come for these winter interludes in search of the "real" Martha's Vineyard. Whether it be truth or propaganda, the message I receive directly and repeatedly from year-round Vineyarders is the need for me to understand that only in winter can I see the island for what it is. I will find, so they tell me, that it is not the playground for the rich and famous that the media would have everyone believe. That's baloney. It's a place where people live from hand to mouth, making do as best they can. And though no one has to lock his doors at night, the absence of crime promises only safety, not happiness.

There are no people more "real" on Martha's Vineyard than the Wampanoags, the island's indigenous people. And, it is truth, not myth, that the early white settlers plundered and pillaged their communities, banished them from their lands, and killed vast numbers of them. Now, hundreds of years later, a small, proud tribal community remains in Gay Head.

One of the first things I do after I arrive on-island for the first winter is to arrange to meet with Beverly Wright, the Wampanoag Tribal Council chairperson, whose own roots go farther back than any white islander's. It's a cold January day, and on my way up-island, I spot a sign posted at the entrance to a wooded area off the State Road in West Tisbury. I pull over and read it.

WILL TRADE THESE 22 HISTORICAL ACRES, FOREST IRRIGATED PASTURE, POND, STONEWALLS, HILLS, ROAD, WELL, ELECTRIC, SEPTIC, SURVEYED, FENCED FOR MINT CONDITION RENTAL PROPERTY. OWNER, BOX 16052, RUMFORD, R.I. 02916.

The sign, except for the phrase about rental property, seems amusingly anachronistic for the Vineyard of today. A trade: twenty-two acres, every amenity but a house, no Realtor. How could it be? I wonder. The property, if it is all that it purports to be, must be valued in the millions of dollars. To match that, the rental property must be spectacular. I laugh as I drive away about the coincidence of coming across the word *trade* in the context of a commercial sign on my way to see Beverly Wright at the Wampanoag Tribal Council Building. The word has a Native American resonance, harking all the way back to the beginnings of commercial relationships between settlers and natives.

The modern-day Wampanoags are business wise and pound sensible. On Martha's Vineyard, where the majority of the remaining Wampanoags live, the tribal leadership works tirelessly on behalf of its seven hundred-plus members for social and economic benefits and rights, either centuries overdue or right in step with the majority society. With federal financing from HUD, they have built a thirty-unit low-income housing complex on land belonging to its trust. This means that some Wampanoags from the mainland will be relocating to the island. A majority of the white community in Gay Head objects to the housing, claiming that it will have a burdensome impact on local services—especially on the school, which will not receive tax revenues from the Wampanoag households. Instead, the tribe has offered impact aid to the school and funding for its own ambulance, fire, and police services. *Aquinnah*, the Native American's original name for Gay Head, is the name of the new development, a part of which is already occupied. Translated, it means "land below the hill, beautiful colors by the sea." (In 1997, the town of Gay Head voted to return to its original name, Aquinnah.)

Beverly Wright's office is in the handsome, glass-front Wampanoag Council Building, which sits overlooking the sea on land above the hill near where the ancient Moshup Trail converges with the State Road, close to the westernmost point on Martha's Vineyard. The building serves as a meeting place for the community and the center for its health and human services, economic development, land trust, natural resources, education, and general administration needs.

Ms. Wright is a paid elected official who is in her third two-year term as chairperson. When election time comes in a small community like hers, her opponent may be a member of her own family. Thus far, she has prevailed in all of her campaigns and presides over an eleven-member council on which she has already served for twelve years as an unpaid member. Today, the council is a growing organization which relies heavily on ever-scarcer federal funding.

"We needed to find other funding resources. We thought about starting small businesses to provide employment and revenue, but we didn't have sufficient capital, so we explored the potential of the Indian Gaming Regulatory Act, which was passed by the federal government in 1988. Native Americans have been in the gaming business for the last quarter century. The act establishes guidelines and regulations for tribal gaming establishments. We thought of opening a casino, not here, too small, but in New Bedford. With the concurrence of the governor, we could take state land into trust and build on it. Governor Weld supported us. New Bedford was a depressed area, and our casino would provide five thousand to seven thousand new jobs, with preference for tribal members. Everyone would benefit. The state would receive a percentage of the revenues. We would be able to sustain our services, and New Bedford would have job opportunities. We've put two years into this effort, meeting with lawyers, public-relations people, state and local officials, developers, and federal government representatives. The complexity of the project is mind-boggling."

By the spring of 1996, the casino project is no closer to fruition, caught in an endless tangle of red tape, and Ms. Wright is more than a year into her third term. (As of January 1998, the casino project was no further along.)

"This tribe is my whole life," she confesses. "Burnout would be easy, but I want to do this for my children and their children to ensure that they will have land, education, and health. It's my time to contribute. We're on the cusp of merging into a huge organization. We've had some really stressful times. Eventually, we won the housing battle, but the issue tore the community apart. I believe in depersonalizing conflict, so we hired a mediator to help resolve our differences with the wider community. There was racism. Whites were afraid of an invasion of 'little brown people.' "

Beverly Wright was born on the Vineyard, a descendant of its true natives. Her grandfather was a tribal chief. Her mother, now in her eighties, has always lived there. But for twenty years, Beverly lived a suburban housewife's existence in New Jersey, visiting the Vineyard in the summertime. Traces of that life show in her person, in the sleekness of her dress and comportment, in the hints of the modern, smart mainland career woman. Evidences of both lives is revealed in her casual, unassuming, friendly manner—professional, but less formal than that of administrators on the other shore. Not until 1976, when she and her husband divorced and she became a single parent, did she relocate to the island for good. Upon her return, she went to work as an administrative assistant to the county commissioners. Without benefit of a college degree, the job gave her experience that would prove invaluable when her time for leadership arrived.

Throughout her tenure as chairperson, Beverly can look back with pride upon her accomplishments. If one were to put Ronald Reagan's rhetorical question to the Wampanoags today— "Are you better off now than you were four years ago?"—the answer would be "yes." The combination of federal help to the tribe and escalated property values on Martha's Vineyard appear to have given the Wampanoags the economic boost they need to survive the brutal island winters. After I depart, I feel heartened by their improving circumstances and by the implication that they represent the belated receipt of partial reparation for their losses. As an outsider, a nonresident of the town, I find it next to impossible to ally with those who give greater weight to school budget and tax revenue shortages than to the long-awaited deliverance of just compensation. Perhaps I would see things differently if I lived there, but I hope not.

I find little evidence of hand-to-mouth living during my routine midwinter breakfast visits to The Artcliff Diner. Sometimes after snowstorms, I don't make it in until my driveway is shoveled out and the roads are passable. In the wintertime, the one-room eatery is packed with regulars, most of whom are men. Over the counter, there are old signs with pictures of food and accompanying prices: hamburgers for a dime, coffee for a nickel, a full breakfast plate of toast, eggs, and bacon for a quarter. The Artcliff has been one of the last holdouts on the smoking front, and because smoke still permeated the diner's air when President Clinton came to the island, he refused to grace it with a visit. That didn't endear him to Pat, the owner, who holds smoky court most mornings with her loyal male contingent. (In

1996, the Artcliff went the way of the other island establishments and banished smoking.)

The wintertime Artcliff is more fun for an eavesdropper like me than the summertime Artcliff. Then it is jam-packed with tourists hankering for good food and reasonable prices—that rarest of combinations on Martha's Vineyard. But being there in winter is like dropping into a neighbor's kitchen and finding your other neighbors already seated around the table.

Pat and I always go through an opening how-to-find-Johnny-Seaview ritual, but one day toward the end of my second winter stay is particularly memorable because she teases me unmercifully about my failure to find him. Admittedly, my unsuccessful pursuit of the man has extended beyond all reasonable parameters.

"You still haven't found him? What's the matter with you? This isn't New York, you know. He's either here or at Cumberland Farms. You just don't know when he's coming. He's not consistent."

"I know," I answer defensively. "Do you know how many times I've gone to Cumberland Farms looking for him? He's never there when I'm there. I'm just about ready to give up on him. There's only so much looking I can do."

"Maybe you oughta have your eyes checked, honey. I told you, he always wears the same red hat, and he's usually here or there. You just can't miss him. Now, what do ya want to eat?" I try not to be hurt that she's forgotten that I always have a muffin and a cup of coffee.

On this day at Pat's head table, the gang is looking at photographs of a birthday party that she has given for one of them at the diner. Besides the Johnny Seaview ribbing I've taken from Pat, there's another reason that this is a red-letter day for me at the diner. For the first time, I'm partially included in Pat's select group. She brings the photos over to my table. One photograph shows the rafters decorated with streamers, balloons, and HAPPY BIRTHDAY messages, and another reveals the ample, naked midsection of party's hired belly dancer, surrounded by admiring men in their seventies. Some of the men in the photo are in the diner this morning trading laughs with Annette, a black woman working behind the counter. I miss a wisecrack that one man hurtles at Annette, who is laughing hard and loud, but I hear Pat turn the joke back on him. "What's the matter? Have you got something against black people?" she asks kiddingly, and before he can answer Annette bellows, "Well, you've got one more day to be nice to me. Tomorrow Black History Month is over." Everyone at the table roars at that one. As the laughter dies down, one man heads over to Cumberland Farms to cash in his scratch lottery ticket. "I guess I'll come here again," he says sardonically on his way out the door. But he would have to wait for three weeks to return, because the Artcliff is closing for most of March while Pat is in Florida. The succession of snowstorms this winter has taken its toll on her. She can't wait to get down South.

I am postponing my meeting with the "real" Martha's Vineyard. Island winters require acclimatizing. They highlight and intensify personal isolation. And, for one as accustomed as I am to a social existence, the long stretches of unbroken silence between breakfast and nightfall are initially unnerving. I suspect that I am afraid that if I go looking for it, I will become unhinged by other people's desolation. So at first, I keep avoiding that possibility. Instead, I look for entertainment, for places where people gather, where there is music, drama, and laughter. For the first few weeks of winter I am a presence at whatever island entertainment venues are open. I frequent the Wintertide.

Throughout the year, the doyenne of Vineyard performing arts, Helen Stratford, performs there. There is a fey quality about her on stage. It has something to do with her clothes—her big floppy hats, billowy vintage dresses and skirts, and jumbles of jewelry—and something to do with her self-absorbed demeanor when seated at the piano playing the wistful melodies she composes. Sometimes she just plays; at other times she plays and sings. Sometimes she is the only act, at others, the opening act, but whenever she is onstage, she looks as if she has an organic relationship to it. One senses that she makes her exits regretfully, a little sorrowfully, with the insinuation that nothing offstage could be as nice as this.

Indeed, Helen's early offstage life had been tumultuous. Her entrance into the world and the childhood that followed were preternaturally dramatic. She was born into a turbulent, fatherless household where she lived temporarily with an alcoholic grandmother, alcoholic aunts and uncles, and an obese, feckless mother. When she was four, she and her younger sister were placed into the unloving arms of the state of New Jersey. For many years, the two girls lived with stern, Calvinistic foster parents who gave them no freedom and held them of little value, and when the foster family moved out of state, Helen, then in adolescence, refused to go. New Jersey, this time, if not a loving surrogate parent, was a creative one. The state had no vacancies in their juvenile facilities, so Helen was sent, at the state's expense, to a progressive boarding school in Connecticut from which she subsequently graduated.

"I learned how to be a bohemian there. It was lucky that I proved to be an excellent student, as well. We called our teachers by their first names. We were given wide berth to express ourselves. My fellow students were classy. They took European trips, and had their own shrinks. Someone was always trying suicide. Well, I was Miss Kmart, three-piece polyester, mistaking my tackiness for classiness. Being artsy was a good alibi, it got me out of a useless attempt to be like them, and eventually, after a few years living and working on my own in New York, it and my good grades got me into Vassar." There, her artistic side blossomed, but once she'd finished college, it wilted, and she drifted. From job to job, man to man, place to place, substance to substance. There was a stint with a theater company in Manhattan, and a consequent love affair with a Shakespearean actor who courted, then abandoned her, broke her heart at just about the time he was due to appear in a play on Martha's Vineyard. "I'd never heard of Martha's Vineyard, but I knew when and in what venue he was performing. I decided I'd go there, sit obscurely in the audience, and have a private good-bye with him from a back-row seat." Helen arrived on the island dressed for New York anonymity—long sequined black gown, black hat, and black pumps, thinking that she'd fade into the crowd.

"Well, you know what the amphitheater here looks like. It's a clearing in the woods. I must have looked like one of the Witches of Eastwick," she exclaims, laughing all over again at herself. Somehow though she managed to accomplish her silent farewell. "After the performance, I was hitchiking to the youth hostel where I planned to stay for only one night. Two Edgartown men picked me up. They owned a huge sailboat and needed a helmsman to sail it to Boston." They trained Helen to take the helm. She stayed on the boat all summer, returned briefly to New York, and then was whisked back to the island by one of the men she'd met on the boat.

Helen's story has a happy ending. She stayed on-island, healed her habits, met another man—her one and only—and set up housekeeping with him and rediscovered her artistic soul. "Music composition brought me back to life. It was like I arose from a stupor." Once arisen, she founded the ongoing Darkside/Wintertide series, held biweekly in winter and monthly in summer at the Wintertide. For her long-running show, she recruited talented island performers, directed the staging, and performed her own work. Her reach extended further. She helped showcase fledgling performers by helping to manage and maintain the Sunday night Daggett Street Cafe performances.

One dollar buys me admission to the Daggett Cafe show, where the off-the-street talent comes to strut its stuff. Helen, dressed as usual in her from-the-house-of-Helen attire, plays the piano first, then presides over that night's variety troupe—poets and writers, musicians, singers, comics, and thespians—and does her best to hold them to time limits. Some of the talent is so-so, some dazzling. A young writer reads a wonderful stream-of-consciousness piece about a remote-control device. And there is originality and derring-do in the performance of a scarlet-haired singer with a beautiful mezzo-soprano voice who croons a witty, autobiographical song—an opus-in-progress about her life in the nineties.

The next day, I have a chance to compliment her. We're seated at adjacent tables in an outdoor café on an unseasonably warm winter day. I look up from a book and find her there beside me. I tell her that I admired her performance.

"Do you live here year-round?" I ask.

"I can't afford that luxury yet. I commute between here and New York. I teach and perform there so I can earn enough money to live here part time. I have a few students on-island now, but I'd need a lot more to live here permanently. I don't like the New York show world. Fame and fortune are not what I've wanted. My work is too personal for New York." She continues in a personal vein, talking about some of her experiences on the Vineyard. Most notably, about a Native American friend who has taken her to historic healing sites all over the island. Occasionally, they've wandered onto property she assumes is private. "Hell, no," he tells her every time. "None of it is private. My people own this island. We've been here for

191

two thousand years." Once he tells her an ancient story of his ailing forebears on the mainland hearing the voice of a wise man directing them to move to the healing place on a yonder island. So his people come to Martha's Vineyard and are healed. "That's how it came to be a healing place," she says emphatically. "It's one of the main reasons why I like being here."

"There's not a whole lotta healing goin' on that I can see," says Hank Giddings, a rock and blues musician on the island. "The people who come to hear me in the off-season, the regulars, they sure as hell aren't healed. I know that there's supposed to be a big recovery movement here, and God knows there are twenty meetings a day in various places on the island. Somebody must be going to them, but recovery doesn't scream out at me. The people I see get trashed, really trashed, and it seems to be OK, like it doesn't have the stigma that it has in the city." And, indeed, when I go to hear Hank at a restaurant-club in Oak Bluffs on a cold winter's night, the unrecovered are well represented. At the bar, beer goes sloshing down gullets at high speed, like pouring bucketfuls of water down dry wells. Hank and his band play on gamely through the clatter of bottles and glasses and the din of barside conversations. Although I'm seated next to the band, a big room's length from the bar, I can barely hear Hank's voice or appreciate the music. I watch the action at the bar. At intervals, the drinkers swivel their barstools away from their beers toward the bandstand as if they're moving on automatic timers. Listening time. Another swivel, back to the bar. Replenishing time. And, around and around, listening and replenishing until the end of the tune, when every stool faces the band. Clapping time.

Hank is the son of a good friend of mine, so the following day he invites me to his house. Over coffee in his living room, he tells me that in the summer his three-piece band has a wider, more music-centered audience. Secretly he wonders why the bar owners hire them in the winter. Wouldn't the customers be there anyway, without the music? Maybe, he surmises, it is his job to get the crowd excited, thirstier. He isn't sure, but he is grateful for the gigs, especially if he and his wife are to seriously contemplate permanent residency on the island. They bought their Edgartown house back when they were both making good money in Manhattan in the winter, he with musical jingles and she as a dancer. But after a while, the jingle business went sour and his wife, Suzanne, got pregnant. So, after the summer of 1995, when Hank was making good money working seven nights in clubs on the Vineyard and playing at weddings and parties, the Giddings stayed on through the winter, supplementing his reduced music income with rent from the rentable spaces in their house. They still keep a low-rent studio apartment in New York, and return there periodically through the winter. The Giddings can't get by without these city jaunts. He does a jingle or two. She teaches a dance class, and with their pockets a little fuller, they return to the island.

Unlike the other artists I have met who unanimously swear allegiance to the Vineyard, Hank and Suzanne are uncommitted to full-time island living. Yes, they like the safety, the unlocked doors, the beauty and mellowness, the cooperative community spirit, but they miss their New York life, and more so when cabin fever strikes and they can't see whichever movie they want or get the citified stimulation to which they are accustomed. Add to that the legendary Edgartown snobbery, which turns out to be as real as it is legendary—a neighbor who never speaks to you, another who keeps reminding you of his importance— and you feel less sure that you belong here. For Hank, it's easier than for Suzanne. He's out more, and has more friends, people who, in contrast with his friends in New York, will always help him out in a pinch: other musicians, artists, and contractors.

"Everybody here's a contractor, even if they call themselves something else. Maybe I should be one, too," he says when we part, then adds as an afterthought, "Make sure you talk to Johnny Seaview. He's not a contractor, but he's the real thing, an honest-to-God island character."

Ultimately, I learn to enjoy, even to treasure, the solitude that winter on the Vineyard affords me. It becomes at once renewing and self-absorbing. Renewing, because it both heightens my awareness and relieves me of the daily stressors I live with in the city—the claims on my time and energy, the demand to serve other people's needs, the allegiance to a schedule, the constant ringing of the telephone and fax, the intermittent fear of bodily harm. Self-absorbing, because it places no restrictions on egocentricity. I feel like an islander, a refugee from the world. I imagine myself poor, ill, unhappy, and think that it might be less painful to be in any of those conditions on this island. I'd be free to attend to my own wounds, to leave all other worldly cares to others. At home in Boston, I set my electronic burglar alarm each night. Here, I don't lock my doors.

It is during the winter that I meet Alice DuBois, a mother with a meager paycheck who had come from Oregon with her two children to the Vineyard. They all wanted to go east. Her marriage had dissolved, and she and her children, like the mallard family in *Make Way for Ducklings*, were searching for a new home near the water. Before she left the west, Alice subscribed to the *Cape Cod Times*, and made up her mind to head for Hyannis. By chance, after she arrived, she responded to an ad for a nanny on Martha's Vineyard. She would not be paid, but would receive room and board for herself and her children. That was in January 1994.

"The woman who employed me had three kids and worked

three nights. I covered for her during work and on three additional days. On my days off, I worked as a bookkeeper at a motel for ten dollars an hour. There was never enough food for all of us, so I was always having to spend what little money I had for food."

Then May came—the cruelest month on Martha's Vineyard. Alice's employer wanted Alice and her family out so she could rent their rooms to summer people. Alice was desperate to find a place to live. She went to a town picnic and met a pregnant mother with two children who was planning to put her baby up for adoption because she couldn't afford to care for it. She lived in a two-bedroom trailer. But those who have the least are often those who give the most. This woman of no means took in Alice and her children for a month. When their children went off to visit their fathers for a month, she slept on the living-room couch so that Alice could keep her bedroom and the other could be rented. Alice contributed whatever she could. At summer's end, another kind woman offered Alice and her children a place to stay in her large house.

Ten months after she arrived on the Vineyard, Alice found a permanent home. Nothing fancy, but big enough to accommodate her family with an extra room to rent out in the summer. Every month, she struggles to pay the rent and her credit-card bills. A car marked FOR SALE with little equity in it sits in her driveway, but it was the value of that car, not the huge sum she owed on it, that prevented her from receiving food stamps and subsidized housing. "With that nice car," the officials said, "it wouldn't look good for us to be giving you food stamps."

The Island Food Pantry and temporary fuel assistance saved Alice from going over the edge. But, according to those like Alice who teeter on it, a Martha's Vineyard edge is not as precipitous as a mainland edge. There are always people willing to lend a helping hand, they say. Still, I couldn't help thinking that if Alice lived on the mainland, her college degree in physics might have offered her a steadier helping hand. Physicists are not in demand on Martha's Vineyard. Despite her bare-bones existence, though, Alice prefers to be where she is.

"I don't have to worry about my kids' safety. I can leave them alone at night. They can walk anywhere on the island at any time. We don't have to lock our doors at night."

Alice's recollections of the death of her cat, not her stories of financial stresses, bring the tears to her eyes. Just before it died, it had borne two kittens who later required hospitalization, round-the-clock attention, and emergency procedures. Alice told the vet she'd beg and borrow, if need be. The kittens were saved, and the vet forgave the bill. The helping hand again.

"Where else would something like that happen?" Alice asks.

Martha Coles, a woman in her forties, is a lot like Alice. She lives with her two kids in a small winter rental house. When May comes and the rent goes up, she moves to a campground and pitches a tent for a $1,650 seasonal plot fee. She has a canvas roof over the family's head, a propane stove, a refrigerator, an electric hookup, and close proximity to the "facilities." If it happens to be a rainy summer, dampness infests everything. Heaven for Martha would be a bigger, off-the-ground tent, more moisture-resistant, with a built-in counter, stove, and refrigerator, but the price would be high—$2,500 for a used luxury accommodation like that. She isn't sure she can ever afford it on her savings from her salary as a licensed practical nurse. Every April she begins the packing process, organizing her belongings, then moving them to a summer storage bin. At this time in February, the next move is not yet on her mind. "Some of that is denial," she says. "I don't like the feeling I get in the pit of my stomach at the thought of moving."

I am amazed at Martha's equanimity, and tell her so. She laughs.

"Look, my kids get to grow up here. They can have real childhoods. The schools are good. It's safe, much safer than Anyplace, America. So, I live paycheck to paycheck. It's worth it. At least I can provide food, clothing, and shelter. I get spiritual meaning from living here. I'm closer to my inner self. It's got something to do with the water. It's cleansing."

Martha goes on to explain how she believes that some preternatural power put her on Martha's Vineyard to partake of its gift of water. From that source, she believes, she was empowered to recover from alcohol abuse, confront herself, deal with stress. And she accepts the gift gladly. Whenever she is upset, she walks by the water and returns to herself.

Brenda Grady like Alice and Martha, is in her early forties, but unlike either, she is childless and an island native. Nor does she share Alice's faith in the island's helping hand. In the course of her adult life, she has made many entrances and exits to and from the island. "Wherever I was, I'd be thinking about the Vineyard, the blues and greens of it, the different colors of the sand, and I'd cry so much that I'd have to come back." On her last return, she was divorced, and for a while, things went well for her. She had a good job, a good year-round rental, and a successful recovery from alcohol abuse. Things were going fine until she was suddenly evicted without forewarning or clear rationale. "OK, so I get lucky, I find another rental, but it's not secure. The landlord can easily kick me out to get a higher summer rental. I can't afford to pay summer prices. I think I'm going to have to leave again, but I'm stubborn about it. This is home to me, but I feel it being taken away from me. The way of life is gone, that secure feeling I had as a child that everything was hunky-dory because I lived on an island where no one locked their doors at night. We were a poor family, living with the bare necessities and hand-me-downs, but I didn't even know it until I was in my thirties. There's no community anymore, just an occasional glimpse of it in wintertime. Eventually the long arm of capitalism will reach out and grab everyone but the rich, and plunk them down somewhere else. I'm next in line. In places like Aruba and New Zealand, business people from somewhere else can't just come in, make their money, and leave. They have to stick around, hire people, not replace them. Here, anyone can come in, set up shop, stay for a while, and leave at the end of the tourist season."

Despite her awareness of the cruel economic realities, Brenda is pulled by a stronger magnet. "This island is my home," she keeps repeating. "It's safe, it's beautiful, and it's familiar."

I tell her that I have heard the word "safe" more than any other word to describe the Vineyard, and wonder if that means that Vineyarders are a fearful lot.

Brenda pauses a long time pondering the thought. "I guess we are," she answers finally. "We think we're safe because there's no crime, because we're protected from it by the water. There's just enough truth in that to make us forget that crime is not the only, not even the worst danger that confronts us."

So Brenda is going to leave. No, she is going to stay. She'll let things take their course. If (a very, very big if) she can scrape together the money to buy a house, have her own door to leave unlocked, that will be security. Then she can stay. Then she won't have to wonder where else she could go to find those blues and greens, that multicolored sand.

Where else? seems to be the year-rounder's perpetual, rhetorical question. Just ask those who have come from Brazil through the urban gateways of New York and Boston and cut their teeth there, laboring in restaurant kitchens, returning in the small hours of the morning to rented rooms. They will tell you that this is not the America they expected to see. It's not the way it looks on their TV screens back in Brazil. Their image of America is easy come, easy go, a joyride on a river of lucre. But what you see on the screen is not what you get in the actual place. Life is a grind in the big American cities, and eventually some of these immigrant Brazilians tire of it and return to Brazil. The Brazilians on Martha's Vineyard have come through friends or relatives who have acted as pioneers, in search of an easier America. Maybe on Cape Cod they'll find it. And while there they ought to take the boat out from Falmouth for a lark, to take a look at this Martha's Vineyard that is all the rage with Americans. Some decide they like it and settle in. They get the word out to friends and relatives in Boston or New York, and they follow, passing the word over telephone lines to their towns in Brazil, and soon a new wave, untested by the American metropolises, arrives direct from Brazil into the ever-growing Brazilian community on the island. For the most part, they will staff the Vineyard restaurant kitchens and hotel laundries just as their predecessors have in the cities. One Brazilian state about six hours by car from Rio, Minas Jerais, and one of its towns of fifteen thousand people, Conselheiro Pena, is home to most of the Vineyard Brazilians. It became the launching pad for a Brazilian community on Martha's Vineyard. Now people come from other states and towns.

No one around the dining-room table at nineteen-year-old Catarina's parents' rented home in Edgartown can agree on how many Brazilians reside here. "One hundred in the winter, three hundred in the summer," says Aunt Marlena.

"No, no," says Catarina, "three hundred in the winter, one thousand in the summer," arguing with her aunt in Portuguese.

"They're both wrong," adds Uncle Reinaldo in English, escalating the argument. "I've been here longer than they have. I ought to know. It's more like two hundred in the winter, five hundred in the summer."

"No," shouts Catarina's young brother and sister. And soon everyone—aunt, uncle, kids, Mom and Pop—are arguing at a fast clip in high-pitched Portuguese sprinkled intermittently with English phrases.

But, as there is no way to find consensus, they move on to other topics. Marlena, a young woman in her thirties, has been on the island for seven years. First came her brother, Reinaldo's friend, then Reinaldo, then Marlena. For her, as for them, her arrival was followed by a chain of firsts. She is the first Brazilian to have worked at an up-island inn, the first to work at a certain pizza parlor. Soon she has a network of friends and relatives on the island. It's a good life, less dangerous in every way than small-town Brazil or urban America. Back in Brazil her family owns land and grows coffee. They have a good life. So, if it's a good life here and there, it's a wonderful life when you combine the two. You make a better hourly wage here, have land there, visit once a year, and if you get sick, you go back there because there's no health insurance here.

Reinaldo came for the excitement of it. Back in Brazil, he planned to be an architect, but his designs for buildings were no match for his designs on adventure. Finished with his undergraduate studies, he was free from studying and ripe for living. And live he did, all over the United States. When he got to Boston, he hit the jackpot—a girlfriend with a rich mother who took the couple on gambling junkets to Atlantic City and Las Vegas, to Florida for the Super Bowl. She even bought them a house near hers to live in and an allowance to live on. If only the girlfriend could have kicked her drug habit, Reinaldo might have found the America he'd seen on TV back in Brazil. After three dream years, he said good-bye to the high life and settled for the working life on Martha's Vineyard. Carpentry was okay in a pinch, but not for the long haul. Australia is Reinaldo's new mecca. He has a cousin there who has struck it rich. "Come on over, you'll love it here," she tells him. Why stay here with a green card and pay taxes to the government? Who needs taxes when Australia beckons?

"Don't think we come over here because we're poor. Only a minority of us are poor, but why not be rich? That's why we come. We Brazilians love money. You have to be dressed to go out in Brazil, no jeans and sneakers for a night on the town. Fancy clothes and cars and jewelry are expensive. See what I mean?"

I see what he means, but just to make sure I really have it, he tells me about a poor cousin on the Vineyard.

"You oughta see her. Wow, does she dress rich—jewelry and fancy clothes. If you saw her, you'd think she was a fine lady."

Dark-eyed, dark-haired Catarina is beautiful, but a fine lady? Not on a salary of $100 a week at a hotel laundry. No jewelry and fancy clothes for her. Catarina's mother would have liked her daughter to finish her education, but Catarina will be getting married instead to a Brazilian she met on the island. Back home, she had been in college, but studying held about as much appeal for her as it held for Uncle Reinaldo. Better to be married and earning money. Her $400- to $500-a-month wages and the approximately $1,000 a month her fiancé earns as a dishwasher make the $300 rent for his house in Oak Bluffs affordable. Further evidence that love, be it budget or luxury style, comes without academic prerequisites attached.

For a small minority of Reinaldo's kinfolk, the money trail leads not to the bank but to the Island Food Pantry. There they are joined on Friday afternoons in winter by other islanders, old and young, predominantly white, who arrange themselves haphazardly, whether alone or in pairs or clusters, on the benches in the church basement. People hold blue tickets as if they are in an audience awaiting a performance. When new people straggle in, the heads on the benches turn in unison in the direction of the newcomers, and follow them until they've taken their seats. But the before-the-curtain buzz is missing here, supplanted by a plaintive hush, a collective disquiet. In the center of the room, at a distance from the waiting audience, a lone man sits behind a table busily sorting and marking papers. His presence lends tension to the scene.

After what seems to be an interminable silence, the man calls for someone to come forward. Shyly and hesitantly a woman approaches the table and presents her blue ticket. Scanning his papers, he locates her name and applies a pencilmark beside it, then, reaching under the table, hands her a paper sack, and directs her to the food table on his right, whispering instructions on allowable quantities. Open cardboard boxes bulging with vegetables and bread sit on the table, and farther to his right, in an open kitchen area, sits a large refrigerator containing perishable foods. Adjacent to it are shelves stocked with boxes and cans.

"Next," he repeats at intervals to the patient bench sitters, then ploddingly follows the same set of procedures with which he'd begun. He is neither unkind nor officious. When one or another appears before him without the blue ticket, he lets him proceed with a gentle admonition for next time. "Just be sure to bring a letter from your doctor, minister, or some other qualified person," he advises softly.

Although it appears at opening time that only a few people need the food pantry, as the afternoon wears on, their numbers swell and people's faces acquire a generic quality. Only one woman's image stays with me. I would recognize her now if I passed her on the street. She is alone on a bench in the back of the room. Her clothes, her posture, the look on her face spell *middle class.* Watching her reminds me that of all the deceptions we Americans allow ourselves, none is more fictitious than our proclaimed lack of class-consciousness. This woman wears her shame awkwardly—head lowered, eyes roving over surfaces, averting other eyes. For a flickering moment, hers meet mine.

They are the saddest eyes I've seen on Martha's Vineyard.

Those sad eyes notwithstanding, if Alice, Martha, Brenda, and the other people in the food pantry are the true faces of Vineyard poverty, then poverty looks less desperate and debilitating here than in any other place in the world. I know it seems odd and perhaps cynical, this comparing of one kind of poverty to another. But the poverty I am seeing makes me dubious that I am seeing it at all. The condition I think of as poverty doesn't look like this. It has a host of accompanying miseries: substandard housing, criminality, untreated illness, child abuse and neglect, addiction, domestic violence. If these concommitant miseries exist on the island, they must be hiding somewhere far from view.

After talking to Ann Wallace, the director of women's support services at the Martha's Vineyard Community Services Center, I soon discover that some miseries are more easily concealed, whether or not they are consequences of poverty. She shows me that there is a dark side to island life, one I'm unlikely to see firsthand. First, she tells me that she's skeptical about the belief, widespread among islanders, that the island is a healing place. "I'm sure some people do find peace and a return to health here, but we in this agency are always looking at cold, hard statistics. On this island, we have three times the state average for people discharged from substance-abuse programs. We have a higher percentage of active abusers. And we have a high rate of sexual assault, which rises dramatically in the summertime. In the winter, we have severe unemployment problems, and many cold, dark days. In one year, out of a winter population of six thousand women, we saw three hundred fifty who were battered. Some islanders have the illusion that because they're surrounded by water, they're protected from earthly woes."

Ann and her staff of four perform counseling, education, court advocacy, and community outreach, and take turns manning the twenty-four-hour hot-line service for victims of domestic violence. They run a volunteer safe home, a shelter program, and provide training for the volunteers.

"The women are in a fishbowl here. Everyone knows their business. Battering crosses all racial and socioeconomic lines. It takes guts for a woman to come forward knowing that anonymity isn't possible. Think of the guilt and shame, the self-blame that accompanies that. And, as if that weren't bad enough, real protection is hard to come by. It's easy for batterers to find their victims on an island this size. That's why we don't have one shelter site. It would be too obvious and too dangerous. While the women are in the safe home, they can be hidden temporarily. If we think anyone is in grave danger, we will arrange for her to leave the island. Otherwise, we work hand in hand with the police and the courts to help us protect our clients. We have court-mandated programs for batterers, but we do not regard victims as mentally unhealthy. We see battering as a cultural problem, as a consequence of a patriarchal society. Battered women who feel depressed have good reason, and we will not be party, covertly or overtly, to the notion that there's something wrong with them for having been battered. Thus, we are not proponents of antidepressant medication."

Wallace, like many mental-health professionals on the island, looks to psychiatrist and Vineyarder Milton Mazer for inspiration in her work. In his book, *People and Predicaments*, a study of life and distress on Martha's Vineyard, Mazer describes the role confusions that plague year-round residents. An economy dependent on tourism is ripe for nourishing a love-hate relationship between year-rounders and summer residents and tourists. During the winter months, the islander is king of the hill, but once summer arrives, he becomes a servant to seasonal kings of bigger hills. He builds and renovates their houses, fishes for their suppers, fixes what they need fixed, and sells his wares to them. Whether he is invited to or excluded from their cocktail parties, his social status is lower than theirs. He can't help but note the disparity between summer wealth and winter poverty, and feel some uncertainty about where he fits on the top-heavy ladder. Neither can he avoid resenting the time-conscious and entitled attitudes that the city slickers import to the island culture. There are the women in white, for example, who seem to presume that their financial contributions to the local economy earn them the privilege of cutting to the front of the checkout line so they can be punctual for their tennis lessons.

"The islanders' entire value system goes out of whack in the summer," Wallace explains, and could well have added that the resulting psychological problems those values engender don't vanish with the season. "From May through September, the women here go out and get three jobs to cover them for the winter months when they're lucky to have one job. They're careful not to offend anyone on whose business they depend, but the rest of us take it for granted that we are free to disagree, to express ourselves honestly. Our work doesn't force us into developing hidden agendas."

Before we part ways, Ann gives me two examples of the aftereffects of the O. J. Simpson trial. One is an ethical dilemma that confronted Ann Nelson, the owner of the island's largest bookstore, The Bunch of Grapes, when O. J.'s I-didn't-do-it book was published. Should she, could she, in good conscience, put it on her shelves, given the high rate of spousal abuse on the island and on the mainland? Finally, she decided to stock it and donate the profits to the Women's Support Services. The other example is about a call Ann Wallace herself received from an editor at a widely circulated magazine. "I wonder if you could tell us if you know of any celebrities on the Vineyard who beat their wives?" inquired the voice from the Manhattan suite.

"That was an easy call," Ann explains. "I just refused to answer."

Judging from my own limited experience, the island does carry an imprimatur of recovery, whether mythical or real. "This is a healing place," people remind me repeatedly, and indeed there are legends of healing passed down from the Native Americans who have designated healing areas around the island (like the one located on Jackie Onassis's estate). And, since many people I meet in the winter have recovery stories, I begin to believe that it might be true. Maybe the island has magical, curative powers. All the stories begin as grim tales of aimless drifting, addictions, adulthoods gone awry, and end in triumph and renewal four miles out to sea at the healing place.

One night I accompany a friend, who is herself "in recovery," to an island A.A. meeting in Chilmark in the hope of seeing healing in progress. (This is one of countless meetings on the island.) There are about twenty-five people in attendance.

"I don't like feeling feelings. I can feel them, but I don't know what they mean," confesses the first speaker, a man whose words are echoed by his successors in the speaker's chair.

"It is easier to be called mentally ill than to be called an alcoholic, easier to be hospitalized than admit to a drinking problem. It's a relief to be mentally ill, to be taken care of in an institution." Another male speaker, another echo.

More chorus and refrain from men of all ages and a handful of women about the uselessness of psychiatry, about their children's alcoholism, about how mental hospitals at least spared you from being a spin-dried detox junkie, about the abundance of pills prescribed by doctors, and about depressions waiting to happen.

I woman I'll call Claire has a judge in her head, a loud, critical voice telling her she's no good at getting sober, that she's a failure. She was drunk last week. "I feel like scrap metal, but I like it better on the other side where you pick up the pieces, not on this side, where you are the piece." Claire hates "tough love." What if she is one of those who can't quit? She will be bitter.

Marty, too, sober for one month, is edgy and restless. "I'm still nuts, still really insecure. I think about drinking every day. If anything, I'm a credible drunk. I'm insane to still be thinking about it."

Ed is a trucker. For many years, he was late on his runs. "Well, he's just been drinking," his bosses would tell their customers. Never said it was a problem. His doctor hinted it, but didn't say it. He had never been in any kind of institution for anything, just Catholic schools where it was safe to drink, and everyone was either an Einstein or an abuser.

All present at this evening's meeting agree that there is nothing as good for alcoholics as going to meetings, every day if you need to. The know-nothing professionals are out of the way, you're among peers, and with their support, you can weather any storm. On a note of thanks, the meeting ends. Much to my disappointment, there has been no mention of Martha's Vineyard, nor any reference to its healing capabilities. The meeting could have been anywhere.

Maybe just for the chance to tell a happy story, to render the unreal real, I want to believe that the island *is* truly a healing place, that those who come here addicted and afflicted do recover. But, alas, I can't. Not because I'm an inveterate skeptic, but because I have put the question to many who *have* recovered (most from alcohol abuse). Unanimously, they say that the un-recovered outnumber them by a wide margin. Like Hank Gid-dings, the musician, they say that there's not a whole lotta healing goin' on that they can see.

During much of my winter's stay on Martha's Vineyard, I keep to myself, partly because as soon as I shovel out my driveway, another storm fills it up again. Not that there aren't winter events to attend. There are activities to suit every sensibility: lectures, dances, bridge games, movies. Often I mark them on my calendar and when the appointed day comes, I find reasons not to go. Too much snow, too cold, too tired, no one to go with (something that never bothers me in the summer months), too many other things to do—like writing this book. The Vine-yard in the off-season suits my physical and psychological re-quirements. As I have said earlier, I find the solitude soothing. I can drive some distance without passing another car, go to Lucy Vincent Beach and have it all to myself, roam the island on foot or bike without interference, read books at night un-interrupted. And I have time left over to talk to people when I feel like it. Still, hard as I try to orient myself to Martha's Vineyard as a winter culture, I am not ultimately successful. It seems to me that winter here is a spell closing in on itself, rather like a long quarantine in a bedroom darkened by drawn shades with bottles of odiferous potions standing on a bedside table. I can't get myself to fall under the spell. Oh, I listen when people talk about the wonderful life in the winter, how one can hear the birdsong clearly, experience the ocean's true intensity, and feel the untrameled earth moving below her feet, that it isn't until all the summer people have left that you can really appre-ciate the magnificence of the place. But to tell the truth, I don't detect any major improvement in my sensory capacities in the off-season. The warm sun on my back, the greenery in bloom, the whiteness of sand against the bright blueness of water in the summertime is sufficiently magnificent for me. (Only one year-round Vineyarder among the many whom I meet actually admits that he likes summer best on Martha's Vineyard. It is Ron Rappaport, the island attorney who defended Edgartown against the Wallace brothers.)

Now and then, though, I do get myself "up" for one or another off-season event, like the public hearing in Vineyard Haven about a Dunkin' Donuts franchise that wants to move onto Main Street. I am curious to see firsthand how townspeople and town government work together on controversial issues. From what I have read in the papers, it appears that most of the townspeople are opposed to the franchise. Angry letters have been written to editors inveighing against the plan, forecasting doom. Despite these objections, some of the town fathers are reported to be supportive of the owner, a longtime Vineyarder. Hearings, many poorly attended, have been held, and now it's the home stretch. The hearing in front of the Zoning Board of Appeals takes place on a biting-cold March night. I enter a small room in a small town building, far removed from the town center, that can only accommodate a few people comfortably and not many more uncomfortably. At one end of the room the board is seated, and in front of them are people packed into the few available seats or leaning on walls, jogs of walls and bookcases, filing cabinets, whatever is available to be leaned upon. The middle-aged doughnut man sits at the table across from the board members, chatting them up, friendly as friendly can be. There is the distinct feeling in the room that after all the correct democratic proceedings have taken place—the reading of letters for and against, to the board, the registering of audience opinions, the answering of audience questions, and finally the vote by the board—victory for the doughnut franchise will be a shoo-in.

First, the letters are read. A lady in Chilmark writes that the doughnut plan represents a corporate takeover of the island. A man from West Tisbury declares that it will make the Vineyard look like everywhere else. Someone else opines that it is a wonderful plan—another example of free enterprise at its best.

Next come the audience comments. The board chairman asks to hear first from the plan's proponents. "I know Bob, and I know how he keeps his shops clean, does a really nice job of it. I think he'll do the same with this place," says one supporter. Another man, a fence sitter, thinks the shop will be fine so long as certain conditions are met.

The opponents follow. "We've already got enough coffee shops. If it's Dunkin' Donuts, it has to have a sign somewhere, and the sign will encourage other franchises. The local coffee-shop people won't be able to compete with Dunkin' Donuts prices. It'll drive them out of business," says a young woman. Trash is the concern of the next few speakers. One is worried about the recyclability of Dunkin' Donuts Styrofoam cups, another about where the store's trash will be dumped. A young man with a foreign accent rises and introduces himself as a spokesman for summer people. "They don't want this place to become Main Street, U.S.A., like it is all down the eastern seaboard. We have to be careful and protective of the rich people who come here. Our jobs are dependent on them." Several people echo his opinion, one man rather more passionately than the others. "I just don't like the product. I don't want to see those wrappers when I'm out hiking, and neither do the summer people. They come here to get away from that."

Finally, the doughnut man has the floor. No, he won't be putting a Dunkin' Donuts sign out on the street, no exterior Dunkin' Donut trademarks anywhere (sighs of relief). Yes, he will be using their paper products inside, and will have one of their signs there (shrugs and groans). Yes, he's thought about trash. He'll have recycling bins right outside the door, and regular trash bins, too. Yes, he'll be selling other foodstuffs as well as the Dunkin' Donuts line (more sighs of relief and mumblings of "Thank God").

Democracy thus respected, a board member, a Mr. Parks, addresses the congregation. "There's no law on the books dictating the number and kinds of shops we can have on the street. There's only so much we can do by law. We can rule out the outdoor sign and outdoor advertising, but that's about all we can do." Then another middle-aged board member speaks.

"Personally, I like Dunkin' Donuts and McDonald's. I feel like I missed part of my childhood not having them around."

An angry voice from the back of the room follows this soliloquy. "Good, why don't you just go to the mainland and get your fast food? That way you'll make room for one more tourist who will help *us* make money."

Things are getting out of order. Mr. Parks rises again. "Well, all I can say is I'm damn glad it's Bob who wants this instead of some off-islander." With that, the discussion ends. The board votes unanimously, 5–0, to accept Bob's plan with the conditions on exterior advertising, and the meeting is over.

There is one winter event I attend that stands out for me among all the events in every season. I will always remember the funeral I attend one late blustery February afternoon. In truth, it isn't so much a funeral as a funeral party. I haven't known the deceased, nor do I know the "hostess." My own audacity gets me there. I have invited myself. I like the way it has been described to me by new acquaintance, Brenda Grady. Through her, I wangle an invitation. On the funeral day, around 5:00 P.M., Brenda and her sister pick me up, and we drive past snow-covered fields, silvery, shimmering trees, and white ponds down Barnes Road onto the Edgartown Road, and from there take a turn into an unmarked side road. I am glad to be the passenger and not the driver, because this is an area called Iron Hill, which is totally unfamiliar to me. We take intricate turns to get to our destination, passing broad white meadows, thick patches of forest, and occasional houses along the way. Finally, we pull into a driveway at the end of a wooded cul-de-sac to the front of a lovely modern multilevel, wood-frame house, aglow with light and brimming with people—all kinds of people from all walks of Vineyard life, gay and straight, black, white, Hispanic, Native American, married, single, old, and young. There is an A.A. presence here, too, which is mentioned when the ceremony begins. In the bright living room reached by steps leading from the front door and in the adjacent dining room and kitchen area, people are eating and drinking, clearly enjoying one another's company. As has been explained beforehand, we have been asked to bring gifts to the "celebration" and to return home with gifts. We place ours on the table, and I am introduced to Val, the hostess, a tall, slender woman with great charm and warmth who shared the house with the beloved woman who died.

During her lifetime, Carolyn Cullen had been a pilot who owned her own planes, airstrip, and flying school on the Vineyard. She had taught many people, known and unknown, how to fly. There were pictures of her around the house and articles about her in scrapbooks scattered among the rooms. She appears to have been a beautiful woman, a passionate aviator and an equally passionate Vineyard lover. I regret that I will never know her except through photographs and eulogies.

The ceremony is a thing of beauty, another quintessential Vineyard experience, but more eclectic and personal than any funeral I've ever attended. It opens with all of us standing in a circle around the living room singing Native American chants (read from a printed paper) to the rhythm of drums. Eulogies are delivered by some of those assembled, lovingly and softly, interspersed with humorous recollections. Tears fall quietly from bowed heads. When Val speaks she recalls Carolyn's love for the island, for its healing powers and its gift of relief from the human propensity to self-destruct; and she speaks simply and eloquently of Carolyn. She ends with poetry, and then the drums sound again, heralding the climactic moment when Val climbs the stairs to a deck overlooking a pond and the surrounding meadow. From there, she chants loudly into the darkness, calling out the spirits. When she has descended, we stand again to sing.

"Now, everyone, please have a good time," she says in closing.

And we do have a wonderful time for a few more hours. I meet an English couple, neighbors of Val's, who live on the Vineyard year-round now that they've retired. "We feel at home here. It reminds us of the Midlands," the wife says.

There is a woman named Joanne who wants to open up a home antique business, but her neighbor, a summer resident, has protested by writing her a letter suggesting that she move out of the neighborhood. When that doesn't work, she goes around to other neighbors seeking support. She calls Joanne's friend, Joe, who tells her, "Gee, I'd like to help you out, but Joanne and I have been sleeping together for five years. It just wouldn't be right."

There are more people and more stories, and then it is time for each of us, on our way out, to pick one of the gifts that the other guests have brought.

Alone at home that night, I think about the "funeral" and how out-of-place and pretentious it would have seemed to me in another setting—in the suburbs, for example, or in the fashionable, bucolic outposts of Vermont or California. But on the Vineyard it is fitting and proper, not just a ceremony of symbol; rather, one that demonstrates pride of place and a sense of communality. I like the values it advertises: connection over division, uniqueness over conformity, and forgiveness of foibles over judgment upon them. Maybe most affecting of all is the link I see being made there between then, now, and tomorrow— a forging of the best traditions of the past with the troubling contradictions of today in an attempt to create an inclusive, harmonious vision for the future.

Over in America, you don't get that in any season; certainly not in a political season.

When it is time for me to go back to America at the end of the winter, I do so with three regrets. I will miss the opportunity it has given me for reflection and introspection. I still haven't found Johnny Seaview, and I am unable to meet the ninety-seven-year-old writer, Dorothy West, in person even though we have a mutual friend who assures me that winter is the opportune time to meet her. When I phone Ms. West, she tells me that she has been deluged with calls and visitors ever since her book, *The Wedding*, set in Martha's Vineyard, was published. As the last surviving member of the Harlem Renaissance and the author of other acclaimed works of fiction and nonfiction, Dorothy West was quietly famous before. Now she is noisily famous, a media darling, and the stampede to her door has been exhausting for her. Unfortunately for me, I reach her just after, not before, this invasion. Dorothy West has lived on Martha's Vineyard for most of her life, so her relationship to it is long and intimate. "I'm ninety-seven, you know, and I can't use all my energy talking to people. If someone's going to write a history of black people on the island, it might as well be me, so I've got to conserve my energy. If I talk to you and everybody else who wants a piece of me, how am I going to get the time and strength for my own project?" I can't help agreeing with her. I know that she would gladly have given me her time if she could. But with Johnny Seaview, it's another story. I leave the island believing that he would go to the ends of the earth to avoid me.

No, winter doesn't call me to a life on Martha's Vineyard. The persistent calm gradually begins to grate on me, as if I am in some unnamed civilization that is either way ahead of or way behind current civilization. I think it's probably way ahead, and that's discomfiting. It makes me want to escape certain pessimistic signals I've been picking up. You-better-watch-out, we-told-you-so signals, such as: (1) Developers will take over the world if you let them, and so will Starbucks, McDonald's, and Dunkin' Donuts. (2) Human isolation is not just an island problem. (3) The gap between rich and poor can get bigger than any American ever imagined; that's why we Vineyarders keep sending all our less-than-rich people over to you on the mainland. (4) Regular people follow celebrated people, hoping to be celebrated themselves, but it never works, so give it up. (5) Ecological danger is real. I should say that I have also received two happy signals: (1) Black and white people can live in relative harmony in a circumscribed, crime-free, unlocked locale. (2) Contrary to what every card-carrying American believes, some taxes do a lot of good, transfer taxes, for example.

So I'm on my way to take advantage of my civilization while it lasts. Besides, I miss my family and friends, and other things: the roar of the traffic, the sound of an army of boots sloshing through snow on Newbury Street; the lights in the skyscrapers, the old CITGO sign, the Charles River; the man on the corner dressed in camouflage talking to himself; the panhandlers, parking tickets. All that city stuff.

8

Summer Again and Again

*I*t's the inner summer child of mine that prompts me to bypass spring altogether and return to Martha's Vineyard in July. The boat on which I arrive docks in Oak Bluffs. Since my rented house is also there, I miss my ritual stop at Bruce's Holmes Hole Car Rental. In comparison with last summer's residence in Edgartown, my new home is a palace—a big old weathered cottage with a long, sagging veranda overlooking a little park. This time, I have invited my family and some of my friends to share the space with me for some of my stay. Although I plan to enjoy a little R and R, I also make a solemn vow to find Johnny Seaview. I've spent far too long looking for someone on twenty-three miles of ocean-locked land. To save face, I tell myself that it's not as embarrassing as it seems. After all, I'm seeking a man who spends most of his waking hours in treetops, and there are lots of trees on Martha's Vineyard. That's the problem—I've been looking low, not high. Of course I couldn't find him.

Meanwhile, I explore my new neighborhood, and am pleased to see that my neighbors are diverse in age and race. Around the corner from where I live, I notice a cheerful gray, red-trimmed house and guest cottage with letters Q.T. hanging in red on the siding of the main house. A bell rings in my head. This must be the home of Q. T. Bowles, about whom Ruth Hatton, among others, had told me the previous summer. "Go see Q. T. Bowles. She's been here a long time. She knows more than anyone about the black community on the island," Ruth had advised, but other activities had interfered and I never followed through.

Little do I know the next morning when I knock on Q. T.'s door that she will become one of my favorite people on the island. I expect a stooped and wrinkled octogenarian to limp ploddingly to the door and peer at me from behind wire-rimmed bifocals. Instead, a sprightly, smooth-skinned, short and slender figure appears instantaneously at the sound of the bell, nonosteoporotic, without glasses, a bandanna around her hair, an extra-long cigarette between two fingers of a slim, unwizened hand. Her moniker suits her perfectly. She *is* still a cutie in her eighties—witty, vigorous, "full of beans" as my mother used to say about her archer acquaintances. Once she invites me into her cozy den, and we are seated there, I ask Q. T. how she got her name. "My mother thought I was cute, so she called me cutie, and then everybody else did, too. I changed it to Q. T., but I've got a real name. It's Olive, just like my daughter."

Hers, I see, is an uncommon brand of charm, the kind that gloms onto one's consciousness and stays there whether in her company or not. My husband and I receive a delightful dose of it one day when we take her to the gallery where his sculpture and the paintings of a better-known artist share the display space. To say that Q. T. is unimpressed by the painter's work is understatement in the extreme. Her eyes take one long sweep of the room where it hangs. Without comment, she moves briskly by the canvases, giving them, one by one, a cursory, averted glance and then, with dramatic flair, uses the gallery's advertising flyer as a blindfold, a divider between herself, the viewer, and all the paintings that are viewable. To my husband's sculptures, in stark contrast, she pays adoring and rapt attention with long lingering looks at close range and distant. She fondles their steel contours like an agile lover, extolls their beauty, asks to be told about the creation of every piece, behaves as if she's in the company of genius. And when it is time to leave, as we exit through the painting gallery, she proffers one last mocking nod and one last flourish of her crumpled flyer. By then, my husband, the reborn Michelangelo, has fallen hopelessly in love.

The walls of Q. T.'s house are lined with her paintings—vibrant, exhilarating depictions of people at play and serious portraits of individuals, the angst of living etched into their faces. She has enjoyed some success as a Vineyard artist, and has exhibited and sold her work at local galleries. All her life, she wanted to paint, but it wasn't until she was middle-aged that she took herself seriously as an artist. "My mother gave me a paint box when I was young. Our family had art in our blood. I had five sisters. Today, all of them are painters, too." Q. T. came to the Vineyard before the war, residing for vacation periods at Shearer Cottage, the infamous, history-laden hotel where black people first resided on the island before housing and hotel accommodations were available to them. In 1953, Q. T., her husband and daughter bought their house and spent summers there until 1971, when she and her husband retired to it year-round.

Although Q. T. had lived and worked in New York, she didn't come to the Vineyard with the same racial legacy that her African-American neighbors brought with them. Her ancestry was British West Indian on her father's side and Scottish on her mother's. "West Indians, full-blooded or mixed, didn't carry race on their backs the way American blacks did." In New

York, she felt the prejudice that her American kinfolk experienced, but not on Martha's Vineyard. There she felt accepted.

Shearer Cottage was an exciting place in its heyday. The owner's daughter, Liz White, had the guests perform in plays on the front porch of Twin Cottages (part of the Shearer complex) for an audience seated on the lawn. "I couldn't act. I didn't know what I was doing up there on stage, but Liz made all of us perform. Come on," she says, taking me by the hand. "I'll take you up there now so you can see what I'm talking about." And off we go up a path and onto an incline leading to the lawn of Twin Cottages—a huge, rambling double-entry cottage with a grand veranda in front.

"Liz would get costumes from Katherine Cornell's auction. [The famous actress, Kate Cornell, summered on the Vineyard and often performed there.] Oh, the plays we put on: *Angel Street*, *Anna Lucosta*, *Lysistrata*, *Othello*. It wasn't until many years later when Liz decided to make a movie of *Othello* that we stopped performing. I was still going strong when I was forty-nine."

So the last curtain call for the unwitting actress became blossom time for the eager visual artist. Her paintings appear each August in the Oak Bluffs art exhibition and competition. Even now she paints, but not as prolifically as before—maybe four or five works a year, a few of which she donates to island benefits.

As soon as I find time, I drop in on Bruce Eliot, and take up a bench. Once again, we start up with our bantering routine. Then I get deadly serious. I tell him that he *has* to find Johnny Seaview for me because my time on Martha's Vineyard is running out. Here I pause to confess that it has begun to dawn on me that I no longer know why I'm looking for Johnny. I suspect that, by this late hour, the *quest* has become more significant than its object. After all, what is he? A character? So what? The world is full of characters. But then again, maybe not. Maybe they are a dying breed as some islanders say, not just on islands but everywhere. And, more important, what if, when I meet him in the flesh, he doesn't live up to his billing, much less to the larger-than-life stature I've given him in my imagination? Of course, I don't let Bruce hear my doubts. I hardly let myself hear them. Memories return to drown them out—memories of unforgettable island characters I knew as a child. My former playmates still residing on Little Diamond Island go one step further than Vineyarders—"Real characters are extinct," they say.

So Bruce promises. "Be here at five o'clock on Thursday," he instructs me.

I have been truthful in telling Bruce that closing time is coming for me on Martha's Vineyard. Hereafter, I would not return in the same guise as before, as the spy coming in from the cold. I'd be just another vacationing visitor without portfolio. I notice a certain sentimentality coming over me. I'm keenly aware of things I've paid little heed to before: the feel of Bruce's rough-hewn benches, the smell of coffee and bread from the Black Dog Bakery, the pleasing clutter on the outdoor tables at the Get A Life Bakery on Main Street, the hum of the machinery at the Gannon and Benjamin boatyard, the dip in the road in front of the Vineyard Studio Gallery. I realize that there are a thousand places on the Vineyard I've never seen, paths I haven't taken, vast stretches of beach I've never walked along, and great gaps in my knowledge of the island. Still, I have a slightly proprietary feeling about it, as if I own it, as if none of it is private. My people, my land.

If I'm leaving a place to which I've grown attached, and don't know when I'll be back, I have the illusion that if I find something I don't like about it, it will be easier to leave it. Easy come, easy go. Sure enough, I find something a couple of days before the Thursday I'm supposed to be meeting Johnny. My husband and I and two friends rent a sailboat and sail around the lagoon. We come ashore on a deserted beach to take a swim and stretch our legs. On the hill above, there are a few houses nestled in among the trees at some distance from the beach with no apparent rights of ownership. Perfect place for a swim, we decide, and plunge into the warm water. With our heads submergd, we don't hear the man calling to us from the beach at first, but when we surface, there he is: slim, middle-aged, wearing rimmed glasses, a shirt, and shorts, holding a book in his hand.

"May I help you?" he calls out, urgency in his voice.

"What?" our male friend answers.

"This beach is private," he says, "but down there [he points to an area a few yards away also bordered by houses] it's public. You can go there." Abruptly, he turns and climbs a steep staircase which is barely visible in the surrounding flora.

It's the kind of moment that begs for a retake, a second chance for the perfect one-liner, the touché. As aware as the four of us are of the rules of trespass and the tenets of private ownership, the incident leaves a rancid taste.

"Yes, we'll have four gin and tonics," my husband wishes he'd said.

This is the least appealing side of the Vineyard, this obsession with private property, and the disingenuous turns it takes. Consider the man's wording, "May I help you?" a patronizing way of saying "Get out of here." The Vineyard papers are replete with more significant examples of the hypocrisy of the highly placed—owners who are avowed proponents of environmental protection, historical preservation, and zoning regulations until any or all of those collide with their own interests. The what's-mine-is-mine, I'm-entitled-to-have-it-my-way posturing comes often in disguise on Martha's Vineyard, greed dressed up in nicer costume.

* * *

How ironic it is that it is none other than Johnny Seaview who gives me something else to dislike about the Vineyard.

Just as Bruce has promised, at 5:00 P.M. on Thursday, leaning on an old Coke machine in front of Holmes Hole Car Rental, is a short gray-haired man in a red cap, who appears, as I move closer, to be holding the daily racing form in one hand and a thorny, short-stemmed rose in the other, definitely not a florist's rose, but a gardener's. The flowers and the racing forms are the biggest part of his legend. He is as well known for his knowledge of horse racing as for presenting flowers—posies plucked from other people's gardens—to the ladies. Minutes before he gives me my rose, he has bestowed a yellow hibiscus blossom on Bruce's girlfriend.

Close up Johnny reminds me of a stripped-down Santa Claus. No red suit or snow-white beard, but the right age (sixty-seven), lively and quick with twinkling eyes, a droll little mouth, rosy red cheeks, and a nose like a cherry. Even though he isn't a big man, I can see that Johnny has a touch of male bravado about him, a guy swagger. I am reminded of a *Martha's Vineyard Times* reporter who has told me how he thinks of Johnny as a throwback to the Humphrey Bogart characters from the forties. "You know, the big-talking, *real* men of that era."

"Now save that rose" are the first words Johnny utters to me. He's laughing as he speaks. "Do what my mother does. She's ninety-two. Lives up in Boston. She always puts a penny and an aspirin in the water. One doesn't work without the other. You gotta use both. She says they work wonders with the tulips I bring her," he tells me in a sandpaper voice.

Immediately, I like the opener. He is an honest-to-God character. I'm ecstatic. At long last, I've found him. We're seated on Bruce's benches facing the sidewalk, and he's talking to me as he's studying his racing forms. The legend also has it that Johnny, born Oliver Perry, was a jockey in his youth, but had long ago given it up for tree work.

"I'm a tree surgeon," he tells me proudly. "I've been climbing trees since forty-nine. All over Massachusetts and down in Florida, too. Came here in nineteen fifty-two. They had tussock moth all over the island. My partner and I would leave and come back in the summertime. One year we spent six weeks on Nantucket and six weeks here fighting Dutch elm. Then we left again. We still go away like we always did, but we live here. I'm over at Woodside with the senior citizens. I climb everyday. You have to study to be a tree surgeon like me. Gotta know all about photosynthesis, alkalinicity, acidity, and the like. You know, there's no vacuum in nature 'cause nature abhors it. You have to study, study, study. Let me tell you, I've been to a lot of Carnegie libraries in my day, learnin' about trees. That's what it takes to be a tree surgeon."

He returns to studying the racing forms.

"What about the old Seaview Hotel in Oak Bluffs? Didn't you work there, too?" I nervously pry. He is marking the forms with a pen.

"Yeah, I started there in nineteen sixty-seven, the year the Red Sox won the pennant. Ha, ha, ha. Lonborg was pitching. I pulled the bar for Loretta. She owned the place. Kept it open in the summer because a seasonal license was all she could get. The hotel had thirty-eight rooms for the guests and thirty-eight for the squatters—the help." He avoids eye contact, but he keeps on talking. "Seventeen years, I worked for Loretta. When I wasn't working the bar, the two of us fixed up the place with the receipts from the bar. Did all kinds of repairs. She and her husband, the doctor, came from New Bedford, but he wasn't much interested in the business. They lived in that big ark of a house, Peter Norton's place over in Oak Bluffs near where the Seaview used to be. My partner and I rented a house behind the hotel. Had the whole place to ourselves. Everyone came to the bar. It was more like a cocktail lounge, 'the' place to go in those days. Stormin' Norman and Suzy got their start there, went on to New York to the big time. I got my name there, never got famous, but the name stuck. The patrons hung Johnny Seaview on me in nineteen sixty-seven, and I've been Johnny Seaview ever since. Back then, those were the days. A glass of beer was twenty-five cents back then."

This is my big moment, I've got Johnny Seaview all to myself, but I'm still nervous. I fumble for questions, ways to keep the conversation going. Bruce and some of his buddies who have gathered around are in my corner, eavesdropping, enjoying it. Suddenly, though, Johnny's name is called from across the street. "Come on, Johnny, let's go to dinner," shouts a gruff-sounding voice from a parking lot opposite us. Johnny doesn't move at first, but his attitude does. A tall, unfriendly man belonging to the gruff voice walks over to us, and as he approaches, Johnny's mood shifts from jocular to jugular in a matter of seconds.

"What's this?" the man asks, pointing to a piece of paper I am holding with questions written on it. "Let me see that," he says gruffly. "Oh God, look at this stuff. All gossip. People here live on gossip. I don't know what's the matter with all you people, asking these questions. Shows how you gotta be close-mouthed on this island. Come on, Johnny, let's get out of here. You don't wanna be talkin' to her."

"That's right. That's enough. You've got what you need. I'm heading out of here," says Johnny with an accompanying mumble—something about failure, and how it doesn't permit any alibis. By then, all traces of humor have been erased from his face, replaced by a surly demeanor. Without further ado, he rises from the bench, adjusts his thick tree-climbing belt, and in a clang of his metal is gone, Santa-like.

I cannot recall ever falling from high to low as rapidly as in that instant, and the more so because Johnny is proving himself to be every bit the character he's reputed to be. The boys in the peanut gallery are disappointed, too. "Can you beat that?" says Bruce, breaking the silence. "Johnny's really a nice guy, but put him under the influence of that one, and it's a whole different story."

"Yeah, did you see it? The way he tightened up just like that when [he] walked over," says somebody else.

And on go the postmortems until closing time at the Holmes Hole Car Rental.

Now I am so angry at Johnny Seaview that I can hardly wait for the few days that separate me from departure. I'm no longer even sorry that I will be missing the mega-event of the season, the event to top all events, Livestock '95. The two Vineyard stalwarts, married to each other once upon a time, are to be reunited on stage for a concert to benefit the Martha's Vineyard Agricultural Society. Carly Simon and James Taylor are the island's darlings, its mascots, the two names spoken in the same breath as "the Vineyard," as though they and the place are the combined, magnificent result of glacial happenstance. They have long connections to the island as summer residents, and their marriage, while it lasted, had a storybook quality. No longer young, but still attractive, talented, rich, and famous, they are the Vineyard's version of prince and princess, untarnished by their divorce, unscathed by scandal, still reigning gloriously, but from separate thrones. And now, after a seventeen-year hiatus, Carly and James will be performing together again, this time for an all-island audience. As soon as the concert is announced, there is a stampede to the ticket outlets. Sold out in four hours. As the planners have intended, people with island addresses hold the majority of tickets, but some do fall into the hands of black marketeers from faraway places.

When my departure day arrives, Johnny's rebuff, if not as intensely felt as on the day it happened, still suffices to ease the emotional impact of leaving. Only after I've said good-bye to Bruce and boarded the boat do I feel a bubble of sadness rising, but I have no opportunity to dwell on it. Something else is happening. Today I am riding back to Woods Hole in elite company, in the spacious wheelhouse of the *Martha's Vineyard* as a guest of her captain, Mark Young, and its pilot, Mike Mazza, two friendly men with long stints at the Steamship Authority. I watch while they navigate the boat out of the harbor. Mike steers, Mark runs the throttles, big brass handles that look like larger versions of soda-fountain levers. Once we are out of the Vineyard Haven harbor, a man with the fortuitous title of able seaman comes up to steer, and Mark and Mike are freer to talk.

"How do you happen to have these jobs?" I inquire of them.

Mark graduated from a maritime academy and shipped out to sea as a merchant marine for ten years before he came to the Steamship Authority and settled permanently with his family on the Vineyard. Mike's biography, I learned, was more typical. Like most of his colleagues, he had risen from the bottom up, through the ranks of the company to the pilot's position, but unlike most of them, he lived on the island. Their jobs are ideal. Merchant marines (the alternative career for them) are away from their families for long periods of time, whereas these men sleep at home every night except for occasional layovers on Nantucket. They work in shifts, scheduling their watches to relieve one another. Twelve hours on the first day, three or four the next. Off for a day and a half, and back around again.

We are breezing along at a brisk fourteen knots toward Woods Hole. For this short run, there isn't much for them to tinker with. Don't even have to fiddle with their fancy global positioning system (GPS—a system of satellites that radio to their antenna, giving them their course and telling them their longitude, latitude, and speed). Their jobs look easy. "Aren't there any problems out here on the water?" I ask.

"Oh, yeah," they answer in unison. "Summer problems and winter problems." In the summer, it was avoiding small craft—kayaks, jet skis—and swimmers. "It's hard to see them in the fog," Mike says. "Fog is worse in the summer because there's more traffic, and it rolls in all of a sudden. Now we have state-of-the-art equipment, our radar screen, for example, but for many years we had about the same tools as Christopher Columbus. Even with all the fancy stuff, though, collisions can happen." Mark explains that steel is the best reflector, much better than wood or sails. "Our screen is one hundred percent accurate in clear weather, but its clarity is affected by sea and weather conditions. Sometimes in rough water you get what we call sea returns on the screen. Reflections of the tops of waves. You have to fine-tune the composition to suppress the intensity, and while you're making adjustments you can miss what's out there." So far, they've both been lucky. No accidents on their shifts. The summer before one minor collision had taken place in thick fog between a Steamship Authority vessel (manned by another captain and pilot) and a fishing boat. "From what I heard, no one was in the wheelhouse of the fishing boat when it happened," says Mark.

They give me a quick overview of the rules of the sea. Only in the harbors do they have the right of way. Otherwise, there is a pecking order. Courtesy dictates that the large vessels make room for the smaller. Anything to their starboard side has the automatic right of way.

Before entering Woods Hole harbor, I want to hear their thoughts about The Problem—the traffic on the Vineyard and the Steamship Authority's contribution to it.

"We stay neutral on that one," replies Mike, and adds, "It's tough on management. The people in Falmouth don't want the town to become a giant parking lot for islanders, and the people on the Vineyard don't want the cars over there. The two places have opposing agendas. It's confusing."

As we approach the harbor, they take to their posts, Mike back to the wheel, Mark to the throttles. The able seaman descends to join the others in the crew, some members of whom have titles and jobs I haven't known existed. In total, down below, there are two ordinary seamen (for maintenance), three other able seamen (for moving cars, flag raisings and lowerings), two porters (freight and luggage), a purser (for tickets and payroll, first aid, announcements), a cook and a mess man, a chief engineer, and an oiler and wiper (engine room staff).

The time has passed too quickly with Mark and Mike. I like them, and I like their brand of boat talk, their attitude of "Can you believe it, we get to do this for a living?"

"You can ride with us again," they say as I'm thanking them and leaving. I surely would, and riding a little easier, too, knowing that I'll be safe in all those able hands. (And, in fact, I do ride with Mark again, in the summer of 1996.)

After I've been back in Boston for a week or so, I find myself wishing that I could be back on the Vineyard at Livestock '95. How could I miss Carly and James singing their famed duet, "Mockingbird," and being part of the ecstatic, dancin'-in-the-meadow emotional outpouring from the audience? I have to content myself with reading all about it in *How Sweet It Was*, the sixteen-page supplement the *Gazette* printed afterward; all about the security precautions (with photos of the officers), the Who's Who in the audience compendium (with close-up shots), the quotes from fishermen, waitresses, and carpenters (no photos), the story of the ambivalent Irish girl who misses the concert, but scalps her ticket for the sum of her plane fare home (no photo), and, of course, everything I already know about Carly and James (with huge photos—Carly with guitar at the mike, James with guitar at the mike, Carly and James dancing, Carly and James holding hands, Carly and James holding hands with their daughter)—all the homespun Vineyard fare that the *Gazette* serves up so inimitably to its readers, the kinda stuff that makes them feel they are there.

More often than I want to when I'm at home in Boston, I think of Johnny Seaview. Reality strikes, or more accurately, sadness and disappointment—the good-bye sadness that I remember as a child leaving Little Diamond in September, packing up a summer's worth of special moments, and the disappointment—the anticipation of something happening that didn't happen, at least in the way that I had wanted.

So it is with Johnny Seaview. I feel as if I've met his alias, the department-store Johnny, not the authentic chimney Johnny. I pout and sulk, act as cranky as a kid who doesn't get the doll she's been hoping to find under the tree.

Just as I am emerging from my funk, who should reappear? The real Johnny Seaview. Perhaps Bruce has cajoled him, yanked at his heartstrings a little, or he has had his own change of heart, but we get together again, Johnny and I. A few weeks after I've left the Vineyard, I finally manage to reach him on the telephone. Over the wires he's more accessible than he is in person. From then on, we talk frequently. And a jolly old soul he turns out to be, and voluble, too.

"I'm not a friendly guy, especially when things get personal. Uh, uh, you get too personal with me and you get the steel wire runnin' right across your butt." I say that I guess I won't be getting "personal" then. Instead, we'll talk about horses or trees or the Vineyard; whatever he likes.

"I'm not a real islander. I just came here to work, that's all. What else is there to do here? In *Medfud* (read Medford) Massachusetts, where I come from, they've got restaurants and people, over two hundred fifty thousand people. Here, they've only got a few restaurants and hardly any people. I like *Medfud* better. Go there all the time to visit my mother. I retired here, that's all, but I still work everyday up in the trees. That's what a tree surgeon does, and I'm a tree surgeon. It's my profession, just like a plumber or a carpenter has his profession."

In one of our conversations, I ask Johnny why he calls himself a surgeon. "You're not always opening up trees, are you?" I ask, and add another question along with it, "Do you climb in the winter?"

"Cripes, no! We don't just do surgery. We're arborists. We open up the trees for photosynthesis, but we plant, too. We change the face of nature. It's an old profession. Of course I climb in the winter. The trees don't go inside, ya know."

He hadn't started out as a tree surgeon. In fact, he wasn't even a high school graduate. "I got a double promotion in high school, though. Nope, I never graduated. I got my education in the world. Wait a minute now, I've got to get my book out, and read you some things I wrote down. Look right here, it's Wordsworth—'The world is too much with us . . . We have given our hearts away.' Here's another one. I don't know who wrote it. 'You have part of God in yourself. . . .'" Usually, he reads the words faster than I can get them down.

"I had to go off and fight in the war, and after I got out, I went 'smoke jumpin' [fighting fires] for a while in Colorado. Then I went into the marines. They trained women, too. Well, in Quantico, Virginia, on the base, I ran into a young girl. She was seventeen. Came from Jersey. We got married. She was eighteen when she had our firstborn. We had another son and daughter before we were through. After a while we moved back to Jersey. She worked for that pencil company, for the people who made those yellow pencils that said Dixon on them. She did one-hundred-fifty-seven words a minute, with a typewriter, not a pencil. I bought a pickup truck, and started studying trees. Spent a lot of time at the Carnegie library. I figured there were only two kinds of work I could put up with—horses and trees. I'd been going to the racetrack since my grandfather started taking me when I was three or four. I'd already done horses for a living, put in three years jockeyin' at Havre de Grace. Never stopped studying about them though. Still do. I go right to the back of that bookstore in Vineyard Haven—The Bunch of Grapes—and look at the books about trees and shrubs and horses. I buy some of them. Did you know that Paul Revere had to change mounts nineteen times on his historic ride? I bet you didn't," he says correctly.

A few years in New Jersey, and it was good-bye to that and hello again to Massachusetts. Johnny and his wife returned to his turf and made a home in Cambridge. He started climbing trees. During the summers, when he was on the Vineyard, his wife stayed at home. Theirs was a long union lasting until she died a few years ago. "She didn't have much use for the Vineyard," he notes. Whenever things bordered on the personal, Johnny would steer me quickly back to the impersonal. "For a while, I owned my own tree business, then I gave it up and worked for other tree men. Been working with the same guys for years now. I started out at seventy-five cents an hour. We went all over the place, wherever we wanted. You say you're from Washington, D.C. Well, we went there, too. Did the bot elders at the Blair House for Harry Truman. He was a great guy, that Truman. He walked all the time. He wasn't like these joggers you see now out at six o'clock in the morning. Frownin' and scowlin'. I've yet to see a happy jogger."

In another of our conversations, we wax philosophical and talk about Johnny's opinion of today's men.

"They don't make them like they used ta. What ever happened to the risk takers? Life is an adventure, and it's a lot better if you take risks. These men today, they don't even take the risk of getting inside themselves." Somehow this reminded him of George Bernard Shaw. "Listen to this, 'In the womb of your mother, your life is planned, but look at a tree...All of its life is planned.' The men now, they're taking us back to the past. They fiddle with computers all day long. Don't even know that they already have computers inside their heads. You gotta study all the time like I do: Ovid, Byron, Plato, Socrates. Socrates said the only fact he knew was that he was ignorant. How about that? I read all the time."

Sometimes, Johnny reels off the titles of books he's been reading. Diane Ackerman's *A Natural History of the Senses*. ("You gotta read that one," he advises. "It's about your senses, tasting and smelling and all that. Can you believe they have a history?) *Think and Grow Rich*, by Napoleon Hill. James Allen's *Acres of Diamonds*. A book called *The Dying of the Trees*. "See, a good education doesn't cost you anything," he said.

And, of course, he has to keep up with the horses. For that, he needs, at a minimum, the daily editions of the *New York Post* and the New York *Daily News*. "Can't get any information from the *Globe*. Only the New York papers cover everything—The Garden State, Pimlico, Thistle Downs. All the big races."

I ask him if he bets on the horses.

"Cripes, yes. Certainly," he answers in a mocking tone as if I haven't one ounce of sense.

Knowing that he holds me rapt, he uses some of our telephone time to turn the spigot on his fountain of knowledge, gushing quotes in long desultory bursts. From Gandhi, "We are involved in a life that surpasses understanding, and our highest business is our daily life." John Gage: "No man is born wise. Time ripens all fruit." From Mary Baker Eddy, "If one would be successful in the future, let him or her make the most of the present." From Zen principles, "Seeing into nothingness is the true seeing." From unnamed sources, "No snowflake falls in an appropriate place. It's there by design." Or, "Take away the cause and the effect ceases."

For Johnny, it's study, study, study; memorize, memorize, memorize. "I memorize everything. I've got one of those *photogenic* memories. I fast and meditate, too. I go into Mandela's entropy. What you don't use, you abuse, ya know."

Usually it is I who needs to break off our conversations. On my end of the receiver, my head buzzes constantly. Before I hang up, I always make sure that I remind Johnny how happy I am to have found him; how I'd been hearing about him for so long from everyone I met on the island; how much it means to me to get to know him.

"For cripes sake. I don't get it. I'm not a social butterfly or anything like that. I don't know why I have this *rep-a-tation*. Here, you want to put me in a book, and in June, the *Globe* put me in a piece they wrote about all the celebrities on the island. Ya know, right there with Carly Simon, Meryl *Street*, Ted *Dancing*, and all those people. There was a whole paragraph about me. I didn't see it until I came downstairs the next morning and found it posted on the bulletin board. The girls at Woodside [the senior citizens' housing complex] put it up there along with my picture. I guess they like me 'cause I bring them flowers whenever I can, ya know. I was up in Boston last week, and I brought a rose to my friend, Darleen, who used to live on the Vineyard. She owns a restaurant down there on Milk Street. Anyway, she made me one of those good *fafala* sandwiches from over there in the East. Lebanon, that's the place. When I got back to *Medfud* though, my sister had my favorite waiting for me. Chicken soup with dumplin's."

"Johnny," I say, when we sign off for what will be our last conversation for a while. "You know how glad I am to have found you, but you're going to have to get me another rose, 'cause that first one died. You see, when you gave it to me I had a penny but I didn't have an aspirin, and like you said, one doesn't work without the other."

*　*　*

Without Johnny Seaview, a part of myself would have died like the rose. He's been roaming around in my imagination for so long that he's become larger than life, a mythical character, a "*celebrity* celebrity." Celebrities often thrive better in an imaginary climate than in a real one. You don't want to meet them, really, because sooner or later, you know you'll find out that they are like you in every way (though generally richer and better looking). But not Johnny. He has to be known in the flesh because he is one of a kind—a tree-climbing wordsmith with a photogenic memory! He doesn't walk the celebrity walk, and for cripes' sake, no, he doesn't talk the talk, nor look the look. And the irony is that in his beloved *Medfud* he couldn't get the attention he deserves. *Medfud* is too big, too busy to take proper notice of him. Just as it takes a penny and an aspirin to keep a rose alive, it takes an island to keep a Johnny Seaview alive. Johnny is Martha's Vineyard's own.

Well, after my coup with Johnny, I get an urge to return to the island again at the end of the summer (with my pad and pencil). Out of the blue comes this idea that I ought to go out fishing for a day with an island fisherman. After all, fishing and Martha's Vineyard go hand in hand. What is one without the other? There are two people I have met in the previous year who are intimately connected with it. One is Mark Lovewell, the fishing columnist for *The Vineyard Gazette*, and the other is Chris Murphy, a conch fisherman.

For Mark Lovewell, the Vineyard's proximity to Cape Cod is a curse—too easy to imitate—and a blessing—a gnawing reminder of how a once-beautiful place can degenerate if it doesn't take care of itself. Mark worries about the island's future and the future of fishing. For years, farming and fishing were the island industries, but the former disappeared and the latter is now disappearing. Still, there can be a future for fishing. "Aquaculture can take over where fin fishing leaves off if fishermen are willing to make the transition. Some already have. Shellfish are plentiful here, and the demand is high."

On shore, Mark foresees a continuing struggle to maintain the island's beauty by resisting mainland-style alterations. "When you live on an island, you have to give up some of your rights. You can't have unlimited water, for example. Our finite resources aren't sufficiently guarded. I don't think it's big changes that will destroy us. More likely to be a string of little changes—a McDonald's here, a Dunkin' Donuts there. The residents, summer and winter, who care about this place are often overruled by the business people. They don't want restrictions. If T-shirts sell well, someone's going to sell them, and they're going to pay top rental dollars for the privilege. Right now this place is promoted as quaint, but if it gets Disneyish, summer renters and owners will stop coming. Already, the rental patterns have changed from seasonal to weekly and monthly. With that shift comes a loss of community. Too many entrances and exits, and before you know it, it's like Atlantic City, Cape Cod, the Florida coasts: catering to the lowest common denominator— warm weather, a beach, a towel, and a shower. That's OK for Florida, but not for Martha's Vineyard."

Mark's Vineyard roots go back to the earliest white settlers. "First came the Mayhews," he explained. "They spread across the island, converted the Indians to Christianity, and stole their land. Next came my maternal ancestors, the Peases. They weren't so virtuous. They didn't bother with religion. They just stole the land and settled Edgartown." The Lovewells' modest house in Edgartown, no doubt, sat on a parcel of the purloined land, but the same could be said about every non–Native American Vineyard house. On Mark's paternal side, the beginnings were also inauspicious. The Lovewell name belonged to an old Maine family renowned for killing Native Americans.

Great-grandmother Pease married a wealthy summer resident, a piano manufacturer from Boston—Julian Vose. Undoubtedly she was a pioneer in fomenting a rash of Vineyard-style "intermarriages"—those between winter and summer people. Her daughter, Mark's grandmother, became his childhood summer guardian. For him, those were halcyon summers. He kept his fond memories for the years he spent away from the island. "I had this incredible affection for the ocean and for Martha's Vineyard. My wife felt the same way. Eventually, I decided that I was ready to go home again."

He worked his way up the ladder at the *Gazette* until he became a reporter and got the assignment he wanted, the *Fishermen's Column*. From the outset, he knew it would be tough because fishermen were notoriously inaccessible.

"What I had going for me was a reverence for maritime history, a talent for singing sea shanties, and a fondness for fishing. For sixteen years I've done that column, but now I also cover the waterfront—sailboat racing, yacht club events, whatever is happening on the water. For my regular column, I had to earn the friendship of the fishermen on their turf. They're independent, self-made men who cherish their way of life and don't like people intruding on them. I've always kept myself out of their stories. There's one fisherman here whose hatred of the press is well known, but photographers love to photograph his picturesque fishing shacks.

"Some people walk right in uninvited, and after they leave he has to rake up their film boxes. For years, I asked him if I could photograph him. He'd never let me, but we developed a wonderful friendship anyway. Whenever I came around, he'd stop what he was doing, and we'd start talking about some fisheries issue. In nineteen ninety-four, Chilmark was holding their tricentennial celebration on the Menemsha waterfront, and the fisherman's sister asked me to sing some sea shanties. When she offered to pay me, I told her that there was something I wanted more than money—a picture of her brother. She knew how long I'd been trying to photograph him. Well, finally, in nineteen ninety-five, I got that picture and ran it with a story about the changing face of Menemsha and the hardships fishermen were suffering. Later, he told me he liked the picture and the story. That meant a lot to me. But I guess, even before that, in the preceding years, he respected me for respecting his privacy, because once, out of the blue, he made me a gift of a hand-carved bird. It's a gift I treasure."

The summer before, when I attended the Martha's Vineyard High School reunion, I met Chris Murphy. I remembered his telling me then that all I had to do was give him a call if I wanted to go out conch fishing with him. Now, a year later, he gets the call. Yes, he remembers me, and yes, I can go out with him. He sets the day, tells me to pack a lunch, and then gives me the bad news. I must be at the dock in Vineyard Haven harbor at 5:00 A.M. The good news is that I'm staying close enough by to get out of bed at 4:45, throw on several layers of clothing, and arrive just as Chris and his young Australian mate are pulling up. The three of us board his boat and set off in chilly darkness. All I can remember before I fall asleep in the cabin belowdecks is the reflection of the moon on black water, still as ice, and the stars sequining the black sky like rhinestones on an evening gown. As we head out to sea, I am awakened intermittently by the rocking of the boat and the sound of water slapping it on all sides. By sunrise, I am fully awake. To welcome a day that promises to be beautiful, I join my companions on deck. Before Chris begins pulling his weirs (traps), we talk some about fishing. What he tells me, not surprisingly, is similar to what I've heard from Mark Lovewell.

"Whatever needed to be done to save fishing was too little

and came too late. The waters have been overfished, so nowadays fishermen look for fish they haven't found before. Hell, only a few men fish for cod and swordfish anymore because there's hardly any left. If I had my way, fishing for cod would be banned for ten years to allow the stock to be replenished, but I doubt that that will happen without an effective lobby for the fishing industry," Chris says. Apparently, he doesn't have much use for draggers. "They're wasteful. They kill the huge amounts of fish that they don't keep, so they're killing off young fish. We use pots. They're much greener. We catch the fish alive, and the stuff we don't want, we put back in. At first the draggers were getting all the scup, but now it's reversed. They're not doing as well as we weir fishermen are."

Finally, after what has seemed like a long journey, we get out into the middle of nowhere, and Chris points out his pots' silver and orange markers bobbing in the water. He slows the engine, adjusts the boat's position, and begins the first of many cycles of hauling, unloading, baiting, and lowering of traps. Initially, it fascinates me to see the catch. The scup flapping wildly in their cages, and the giant (and some not so giant) gray conch shells lying peacefully on the bottom of their pots. After a while, though, I pay less attention to the fish and more to the job. It looks like grueling, tedious, repetitive work, and it makes me wonder how men do it, especially those more senior than these two. (Chris is in his forties, and his mate is twentysomething.) By my reckoning, even with the help of electronic winches, one needs, at the very least, arms of pure brawn, a sound heart, good lungs, and a strong stomach. Fortunately for me, this is a calm day at sea, but for fishermen, there are countless days when the sea is angry and the air frigid. I have no doubt that, at these times, fishermen's bodies take a heavy pounding. As much as I don't envy them their work, I marvel at their ability to do it.

Never mind that I have neither scup nor conch on my table (most of it goes to South Korea). From now on, I will be more appreciative of all the seafood that I do eat.

In between markers, Chris tells me a little about himself. He grew up in Chilmark on the Vineyard, the son of a fisherman who later gave up fishing to become an artist. As a child, Chris went out on different boats. With a chuckle, he recalls the swordfish boats he's been out on. "Some of those men didn't take it seriously. They'd go out for a while and come back in. The serious ones stayed out for two weeks at a time." When he was of draftable age, during the Vietnam war, he got a deferment by joining the Peace Corps to fish in South India. Today, Chris still lives in Chilmark. His wife is a teacher, his two children are in college, and he serves on the town planning board, "dealing with subdivisions and things like that. Unfortunately, the towns do too much reacting and not enough planning." In general, he believes that winter people are more tolerant of change than summer people, except for the burgeoning population of retirees who are more conservative than the other year-round residents.

At 3:00 P.M. we start heading out of Vineyard Sound, ten hours after we left Vineyard Haven. It's been a long day, and I'm exhausted even though I haven't lifted anything heavier than my lunch bag. For the hourlong return trip, we talk fish talk again, and I learn some of the rules of the water. I learn that Chris is allowed two hundred, but has only one hundred pots in strings of ten. He is required to set his pots from east to west. And although pots are supposed to have the right of way, he's lost thirty-five pots this summer to ferry boats because his pots cross their lanes. And I learn some of the economics and geographics. For starters, Chris receives fifty dollars per tote from the fishery. Today he may have six totes. He needs ten to make a profit. A thousand dollars a day is a really good day, but it's rare. It costs him forty dollars for bait for every one hundred dollars worth of fish. He used to fish out of Menemsha until two years ago, but now it's better in the sound. When he was younger, he fished farther away, off Georges Bank. Finally, before we dock, I pick up a few snippets of information about what radar screens reveal. They can be used to show schools of fish on the bottom. Mostly they show whether the surface is rough or smooth and suitable for dragging a net.

At the end of that day, I say good-bye again to Bruce, knowing that this time the interval between leaving and returning will be longer than it has been before. On the boat to Woods Hole I think about how much I will miss *looking* for Johnny Seaview, snooping around for stories, sticking my nose into other people's business, because those activities have given Martha's Vineyard a special texture and meaning for me. For most people, the Vineyard is a beloved place to stay. For me, it's a beloved nomadic way station, a familiar place to visit, a place from which to disappear and reappear. Here today, gone tomorrow, back again another day, any day, someday. I've grown to like my relationship with the Vineyard. Although it doesn't call to me in the way that I have been hoping to be called, in that "You must live here; you do not belong anywhere else" way, it does embrace me when I arrive without demanding that I stay. I am appreciated, but not obligated. Only recently has a memory come back to me that I'd forgotten until now. I now remember how much I hated the feeling of obligation I had as an adult about returning to Little Diamond Island. It was as if I had no choice but to come back summer after summer, year after year. My fellow islanders seemed to expect that I would return as they did, as if it was part of the natural cycle of life, like aging. Except it wasn't natural to me. I wanted to be a visitor there and a traveler to other places. And that is how it's been ever since I left.

So, it is sad to say good-bye to Martha's Vineyard even

though I will always return to it. It's not the adjectives about the island—beautiful, picturebook, idyllic—but rather the verbs that define it for me, all the things I've *done* while I've been there. Martha's Vineyard is beautiful, and I want it to stay that way, but in the end it isn't its beauty that is the draw for me. Nature scatters beauty willy-nilly over the planet, near or far, wherever one wants to go to find it. And I'm not drawn to the island because it is trendy and oh-so-voguish. Those features imperil it. Not the calm of it either. I'm too citified, too restless to be held by that. What will be the beacon, then, now that my verbs are spent?

It is a noun that will call me. It is the colors of Martha's Vineyard. The different colors of the people. The blues and greens of the sea and land will pull me back the way they did for Brenda Grady. I can hear her words still:

"An island is the real world in microcosm. You can see how the real world works from watching island life. Every day, I see the faces of those pushed out by capitalism—the working and middle class, people I've known all my life. That is painful for me because I remember the incredible feeling of safety that I had in childhood, that feeling that because I lived on an island, all was right with the world, but of course it was an illusion. There's only one truly inspiring thing about this island, one worthy of a hallelujah. That's the racial scene. It offers lessons for the rest of the world. No one race is the real enemy. The real enemy is capitalism gone amuck. You can see it. I can see it. Everyone can. So, tell me, why can't the politicians see it?"

As it turns out, Brenda Grady couldn't wait for the politicians to correct their vision. She has joined the exodus, but, like me, she will come back often, not just for sentimental reasons but for another specific one: to see whether we like the sequel to the story.

When we come back, we'll both be watching the island's tribunes to see if they will have the penny *and* the aspirin to keep the rose alive.